Price Per Barrel

By

Marc Gregory

Published by:
Stand Publishing Inc.

www.facebook.com/mgregoryauth

Distributed to the trade by Ingram Book Company

Other books By Marc Gregory

Alternative Energy

Alternative Energy II - Blow Me

Price Per Barrel

Quantum Avidya

MARC GREGORY

1

Albert Doyle wiped the sweat from the top of his balding head as he glared at the high-noon sun. The temperature on this mid-August day had climbed to a sweltering forty degrees Celsius. That combined with dense humidity had him cursing the blasted land of Eastern Texas as he placed his hat back on his head. His large, bulky mass was not made for this climate; it was better suited to insulating him during Canadian winters.

The wait gave him time to think about how he wanted to retreat to air conditioning and a frosty pint of beer. But he had travelled a long way for this opportunity, and patience was a skill painfully acquired during his lifetime of service in Northern Alberta.

He turned in his mounted seat, which was fastened to the back of a customized flatbed truck specifically designed for the hunt.

"Hey, Pedro," he whispered in a gruff baritone, "how fucking long's this going to take?"

The Mexican field guide—whose name was Dimas, not Pedro—gave him a stoic look, placed a finger to his lips, and nodded toward the treeline.

Albert turned his attention back to the target. In the distance, he heard the growing commotion of the hounds. Dimas pointed at some brush off to the left, and Albert raised his rifle and peered through its scope.

The brush rustled violently, then out jumped the prey, shrieking and squealing. Albert had been practising for months and got the shot off clean and

1

fast, dropping the bounty in a single squeeze.

He lowered the gun and watched in silence as the Mexicans working the trees ran to collect the trophy boar. When they had dragged it clear of the brush, Albert got down from his seat to gauge its size.

"What the fuck is that?" he said, turning to his guide while pointing to his kill.

"What do you mean, señor? It is your boar."

"No! No fucking way, Paco! I paid your boss big money! I told him I wanted the big one and paid over and above the posted cost! I want a fucking beast, not a pig that builds its house from straw."

Dimas turned away from Albert. He removed the bandana from his head and wiped his face, rolling a toothpick below his moustache. "What was it you say you do up there in Canada, señor?"

Albert puffed out his chest. "I'm the president of the oil sands division for Northern Lights Energy, the biggest fucking oil producer in North America— that includes the good ol' USA!"

"Hmm, oil sands, huh?" Dimas pulled the toothpick from his mouth and twirled it in his fingers as he stood on the side of the flatbed, peering toward the brush. Sweat beaded on his olive skin and darkened his black muscle shirt. He hiked up his torn and stained blue jeans as he turned to Albert. "I understand that you probably have paid a lot of money to Señor Garza. Of course you want to shoot a 'beast' as you say, but the problem is"—he looked side to side, raised his palms, and grinned—"I do not see Señor Garza out here. So where is Señor Garza? Señor Garza is a nice man, but he does not know the pigs. We are the ones who know the pigs."

He fanned his hand toward the three helpers tending to the carcass. "We know where the pigs are. We know how many and how big." He turned back to Albert and looked him square in the eye. "We are the ones, señor, who can get you what you desire. We know where to find the beast!" He clenched his fist in front of Albert, the exclamation point in his sales pitch.

"We are the ones with all the knowing, Señor Doyle, but Señor Garza, he does not pay us very well. We put our lives on the line every day chasing the pigs, and the big ones are very dangerous, but we get very little in return. Garza plays golf all day and gets all the money." He produced a childlike pout. "Payment to Garza gets you on the truck, but the real business happens out here."

MARC GREGORY

Albert understood all too well what was taking place; the industry back home was dripping with slick palms. This was his first adventure of this nature, and his guide had just enlightened him on his mistake. He should've paid the minimum to this Garza and then negotiated the final deal with the actual field guides. He hated being taken advantage of, but money wasn't an issue for him, and this whole trip was expensed to the company anyway: he would just chalk it up to being a learning experience. In any other situation, he would've had the little fucker dig his own hole and then buried him in it, but Dimas held all the cards, and Albert knew what he wanted.

"All right, you win," he said with a scowl. "But before we get talking *el deniro*, we should discuss how big of a pig."

Dimas yelled out something over his shoulder to the others, and Albert sensed the tension in the group ease.

Dimas grinned. "Well, Señor Doyle, we keep a few just for special clients. We can go anywhere from two hundred pounds all the way up to one thousand." He paused, letting the options sink into Albert's greedy little head. "But if it is the beast you want, we have been saving one very special pig. He is truly a beast—the king of the beasts! We can only guess at what he weighs, but I will put him at over one thousand pounds, maybe twelve hundred. What do you think?"

Albert had to admit his guide knew exactly the kind of man he had on the line and how to negotiate with him. He took a minute to stare into Dimas's eyes, looking for the hint of a tell that he might be full of shit. But Dimas never flinched, and Albert could see this taco was a man of his word when there was a bankroll on the line. "How much for the king?"

The guide grinned and stood tall again, placing the toothpick back in his mouth as he turned back to the trees.

***

Seventy-five hundred dollars later, they were bouncing down the road on the back of the truck, the one-hundred-pound appetizer left behind to rot. The crew was busy forging an attack strategy, mapping out escape routes in case anything went wrong. Albert licked his parched lips as he watched the men, the fear in their voices—fear for their lives—giving him an even bigger rush. These men were his, bought and paid.

The moment the truck stopped, the crew began gathering the required tools and sent Albert back to his perch, advising him to buckle in.

3

PRICE PER BARREL

Dimas moved to the back of the kennel trailer in tow, where the dogs were salivating hysterically. With a couple of last commands shouted to the crew, he pulled the pin on the gate and the dogs took to the brush, barking and yelping madly.

The men followed behind, and as the last man disappeared, all fell silent. Albert's heart pounded while he scanned the brush, keeping his eyes trained through the scope on his polished Winchester .30-06.

It was only a matter of minutes before barking exploded from the dogs, followed by some shouting from the guides. Then a shrill screech sent an icy chill down Albert's spine. It was like nothing he'd ever heard before—more of a high-pitched roar than a squeal. Next came a terrible scream from what he assumed was one of the guides.

His heart pulsed harder and sweat raced down his face. He'd just taken his hand off the trigger for a second to wipe his forehead when he heard the horrible screech again. Only this time, it was much closer. Then more frantic barking from the dogs, and the brush suddenly parted directly ahead, the monster bursting through with the speed and power one would expect from a charging tiger.

It was as big as a bear.

Albert squeezed off a shot as soon as it cleared the brush, but he didn't see where he'd hit and the boar didn't miss a step. It took no time for it to cross the distance from the brush to the truck, and the safety of Albert's perch became a farce.

But he was the hunter here, not the pig below him. He thrived under pressure. He unbuckled and stood from his seat, stepping to the edge of the truck bed. With seconds to spare before the beast would be on top of him, he raised the scope again, sighting the swine between the eyes. He felt its rage. Heard the heaving snort of its breath. Saw its frothing mouth.

Only one could win.

"Here, piggy, piggy," he whispered as the ogre leaped…

BANG

The stiff mass barrelled into Albert, knocking him across the truck and off the other side. Another bullet cracked from the gun when he hit the ground with a solid thud, the wind knocked from his lungs.

The crew of guides came running from the trees, minus one. They surveyed the scene. The king was dead, its hind legs hanging from the side of the truck bed.

Dimas ran around to the other side of the truck and found Albert sprawled on the ground, drenched in sweat and gasping for air.

"Did I get him?" he wheezed, exhausted from the adrenaline dump.

Dimas smiled and reached a helping hand down to Albert's. "Yes, Señor Doyle. You got him."

Back on his feet, Albert watched Dimas give a strong nod to his partner across the truck bed. The man returned a more solemn nod, hung his head, and walked back toward the trees.

In all the excitement Albert had forgotten about the terrible scream he'd heard during the roundup, but the echo of a single shot fired only moments later jogged his memory… Only one man returned. They loaded quietly into the truck.

Albert had to hand it to the guides. *Say what you want about the Mexicans, but when there's business to be taken care of, they don't fuck around. My kind of people.*

Albert turned to Dimas on the journey back to the ranch and said, "Hey, Paco. I want to talk to the taxidermist before he touches this pig. I have specific instructions for this one." He produced an envelope full of cash from his pocket and handed it to Dimas with a smile. "Good job today." The smile was full of respect.

PRICE PER BARREL

2

Emma dusted the bottom ledge of the picture frame hanging in the main foyer of the administration building at Northern Lights Energy, north of Fort McMurray, Alberta. She made a special stop at that particular painting early every morning, before the crowds of workers polluted the hallways. It was a portrait of the late George Kennedy, who had served as president of the firm from 1987 to 2001.

Fifty years ago, when Emma turned eighteen, her uncle got her a cleaning job at the plant. Within a year, her affair with George had started.

She smiled, admiring the oiled portrait—George's blue eyes and charismatic smile. He passed away shortly after retirement; it seemed to be a trend with the oil sands personnel. Like a heavy addiction to something that is wrenched away suddenly. But even with his passing, she could still never speak of their secret time together. He was a brilliant man and should be remembered as nothing less. It was no fault of his that his wife had fallen ignorant to the fact he was a man with needs. It was her loss, though. Emma had been more than happy to fill that void.

Her thoughts drifted off to the beginning, to when they first met and flirted every morning while she cleaned his office. They were much younger then. Her nineteen-year-old body was firm and its curves drew the attention of all the men, young and old. She knew; it was not her first game of temptation. And just as George had needs, she also had an agenda.

Their time together was beautiful: she tended to his needs and he took care of hers…

6

MARC GREGORY

The doors to the foyer opened as someone exited the building, and the warm early-September breeze rushing in snapped Emma back to the present. She turned from the painting and made her way down the hall to the staircase. She climbed to the top and then continued to the office at the end. She gave the plaque on the door a quick dust, her chest swelling with pride as she read the inscription.

PRESIDENT ALBERT DOYLE

Emma knocked.

A muffled voice from the other side barked, "Come in!"

She opened the door slowly and poked her head through.

The large brute of a man turned from his grand window overlooking the plant. His stern look quickly turned to a pleasant smile, and he rushed over to give Emma a light peck and then bury her in his arms. "Good morning, Mother."

"Good morning, my handsome son."

3

Charlie Bidwell threw his luggage into the overhead compartment above row 12 on his flight departing from Calgary. He looked back up the middle aisle for his wife, Margaret, who was busy taking her time apologizing to any passenger who had suffered a blow to the head from her oversized carry-on.

An amused smile broke out on his face. "C'mon, Marge." When they first started courting, these little inconveniences of hers brought his blood to a boil. But after thirty-five years, they had learned to cherish each other's quirks. He muscled her bag into the overhead storage. "God Almighty, Marge! I'm not sure what scares me more, the plane crashing or the overhead compartment failing on us."

She slapped his round belly. "Oh, hush, Charles!"

Charlie slid his way into the middle seat. He had learned to let his wife have her spot along the aisle. Even though the flight was just over an hour, she would surely visit the bathroom no less than three times.

Charlie looked over at the young man who had already taken the spot at the window. "Well, hello, young fella," he said, interrupting the boy's daydreaming. "My name's Charlie, but you can call me Charles or even Chuck if you'd like." He held out his hand.

The boy seemed quite timid at first, but one look into Charlie's friendly eyes and he happily accept his hand. "I'm Oliver—Oliver Hynes—but my friends call me Ollie."

Charlie sensed relief emanating from the boy, as though he had not related to another human for some time. He judged from Ollie's accent that he had already travelled some distance.

"Ah, is that a hint of Easterner I hear?"

Ollie blushed. "Yes, sir. Newfoundland." He lowered his head and turned away.

Charlie knew a lot of crude jokes were aimed at the Newfoundlanders who travelled out West. And they were easy to pick out with their accents. But Charlie wasn't so critical. The folk he'd crossed paths with all seemed like decent people. Some were hard workers and some not so much, but that was the same everywhere. He sympathized with anyone who left their home and travelled great distances to work in new environments. Took a lot of balls, in Charlie's mind. Usually Easterners travelled to Alberta in packs, but Ollie appeared to be alone. Charlie continued his effort to make the young man feel more comfortable; seemed he could use a break.

"Newfoundland, eh? I've never been out there myself, but I know a lot people from there and I hear it's beautiful. Love to visit some time—it's on the bucket list." He smiled as he arranged his full figure into his seat and buckled in. "Pity they can't get some more industry going out there so people wouldn't have to leave such a paradise to come work in the sludge out here. I'm guessing that's what brings you out this way, eh? The great and powerful oil sands. Gonna make your fortune?"

"Well, yes, sir. It's not all 'bout the money though. My gran's sick back home, see. She's got the Parkinson's, real bad. I've done all I can to help on my own since my mom passed, five years now. She was a good woman, my mom—hard workin'. I had to leave school, but I wasn't much good at it anyhow." He snorted a laugh. "I worked at whatever I could find through town—St. John's, where I'm from. She's been pretty well stuck in bed, Gran. Hasn't walked for a few years. But I sets her up in her wheelchair and take her out. She needs help with pretty near everything from bathing and getting dressed. But I was doing well by her till she got sicker." He leaned forward in his seat, rubbing his hands together anxiously. "But now the doc says she needs more than I can do, and she's needing money to get her better. Lots of treatments of sort. I hate leaving, but I gotta do everything I can. She's all I gots left for family."

The plane fell silent as the captain came on the intercom to announce departure.

Charlie leaned back while they taxied to the runway. Interesting that he would end up seated beside a young man in a somewhat similar situation to his own. At first impression he'd mistaken Ollie for a shallow young man in search of the good life, as was the intent of most guys his age heading for Fort Mac. But the reality of his predicament quickly shed the stereotype. Charlie looked over at the boy's bright-blue eyes and unkempt blond curls. He was dressed respectably in a plaid button-up shirt, which he'd tucked into blue jeans that were wearing thin at the knees. *A good-looking kid, but it's the small details that tell the truth*, Charlie thought as he looked down at the boy's scarred, callused hands with some slightly disfigured fingers. Ollie seemed old beyond his years, yet still full of innocence.

As the plane lifted off into a steep climb, Charlie realized Ollie had turned a sickly green shade, his fingers gripping both rests.

"You all right, son?"

"Pardon me, sir, but I don't travel too right by air." Ollie's lips drew tight and his cheeks ballooned.

"Oh shit! Hold on now, boy." Charlie frantically searched the pocket on the back of the seat until he found a complimentary travel bag. He quickly passed it to his new friend, who turned away while he made sure he got his money's worth from the bag.

"Is a good thing we met on this flight, sir. Not much left in the tank. Sorry to be of trouble." He lifted the bag to his mouth again and bent over, his body tightening and lurching as he heaved.

"Nonsense, son." He patted Ollie on the back as the plane levelled out. "What a horrible way for you to get across the country."

"Yes, sir, I agree. But it's the fastest."

Charlie turned to his wife and nudged her with his elbow. "Marge, you got something in your purse for this young man?"

She peered around him to the sick boy. "Oh dear! Yes, I'm sure I have something that'll help." She rummaged through her handbag, then handed a package of pink pills to Charlie. "Here, should fix him up good as new." She smiled.

Ollie quickly washed two of the pills down with a bottle of ginger ale he had brought along.

"Thank you kindly, ma'am." He smiled weakly. "You see now why I haven't made much friends so far."

"Nonsense, son, it's just a little air sickness. We all deal with it at some time." He continued rubbing the boy's back. "How you feeling now?"

Ollie took his hand away from his stomach and nodded, then fell back against his seat with a gasp. He turned to Charlie. "So, where you come from, sir?"

"Oh, well, we're moving up from Calgary to Fort Mac for the same reason as yourself. I guess, why would anyone go there otherwise?"

"Seems a bit odd, sir. Isn't there a pile of work around Calgary?"

"Yes, you're right about that. What happened, you see, is I was working for a division of Northern Lights Energy. You know, the big oil sands company?"

"Oh yes, of course I heard of them. They're one of the biggest, eh?" Ollie's excitement visibly grew, as if he realized he was sitting beside a man of greatness.

"Yes, right, they owned the small gas plant I worked at for over thirty years. Then another company bought them out. So I was given the option of taking a buyout package or moving to work in the oil sands plant for my remaining five years… We hope it's only five more years." He winked.

"Why wouldn't you just take the package?"

"That's the interesting thing, Ollie. It's seems we're kind of in the same boat." Charlie tilted forward and reached into his back pocket, then pulled out a wallet and removed a small photo to show Ollie. "See here, that there's my grandson, Summit." The big man smiled proudly.

Ollie raised an eyebrow.

"Yeah, the name's a little strange the first time you hear it. My son ran away to the BC coast when he graduated from high school. Turned into some type of almost hippie. Seems crazy, but I admire him in ways, when I look at all the amazing things he's done—climbed mountains, surfed big waves, and met a whole world of people. Then he fell in love with a beautiful woman, and they made a Summit." Charlie smiled. "He's a photographer and she's a writer, both still waiting for their big breaks, but they make a decent living. Then last year, our little Summit was diagnosed with a rare type of leukemia. They're basically self-employed, so the health care system will take them only so far, and we all want nothing but the best treatment for the little guy. They have a really good specialist out there in Vancouver. Northern Lights has some special project going on in Fort Mac where they could really use my help. Some kind of compressor project. So, when they presented me with the option, I accepted on the grounds that I could sign up Summit under my benefits package, which is one of the best offered by any company. They agreed, so here I am." Charlie filed the photo back into his wallet.

"I'm truly sorry to hear about your grandson, sir. I hope for the best for your family."

The conversation turned to a silence.

Eventually Charlie smiled, brushing aside the gloom that had settled. "So I guess we're both in on the same mission, hey, young feller? For the ones we love."

Ollie held up his bottle of ginger ale. "To the ones that matter!"

"So, do you have a job lined up, or a place to stay?"

"I have a place with my cousin's friend. Said he's got a cot he can set up for me and a job with a company. Not sure of the name. Something about running a disposal truck. Doesn't matter much as long as the money's there."

Charlie nodded. "Well, we wish you the best of luck."

4

In the same sky, headed for the same destination, was the smaller, sleeker, high-luxury company jet belonging to Northern Lights Energy.

Flying out of Las Vegas, the two lone passengers were heading north not to find their fortune but rather to settle into it.

The young woman was a native of Kelowna, British Columbia. Fresh out of college, she craved excitement in new surroundings and had found all that and more in the booming city of Calgary, Alberta. She pranced up and down the aisle of the jet, admiring all the pleasantries and twirling her butterfly-print sundress innocently. Her long, dark spiral of hair, which was complemented by four tightly-wound braids, draped silkily over her bare, finely sculpted and tanned shoulders.

Toward the back of the plane, a man admired his newly acquired fiancée's every flirtatious move while he sipped Scotch. His path had been laid out for him since birth. The only way to fail would be for him to choose to do so. But he despised his upbringing, wanting nothing more than to break through the mould. So he'd headed for Calgary as soon as he'd graduated from high school, attending university for no other reason than to keep his parents happy so they would continue to fund his lavish lifestyle. While he earned his bachelor's in business management, they set him up in a plush condo with a million-dollar view of the downtown skyline.

He took on a couple of roommates for entertainment purposes. The parties were wild and the booze, drugs, and woman plentiful. But the scantily dressed women were too easy, literally falling over with their legs in the air at the sight of his dark and chiselled features, steely demeanour, and promise of a lifetime of luxury. Like most, he appreciated a challenge.

And that's exactly what he found in the sultry young woman before him, Miss Vicky Bellham. They'd met down in Prince's Island Park on a hot summer afternoon the previous year. A band was playing while she lay reading a book on a blanket in the grass by herself—chest down, perched up on her elbows, a bikini top laid loose beneath her. Her breasts touched the ground just enough to hide her nipples, but the fullness of her could be witnessed from the side as he and his friends passed by. A semitransparent white dress hung to her mid-thigh, revealing not one line of anything beneath.

She giggled as they passed, and the sound teased his heart.

He grabbed a couple of beers from the cooler they were hauling. "I'm so going for this!" He turned back toward her, watching her legs tangle together playfully in the air.

He walked over and lightly brushed the frosted bottle against her golden back. She squealed softly and twitched, but not enough to reveal herself. She looked over her shoulder with a perfectly flirtatious smile and invited him to join her, but only after he helped secure her top. They drank, smoked a joint, and enjoyed the warm day. He'd never had eyes for another since.

He didn't have the time. It had been a long year since that day, with many wild adventures as he showed her the good life. In return, she taught him what it was like to have to work for something he wanted. The thrill of the chase. She was wild and beautiful, and she enjoyed attention from all her admirers, driving him mad with jealousy. But he could never quit her. She was an addiction like none other: a long powdered line of cocaine with a pinstripe of Viagra.

He had gone straight, convinced she was the only one for him. But Vicky continued on her path, doing whatever whenever she pleased, resulting in him waiting up late for her to return home or in him engaging in tussles at the bars with men who were trying to make their way with her. She was a seasoned player who had him wrapped around her finger, seemingly oblivious to any instigation on her part.

It was the last thing the young man wanted—to return home. He'd had dreams of travelling the world and tasting many exotic fruits, but now all he

wanted was her. And the best way to a woman's heart is with money and power...
so he was raised. Returning home would put him on the fast track for both. He
was one step closer to securing her now that she had accepted his proposal in
Vegas. The next steps were to surround her in comfort, then get her pregnant.
She needed a baby, some grounding. The games she played were to get him to
commit, so he would give her what she wanted.

His blood began to boil as he pictured his father welcoming him home with
open arms. And that name. How he cursed his parents for plaguing him with it.
Albert Doyle Jr. He'd shortened it to AJ when he went away to school, but surely
his father would be announcing him by his full birth name now that he was to be
a professional.

POP

AJ broke from his trance when a cork popped from a bottle of champagne,
which his bride-to-be was letting spill all over the floor in front of him.

"A-a-a-a-llllbe-rrrrt," she teased. Swivelling her hips from side to side, she
held an overflowing glass in one hand as her long eyelashes fluttered over her
captivating jade eyes.

"C'mon, Vic, don't call me that, you know I hate it."

"Oh, don't be such a shit. Besides, I think it's sexy, *Albert*." She bent at the
waist and ran a finger up the inside of his thigh, taking notice of his focus directly
down the top of her dress.

"Albert!" She slapped his leg and straightened, holding the neck of her dress
closed. She bit teasingly on her lip. "What were you looking at? You are a naughty,
naughty Albert. I'll have you know there's a lot more to me than my breasts!" She
giggled and turned around, placing her hands at her hips and then letting each of
her fingers take a turn hiking her dress up until her bare ass was right in his face.
"How about this, Albert? Do you like this too?" She smiled wickedly over her
shoulder, spread her legs slightly, and arched her back.

AJ swirled his drink and grinned from ear to ear.

"How about this, Albert?" She hooked a thumb in the side of her thong and
slowly pushed down. The silk string peeled away from between her taut cheeks
until she was bent fully over. "Do you like this?" She dropped her panties and
turned back around. "You know, Albert," she said, reaching down to his zipper,
"I've always wanted to join this certain club, sweetie, but you have to come with
me or they won't let me in." She pouted, then began tugging at his pants.

"Vic…Vicky!" He struggled to get away from her. "I'm pretty sure they have cameras on this thing."

She grabbed his hands and forced them back up over his head. Pinning him to the seat, she mounted him, looking famished. "C'mon, Albert, you know I don't like it when you play shy." She pulled up her dress and positioned herself on top of his rock-hard shaft, then thrust herself down around him, fully and instantly. She let go of a loud primitive moan as his glass fell to the floor.

5

Albert Sr.'s whole façade softened at the sweet sound of his mother's voice saying good morning. As great as he was in his own mind, there could be no other soul on earth as strong or wise as his mother. He knew the hardships she'd faced; she'd told him the tale many times when he was young: How she'd fallen madly in love with his father, a strong and honourable young man by the name of Francis Doyle who'd captured the eyes of all the ladies and yet chose her. How she'd gotten pregnant at a very young age, but his father had stood proudly by her. How he'd quit school and in short time taken charge of his own fishing boat. How he'd provided a good living for his young family until the fateful night he was caught at sea in a violent storm and fell to a watery grave. How, battered but not beaten, she'd packed up and made the long journey to Fort McMurray to provide for her son, the way his father would've wanted.

Whenever a young Albert had asked more about his father, his mother would break down in tears. Eventually, he quit asking. He'd never met the grandparents on his father's side because they'd exiled his father from the family after finding out about the pregnancy, saying his mother had destroyed what would've been their son's bright future. So, fuck 'em, Albert decided. He had only one picture of his old man, in which he was standing on a dock beside a huge trophy tuna. He was a large man, strong and gruff-looking. The no-bullshit type. That picture had a special place in Albert's office, overlooking the view of his empire. Though they had never met, Albert and his father had their private conversations from time to time. He was a hell of a man, his dad.

On nights in the small bedroom Albert had shared with his mother as a child, she would lie with him, caressing his hair and telling him about his brave father and how he would grow up to make them so very proud. And he had done just that. He'd gotten a job with Northern Lights at a young age, and the former president, George Kennedy, took him under his wing and groomed him for greatness. It seemed to be his destiny. Albert really had no other explanation for his good fortune. Some people were just built to succeed.

"Good morning, Mother," he replied. Releasing her from his strong embrace, he sighed heavily and turned back to watch the sun rise. "Guess who had a surprise announcement for me this morning, over the phone. It seems he proposed to this girl of his, this… Vicky, during their trip."

***

Emma glided to her son's side and placed a supportive hand on his shoulder. "Really? Well, what is this young lady like? Is she a good woman?"

Emma was frazzled at the suddenness of the news. They were her boys, and any woman wishing to be part of their life would need to gain her approval. AJ was a good-looking young man full of hormones and with power and money behind him. She had suffered many a sleepless night waiting for the announcement that some young floozy had trapped him. Temptation would knock at his door relentlessly. She didn't want the boy to fall victim like his father had. Sure, her daughter-in-law kept a good house and had provided a grandson, but she was otherwise useless. The Doyle men were nothing short of great, and they needed strong women who would not judge but rather accept and cater to them. Emma could never understand why Albert had never left his marriage, other than his strength of character. He was a good man, standing loyally beside the one he had vowed to love to the end. Was there such a thing as her doing too good a job of raising him? She reached up and brushed some lint from his dark suit jacket.

Emma had done well for herself over the years, financially, and could have been long retired. But what is a woman without purpose? Her job running the cleaning crew was a mindless task, but it allowed her to be there to provide Albert with strength and guidance.

"I don't know anything about her, Mother." Albert continued to stare out the window, arms crossed and stroking his chin. "Never been introduced. And AJ rarely speaks of her to me. I suspect they've been living together for some time."

Emma smiled. "Well, son, it's nothing we can't get through together. The good news is, he's finally coming home. If his young love proves troublesome, I'll be quick to get the reins on her. Don't worry, your mother has her ways." She turned him to face her and held him tight, patting him on the back.

RING RING

Albert hastened to his desk and picked up the receiver. "Yes, what is it?... What! Fuck me! Don't touch anything, I'm on my way!"

Emma watched her son's presidential instincts take over as he slipped into panic control.

"Get security to close the entrance gates! No one else is allowed on site, and no matter what, don't let any media reporters through!" He slammed down the phone. "Shit! Mother, there's been an accident, I gotta go!"

"What is it, son?"

He straightened himself as he looked in a full-length mirror. "I can't explain right now, I have to get down there." He stormed out of the room and slammed the door behind him.

6

As the plane touched down, the Bidwells shuffled around to gather their carry-on luggage, then followed the line to exit the aircraft. The terminal was small and crowded, making the gathering of the rest of their stuff from the baggage carousel enough of an adventure for Charlie to consider throwing his shit back on the plane and heading home to Calgary. With all the rumours about Fort Mac, few, if any, were positive. Crowded and undersized, none of the infrastructure was sufficient to support the boom. Immigrants from all over the world flocked there, crime was high, and bring your own woman 'cause the male-to-female ratio was ten to one.

Stepping outside, they were greeted by an unusually hot September sun and a landscape strikingly different from the southern prairies. Charlie smiled at the lush forest, closing his eyes and breathing in deeply. But it wasn't the fresh smell of a mountain forest. The strong scent of asphalt was filtering through the intertwined fingers of green leaves and branches. He wrinkled his nose and opened his eyes.

Marge had moved down the walk toward a man standing beside a limousine, holding a sign saying NORTHERN LIGHTS – BIDWELLS. She wasted no time wheeling her bag down to the smiling chauffeur. "Look, Charlie! They got us a limousine!"

Charlie hurried to catch up. "Yes, dear, that's great!"

While the driver heaved their bags into the trunk, Charlie looked back at the new friend he'd almost forgotten in the commotion.

MARC GREGORY

Ollie was pacing the walkway, talking to cab drivers. A large green military-like duffel bag hung heavy from one shoulder, and a backpack from the other.

Charlie turned to the driver. "Hey, listen, bud. Is it possible for us to give a ride to a young man I met on the plane?"

"Is he with Northern Lights?"

"Well, no, but he's a good kid. Just thought we could help him out. You know, give him a warm Fort McMurray welcome."

"I'm sorry, sir, but I can't take on any passengers that aren't for Northern Lights."

Charlie dug into his wallet and produced a twenty. "I'll toss a little something extra your way. C'mon, it's not as if we don't have the room. You don't tell, I don't tell." He moved his fingers along his lips in a zippering motion.

The driver looked at the bill. "*Pfft*, twenty bucks? This is Fort Mac, man, twenty bucks don't get you shit up here." He realigned his cap and accepted the bill. "Get him in here and let's go."

Charlie smiled as the driver folded the money. "Thanks, you're a good man. You're gonna donate some of that to charity, right?"

"Hey, thanks for the reminder. Charity's working the brass pole down at the club this week."

Charlie turned down the walk, muttering, "Cocky, smartass punk... Hey, Ollie!" He smiled when the boy looked over. "C'mon, son, we'll give you a ride."

Ollie trotted over, his eyes bulging when he saw the limo. "Oh wow! Really? You didn't have to do this for me, sir."

Charlie slapped him on the back. "Oh, it's not a problem at all." He heaved the boy's bag into the trunk and slammed the lid shut because the driver was neglecting his duties, even after the generous bribe. "There's more than enough room."

They filed into the back of the car to join Marge, then Charlie gave the driver the address Ollie handed to him and then fumbled with the button to raise the privacy glass. As the car pulled away, he busied himself by exploring all the luxuries of higher society. He was going to get his twenty bucks' worth. He opened the sunroof and the fully stocked fridge. He pulled out three glasses, then let the cork fire from a bottle of bubbly and toasted to their bright future in the land of opportunity.

Over the river and through the woods, Charlie took in the scenery and

21

found the landscape truly breathtaking. He'd heard all the negative stories of the mine areas. Never once in his memory had anyone described Fort McMurray as beautiful. Everything was so lush, so green, even the rivers flowed the colour of herbal tea. Then the woods opened up and the traffic grew thick as they headed through an industrial park. Paradise was theirs only for a moment. Dust and diesel fumes cloaked the car. Tires screeched and horns blared.

Through the traffic and down a hill into a valley, pockets of trees popped up on the roadside, and he caught glimpses of small shanty-like dwellings made of tarps and trickles of smoke from a smouldering campfire.

In the downtown area, the driver stopped in front of a small rundown house. The yard was unkempt, with an old rusted-up Chevy truck on blocks in the driveway.

Ollie grabbed his backpack. "I guess this is it."

Charlie sat stunned. What must it be like for this young man to travel so far from home and to have to live in that, with strangers? He would've liked to ask Ollie to come stay with them, but the house they were in was a company house, on loan to them until they could find something of their own, and the company had a strict policy on guests.

"Wait!" Charlie grabbed Ollie's bag and ripped back the top zipper. "Here, son, you take all this shit with you." He grabbed all the complimentary snacks and drinks from the fridge.

"Oh, sir, you's shouldn't."

"Nonsense, son, they can afford it. Now, you take care, you hear? Hopefully I'll see you out at site sometime."

Marge passed Ollie a slip of paper. "Here's our phone number, dear. If you should ever need anything, you give us a call, all right?"

Tears welled in Ollie's eyes and his jaw clenched. The boy reached over and gave Marge a hug, then shared a firm handshake with Charlie. "Your kindness reminds me of my gran back home. Thank you both, best of luck to you."

The driver knocked on the passenger's side window. "Hey, got a schedule to keep."

Ollie opened the door and gave one last goodbye, then climbed out.

The driver plopped his duffel bag onto the sidewalk. "Welcome to Fort Mac." He tipped his hat, then chuckled his way back into the driver's seat.

As the limo pulled away, Charlie watched Ollie make his way down the front walk to the house. A nervous tension built in his gut for what Fort McMurray had in store for the young man.

They drove back to the main drag and across the bridge over the Athabasca River to the north side of town. Up the hill and out of the valley, they entered a newly developed area and pulled into a gated community. The sign on the outside of the stone fence read Northern Lights Estates.

Charlie surveyed the world within the gates; the word *Estates* felt misleading. *Chicken Coops* would be a more accurate. The community consisted of townhouses stacked side by side with a small single-car garage on the bottom floor, then two equally small floors above. And stairs. Lots of stairs… Charlie hated stairs.

Maybe he'd been spoiled, but he liked his space. Their previous house in Calgary was on a half-acre, just inside the city limits. It wasn't the Ewing estate, but you couldn't smell the neighbour's breath either. He sulked at the thought of their house, their beautiful house. So many years, so many memories. They really hadn't wanted to sell it, but with their grandson in his situation, it was good to have some extra cash on hand. They'd been researching some highly specialized clinics in Europe. There wasn't anything they wouldn't do for him. Things had to start turning around soon. There was a point of no return for people like him. Charlie sniffed back a tear as he recalled the smell, the sound of family, and the welcoming creak in the floor of the entranceway. It was the exact same pitch his recliner made when he kicked back to relax.

This place! It looks like the house Harry Potter grew up in.

The driver dropped them off at number 34, unpacked their gear from the trunk, and handed them their keys.

The two Bidwells wheeled their bags up the step. Charlie jiggled the key in the deadbolt, then opened the door and lifted their things into the very small landing. He searched the wall until he found a light switch. The lights revealed the door to the garage to their right and a long, narrow stairwell directly ahead.

"Well"—he turned to his wife—"welcome home, dear."

7

After a smooth landing, AJ and Vicky were escorted off the plane by the captain, who couldn't take his eyes off Vicky. AJ believed it was something one had to deal with when he chose to enter a relationship with one of such physical beauty. He was still a little heated from his initiation into the mile-high club. He had little doubt that the whole episode was streamed to the pilots through the cabin surveillance equipment. His fiancée's careless attitude toward voyeurism was a turn-on in the heat of the moment, but after the package had been delivered, he always felt a strong sense of regret.

AJ and Vicky followed an attendant through the private wing of the airport to the waiting limo out front. AJ assisted his love into the back of the car while the driver helped the attendant load the luggage into the trunk.

AJ looked through the rear window to see the two blue-collars whispering and laughing. He couldn't help suspecting stories were being shared about their high-altitude romp.

"Baby, what's wrong?" Vicky asked, giddy with excitement. "Didn't I finish you off up there, tiger?" She leaned across the seat with a sexy growl as the car pulled away from the curb. "You still seem tense." She bit his bottom lip, looking seductively into his eyes. "Should we go another round? We can just make up our own club." She giggled and fell back into her seat, legs spread under her little sundress.

"You finished me just fine, sexy." He smiled and playfully slapped her legs shut. "I need something to drink." He searched the fridge. "What the!" He leaned back and hit the button to lower the privacy glass. "Driver, what the fuck is going on? There's nothing to drink?"

"Pardon, sir? The fridge is fully stocked with an assortment of beverages for your drinking pleasure."

"Oh really? Seems to me maybe you've been doing a little pleasure-drinking of your own, hey?"

The driver was stuck for words. "My apologies, sir. No, of course I would never drink on the job, sir. I'll fix this immediately." He made a short detour to the nearest liquor store.

While he was inside, a small group of young Indigenous boys gathered around the fancy car.

"What do they want?" Vicky asked nervously.

"Nothing, honey, they're just a bunch of Indian kids checking out the car."

It was the last straw when one of the boys pressed his face up against the tinted window to try to check out the interior. Vicky squealed and covered her cleavage.

AJ grasped the door handle and slowly pulled back the lever, then threw the door open with explosive force, sending the kid tripping backward onto his ass.

AJ jumped out of the car and made himself appear as big as possible. "Did you get a good look, you little shit?... Hey!" He stood over the boy with fists clenched. "Now fuck off!"

The boys scattered in all directions. Some laughed and turned back to flip him the finger.

The chauffer came out of the store with a bag of booze. "Yeah, get out of here, you kids!" Jogging carefully with the clinking cargo cradled in one arm, he waved his free arm as if shooing a flock of pesky gulls. "I'm so sorry about that, sir!" He laboured for breath. "Here, let me help you back into the car. I'll pour you some drinks. I'm just very sorry. These kids 'round here should be locked up!" He popped the cork in the parking lot, then filled a couple of champagne glasses for the VIPs and placed the remainder in a bucket of ice. "There you go, folks. Welcome to Fort Mac." He smiled.

"'Bout fucking time," AJ growled back. "Now get us the hell out of here before those kids come back and burn this car down. They scared the shit out of my fiancée, you know!"

PRICE PER BARREL

"Yes, of course, sir. Right away, sir." He closed the door.

The couple were also set up in company-provided housing, but not the gated chicken-coop community with the Bidwells—they were in the newly developed downtown condominium high-rise called Riverview Tower, compliments of the president.

The driver pulled into the underground parking garage, where they were met by a doorman with a trolley who escorted the passengers and their baggage to a private elevator containing only three buttons: lobby, parking garage, and penthouse suite.

The condo was beautiful, with expansive windows, a huge balcony, and a hot tub overlooking downtown and the river valley.

AJ thanked the baggage boy, then locked the door behind him. He turned and smiled at Vicky. "Well, what do you think? All compliments of the company."

"Oooh, this is beautiful." She ran around and explored every room." How long can we stay?"

"As long as we need. And look here"—he grabbed a set of keys with a Porsche emblem off a hook beside the door and held them out for her—"something for you to play in while I'm at work."

She snatched the keys from him, bouncing up and down. "Oh, AJ, this is all like a dream! Can you believe it's really happening?"

She ran out to the balcony while he examined the rest of the suite. When he returned to the main living area, she caught his attention through the window as she stood by the hot tub. She seductively slid her shoulder straps off one at a time, letting her dress fall to the deck.

He grinned.

8

Albert Doyle rushed to the site of the accident in his jet-black, company-issued Cadillac SUV. Along the dusty trail to the tank farm, the colossal, rusted bare-metal storage tanks that populated the area came into view.

When he arrived, the scene was chaos, with emergency vehicles clogging the access roads. He parked in the nearest available spot along the side and walked the rest of the way. The situation demanded his immediate attention.

He spotted the tall, gangly silhouette of the head supervisor against the morning sun and beelined straight for him.

The technology for building the tanks had been around for years and it was rare to have anything catastrophic go wrong, but this project was the first of its kind in some ways. And it was under heavy public scrutiny.

There was a lack of skilled labour in the area, and most contractors had refused the job due to the media flogging they would receive. So Albert had found a loophole in the labour regulations to allow a contract company to bring in Asian workers specifically for the construction, and then he hired a young company, Boreal Mechanical, who had just started up in the area and were looking for their big break. The deal was a win-win situation for Northern Lights because working through a third-party contractor would nullify them of any responsibility should something go wrong safety-wise. And with the contractor employing Asian workers, the bill would be less than half that compared to a contract utilizing domestic employees. It pissed him off tremendously that all these Canadian

PRICE PER BARREL

Union workers who were still trying to solve the marvel of Velcro expected to earn no less than six figures for basic labour positions.

"Bill, what the fuck is going on here?" Albert snorted at the man he had personally appointed to lead the team.

Bill Tisdale turned to Albert. His face was crusted with a dusted sweat, almost to the point of mud. He removed the hard hat from his head, revealing his long, scraggly silver hair, and produced a pack of cigarettes from his pocket. He knocked one loose against his hand, then placed it in his mouth and struck his fancy Zippo lighter against his leg.

"It's not good. Some of the supports for the top of one of the tanks failed. Emergency crews have counted twenty-two fatalities already. It's really hard for anyone to be down there right now."

The storage tank was massive, the diameter of its floating roof measuring over four hundred feet across. Made of heavy-gauge steel, it weighed hundreds of thousands of pounds. Northern Lights had done little to share procedures with the contract company because implementing their North American ways would've only inflated the cost and slowed down progress. They had accepted the low-dollar bid, made sure the vendor's safety standards were up to the required Canadian regulations on paper, and then wiped their hands clean.

The Asians had gone to work the only way they knew how: supporting the load with hundreds of wooden posts. Bill had approached the higher-ups with his safety concerns, only to find little interest, and then had watched the Asians' success and efficiency with much surprise. But really, it was only a matter of time.

"Fuck me!" Albert said as a team of paramedics wheeled past a gurney carrying a full body bag. He watched Bill's hand tremor frantically as he lifted the cigarette back to his crusted mouth. His complexion had turned a sickly white. "Any of our guys hurt?"

"No, not a one. I instructed all our people to stay the fuck away from here. Good thing too."

Albert nodded. "That clears us from any liability. Any reporters on the scene yet?"

"Not that I've seen. I told onsite security to lock this place down tight. But you know the world today, all these fucking smartphones and shit. Probably plastered all over YouTube already."

"Fucking internet." Albert rubbed his chin. "All right, here's how we'll play this. We can hold off the media for only so long, and we don't want to seem overly eager to hide anything; we have to keep our public-friendly appearance up. So send a guy to the gate to escort some of the local reporters to the scene. Only the local guys for now—give them first crack at it, make it appear like we support them. Let the photographers get all the pictures they want, snuggle up to them, treat them well, maybe order some food in. And throw everything at Boreal. I want the bus to run them over, then circle for another round. Say stuff like, 'they guaranteed us safety first'—all that shit, right!"

Bill turned his gaze back over the chaos and remained silent for a minute. He blew out a white cloud, then tapped the ashes to the ground. "Yeah, I know… all that shit."

Back at the office Albert wasted no time making a call to a local reporter. He couldn't stand the guy, but he kept his palm well greased for just such occasions.

"Nick, Albert Doyle here."

"Holy fuck, where the hell are you? Hiding somewhere, if you're smart. I'm down at the tank farm. This place is a media circus."

"Yeah, I know. Listen, I'm ready to make an official statement on behalf of Northern Lights Energy."

"Fuckin'eh, let me get my pen… All right, let her rip."

Albert cleared his throat. "The tank farm industrial accident today was a result of poor safety practices on the part of third-party contractor Boreal Mechanical. Northern Lights Energy was reassured by said contractor that the project would be carried out in a safe and timely manner despite the use of foreign workers. Northern Lights is disgusted with the lack of due diligence on the part of the contractor that resulted in several fatalities and injuries. As of today, Boreal Mechanical employees and equipment will be escorted off site and refused any further contracts. Northern Lights will also be looking to press charges against Boreal for criminal negligence."

"Holy fuck, going right for the throat, hey?"

"Oil sands work can be dirty. If you don't want to get any on you, go sell shoes. Just make sure we look clean, or no more box seats at the Oilers games."

"No more box! And the ladies?"

"If you're referring to the whores as ladies, then no."

"All right, you hard ass, I'll take her through the wash and spit shine her for ya."

"Good man." Albert hung up and leaned back in his chair. He had it handled as best anyone could. He thrived in these situations. Even so, the stress boiled him.

With a sudden surge of madness, he leaped from his chair, grabbed the monitor from his desk, and hurled it against the wall. He fell into his chair somewhat relieved, but he needed more. He pressed the intercom button on his phone.

His secretary answered. "Yes, Mr. Doyle?"

"Call for Mary-Ann to come to my office. I've got a bit of a mess here needs dealing with."

9

A tear of pride came to Emma's eye as she watched Mary-Ann Kibbnok, a young lady recently assigned to work under her. The girl reminded her of herself so many years ago. A beautiful Newfoundland girl relying on nothing more than hard work and determination to make it in the world.

As Mary-Ann hauled her cleaning supplies down the hallway, all the men turned their heads in unison to check her out. One attempted to stop her and strike up a conversation, but Mary-Ann politely brushed him off.

The scene took Emma back to the summer of '63 in her hometown of Corner Brook, Newfoundland, a small port city on the west coast of the island known as The Rock. At the age of fourteen, her newly blossomed body and long blonde hair created the allure of a real-life pin-up model. The boys flirted with her and she was ready to take an interest in them—a particularly strong interest in one Stephan Parsons and one Andrew Tucker. Stephan fit the tall, dark, and handsome persona and Andrew was the curly blond surfer type. At sixteen years old, they were the stars of the high school baseball team and were held in high respect by the citizens of the town.

They were voted most likely to get the hell off The Rock, and moving far away from her drunken, abusive family was something Emma dreamed of, more than anything else in life. So she played the tease, and they were quick to chase her bait. She came to their games and cheered them on, and they invited her to hang out afterward. Stephan was her first. She remembered that night on the beach.

They smoked a bit of marijuana and shared the six-pack Andrew had snuck from his old man's fridge. Stephan assured her Andrew was passed out as he lifted her dress and slid her panties down and off her ankles. It was such a magical night, and she felt one step closer to escaping from her hell with her white knight.

Emma blinked and brought her mind back to the present. Mary-Ann was a good girl, and Emma wanted to give her a chance in the world. So she had given the least demeaning tasks to the girl, like cleaning managerial offices rather than tradesmen washrooms. Mary-Ann had performed the tasks assigned to her with incredible thoroughness, actually removing entrance mats and desk items to sweep and dust under them. After several positive comments from the managers, Emma, for the first time in her life, had stepped aside and handed off her only remaining personal cleaning task to the young woman: tending to the office of her son, the company president. Emma herself had escorted Mary-Ann up to the presidential palace six months earlier. Albert was a good man. He recognized hard work, and she had known that after he got a look at the girl, he would do right by her by getting her on permanently at Northern Lights, with full benefits and pension.

"Oh, Ms. Doyle, I'm very nervous. I'm much more comfortable back in the managerial offices. I'm not sure I'm ready for this?"

Emma had smirked. *"Nonsense, my dear, you'll be fine. Just do what you normally do. If I didn't feel you were ready, I wouldn't give you the job."*

She had stopped Mary-Ann before the grand double doors leading to the office.

"Remember, we always show respect to the president before entering by polishing the nameplate." She had taken a small dust rag from her apron pocket and rubbed lightly at a smudge on the placard. Then she had turned to Mary-Ann and held her in her arms. She felt the tremors of nerves in the girl`s body.

***

To many, cleaning the office of a company president would seem demeaning, but Mary-Ann wasn't stupid. What stood before her wasn't just a dirty office, but a chance to fulfill her dream of a life of security through money and benefits for her mother and disabled father.

She had hoped Emma would stay with her and supervise her work, but she had simply led her inside, then turned and left the room, closing the door behind her.

Alone, Mary-Ann had taken a moment to admire the lifestyle of presidency. The wall directly across from the entrance consisted of floor-to-ceiling windows. A large darkly stained desk sat in the middle of the room. Numerous mounted hunting trophies hung from walls or stood on stands throughout the room, and a stuffed wolf stood tall in one corner. On the desk sat some pictures of the president enjoying times with other men in suits and ties, and another hunting photo of himself squatting beside a giant boar while shaking hands with a smiling Latino gentleman. She looked up from the photo and scanned the room. She saw fish, deer, and a moose, but found no stuffed animation of the beast.

Her curiosity fed, she had returned her focus to her task. She would do her best job as quickly as possible; being in the room alone gave her the jitters, and she had no desire to meet the president.

***

As Mary-Ann cleaned his office for the first time, Albert returned from the field, where he'd had a rough, hot morning of playing tour guide to some Middle Eastern investors. Nothing pissed him off more than having to ride around with a couple of camel jockeys. Just being around them and having to listen to their gibbering, terrorist banter was enough to add a spot for them on his trophy wall. He stopped at his office door and chuckled at the idea, then wiped the sweat from his brow and threw open the door.

Oh my! What's this little treat?

He was accustomed to walking in on his elderly mother cleaning his office, but to his surprise, bent at the waist before him, dusting his desk, was a firm, round bum.

He cleared his throat.

"Oh!" The tight ass jumped and turned, and the pleasant behind transformed into a set of large breasts. "My... s-sir!" she stuttered. "I wasn't expecting you to—"

Albert gave a confident and nurturing smile. "Easy now, miss." He lightly grasped her hand, turning it over top of his in a submissive gesture. "It's perfectly all right, I'm just as surprised as you. It's usually Ms. Doyle who cleans my office." He smiled tenderly.

"No— yes— I mean, yes, sir. I realize... but today she brought me up to clean your office. I don't know why, I didn't ask."

Albert chuckled sweetly and patted her hand. "Calm your nerves, my dear.

If Ms. Doyle assigned the chore to you, that says something. Please don't let my presence disturb you, just continue on with your business."

"No, Mr. President. I mean... I'm finished."

"Well, you don't have to run off so fast, calm down and have a seat."

"Thank you, sir. That's very nice of you, but I really must get going and report back to Ms. Doyle, sir." She backed slowly toward the exit, then bowed nervously before drawing both doors closed behind her.

Albert smiled as the beautiful young flower left. Physically, she was perfect for the job. Like a servant brought before her king for the first time. A good young woman brought up the proper way, learning how to take care of her man. He gave thanks to his mother silently in his mind.

He had scanned the office and found not a smudge or spot of dirt. Then he had done a more thorough inspection, lifting things off his desk and looking for telltale cobwebs on his trophies. Nothing, not a speck—even the teeth of his wolf seemed to sparkle. A good beginning to a very promising relationship.

***

In a week's time, Mary-Ann had become the only cleaning personnel, aside from Emma, who was a direct employee of the company.

"You're something special to be given a permanent position with Northern Lights, m'dear," her mother had said, wiping away tears. Her father, disabled by a hip injury after a fall on an oil sands job years ago grasped her hands. *"We have it made now, so mind your manners and do as you're told."*

She was given a supervisory position over the other contractors and relieved of all her cleaning duties, except for one—the presidential office. That job had been permanently handed over from Emma to Mary-Ann at the request of the president himself. She was to do a thorough cleaning every morning before he arrived, and be at his beck and call for anything that came up during the day.

On the first morning in her new position, Mary-Ann was just finishing up when she heard a soft creak from the door. She turned to see Mr. Doyle smiling gently at her.

"Well, good morning, young lady. It's nice to have you back. I hope the company bullshit didn't bore you too much?"

Mary-Ann was surprised to hear him refer to the company orientation as bullshit. "No, sir, I found it all very interesting, actually."

He chuckled. "Mary-Ann, so young and innocent to the world. I suppose if you've never been subjected to it before, it may seem exciting. I can't remember how I felt the first time."

"Yes, sir, I suppose it was a while back for you." She headed toward the door. "I apologize if I missed anything this morning. I was rushed slightly as I didn't get my assignment till just before you were due to arrive. I'll do better from this point on." She smiled politely.

Mr. Doyle closed the door and walked toward his desk. As he passed by her, he took her hand gently. "Please don't rush off on my account. You're one of us now. Time for you to relax and enjoy working life a little, you've earned it."

He led her to a chair across from his desk and motioned for her to sit, then went to his small personal bar and poured himself a Scotch. He moved to the window and loosened the tie from his neck. "Traffic was hell this morning." He looked back at her and smiled, then motioned her to his side. "C'mon over and have a look at the plant. It's quite the view here. Keeps me motivated. Reminds me of why we're all here devoting our time and energy."

Mary-Ann did as instructed. In all the time she'd spent in the office, she'd never taken a moment to have an honest look out the window.

"It's the best view of the plant from any point. I had them relocate the office building here after I stumbled upon this view during one of my helicopter tours." Mr. Doyle placed one arm over her shoulders and waved the other arm across the landscape. "Look at this, Mary-Ann! We're literally changing the face of the planet."

She kept up her polite smile and remained silent. She figured if the president of the company that employed her wanted to brag a little, best just to let him go on.

"You know," he said, "a lot of people think being the president is the best job in the world. But the reality is, the position is very demanding, almost suffocating." He grinned, then slid his arm from her shoulders and moved behind her, lightly pressing his round belly against her back. He continued his soliloquy.

"All those people—literally thousands of people—depend on me every day for their jobs. To put food on the table and a roof over the heads of their families. Millions of barrels of oil a day pass through this facility to power the world.

"I'm aware they all think my job is just private jets and dinner parties. But the truth is, not just anyone can do this job. It takes a man of special ability, of certain character. This position would crush a lesser man and spit him out like a piece of chewed meat. But I'll admit to you that I can't do it all by myself. I have to be careful and handpick the people I keep by my side, in close confidence. We take care of each other here in the company. People take care of me, and I take care of them. That's why when I came into the office that first morning we met and saw what an incredible and caring touch you took in cleaning my office— well, I knew if I could help you out and solidify your future, then you would surely return that kind gesture to me."

His hand slid around her waist to rest gently on her stomach, and a sharp chill shivered down her spine. Like a giant bear, his paw spanned from her waistline to just under her breast. His warm stomach pressed hard to her back, then he leaned back, and the tinkling of ice on glass signalled that he had set down his drink.

He spun her around and she looked up, surprised, into his round face, where a devilishly sweet smile lingered.

"Isn't that right, Mary-Ann? I take care of you and your family, and you'll take care of me and play a key part in running this empire." He wrapped both his arms around her and pulled her snuggly to him, her eyes barely reaching the level of his chest.

He pushed her gently back. She felt the edge of the desk press up just below her buttocks.

What was happening? All of it so fast. What was he asking of her? She'd never fathomed anything like this ever happening to her, especially with the president of the company. Could she stop him? Would it be right to stop him? What would be the consequence?

Mr. Doyle's excitement grew visibly when she offered little resistance while her thoughts whirled. He must have read it as permission because he reached down and untied her apron, then slid his hands up to her breasts and transfixed her with his powerful gaze.

"Be a good girl for me, Mary-Ann." He pushed her lightly back.

Maintaining eye contact, she slowly fell back to rest her head on the desk, paralyzed with uncertainty.

She heard her father's voice. *Just do as you're told.* Saw her mother's tears of joy. Visions of her bright future raced in her mind. To cry out would crush it all. What chance would a young Newfie girl have against the political brilliance of a company president? Maybe it was wrong, or maybe it really was the way these things were?

MARC GREGORY

So fast… his breathing grew nasal, his eyes began to bulge. Lifting her dress, he pulled her panties down and let them fall to the floor.

Her once-proud president of prestige and dignity now grovelled before her, fumbling with his pants while holding her in place with one paw. He grinned selfishly at her, and suddenly all she could see were his stained yellow teeth, the wrinkles bordering his flushed chubby cheeks, and the thick dark curls of his nose hairs wrapping around the rims of his nostrils. He had transformed before her from a man of greatness into… into a pig! A big, disgusting, snorting pig!

She cringed in horror at the beast over top of her, and her instinct to fly kicked in. But it was a moment too late. As she heard the finality of a lowered zipper, he grabbed her waist and she struggled and pushed on his forearms to free herself. The chase clearly fuelled his fire and he pounced on top of her, overpowering her with ease. She felt like a rabbit in the clutches of a lion as he thrust into her with a wicked groan.

She squealed and squirmed but the damage was done. Someone she had trusted had stripped away the sacred gift she'd been saving for the white knight who would one day ride into her life. She placed her open palms over her face and burst into tears. Her body heaved as she struggled for breath between sobs. She could close her eyes and erase the vision, but the worst of it was the sound—the grunting and snorting… and the feeling.

Minutes passed like hours, and she fell into limp shock on top of the desk. She turned her head to the side so she didn't have to look at him. In her line of sight she found another who had made the ultimate sacrifice to this inhumane creature: a full-sized pitch-black wolf on display for Mr. Doyle's entertainment. She could see his soul in those eyes. She could feel his anxiousness. His mouth hung open with bared teeth. The wolf could see all and hear all and he wanted to end her pain, and end him. The wolf would make him pay. Somehow, someway, he would pay.

Mary-Ann managed, through the tragedy, through all the tears, to conjure a slight smile for her new friend. *Thank you, wolf, you are very beautiful.*

***

I am a god! Albert thought, praising himself.

The first thrust was euphoric, especially because she decided to struggle at the last moment. He pinned her down and pushed inside her. She didn't have the power, he had the power—all the power; they would sacrifice for him… all

37

of them. He lifted his gaze from Mary-Ann. Standing tall, he looked over the landscape, at the machines and people picking away at the land. Then he looked down again to see the blood of her innocence flow from her, down onto him. The smell of her hit his nostrils, and like a pack of hyenas in a feeding, he ground into her with all his mass. She had become his latest and most prized trophy.

When the adrenaline rush passed, Albert felt the crash coming. Besides, his prey had stopped crying and squirming and so the hunt had dulled.

He pulled out and grabbed some tissues from a box on his desk to wipe up a bit before yanking up his pants.

He helped Mary-Ann up to a sitting position and kissed her lightly on the forehead, then smiled again. "Thank you, Mary-Ann. You've been very good to me and I'll ensure there's a special bonus in your paycheque. Now, we have a bit of a mess here, I see. You maybe should've said something about your experience, or lack of. But it was an honour to be that man for you. Here, tie this shirt around your waist, then go home and take the rest of the day off. I'll tell Mother you took ill." He put a hand on her shoulder and smiled into her tear-stained eyes. "I'll take care of you, Mary-Ann. We'll take care of each other." He winked before he disappeared into his private washroom.

10

Ollie Hynes paced around his lunch box, which sat on the curb in front of the house he'd stayed in the night before. The tension of all the unknowns was weighing on him as he waited for the truck he was told would pick him up at the dark-morning hour.

He grasped the small cross hanging from a chain around his neck—a keepsake, passed to him by his deceased mother. He repeated to himself, "Stay strong, Ollie, you can do this. Do it for your mom, do it for your gran."

He heard a screech, a low growl, and a few sputters, then around the corner came a red late-eighties crew cab truck, which pulled to a stop directly in front of Ollie. Out the driver's window hung a hand, attached to a smouldering cigar. The operator poked his head through the smog.

"You Oliver Hynes?" The voice was gruff.

Ollie nodded.

The driver looked him up and down. "Well, you ain't much to look at, but we're in a pinch, so I guess you'll do." He broke into a grin. "Name's Red!" He switched the cigar over to his other hand and reached for Ollie.

Ollie shook the man's hand.

"They call me Red because I had red hair." He lifted his cap to reveal a bald head. "It ain't so red anymore, it just ain't. Hop in the back seat, kid, time's a wastin'."

Ollie grabbed his lunch box and hopped in the rear door. Two other men were inside. The guy beside Ollie looked Native, and Ollie could tell he was a large man by the way he took up space. He looked Ollie over with a hint of suspicion, then offered his hand.

"Ken Lakefield." The accent confirmed his heritage.

Ollie nodded politely and accepted his hand. It looked like an adult shaking the hand of a newborn.

The man up in the passenger's seat turned around to face Ollie. He was a slender old man, with long grey hair tied back in a ponytail and a large bushy moustache. He had a weathered look but seemed high-strung, as if sitting still in the truck was a challenge. Judging from the oversized go-mug he was holding, Ollie guessed it was due to an early-morning caffeine buzz.

"Name's Neil Abbott, but the guys call me Honey." He winked and offered his hand.

Ollie shook the man's hand. "Nice to meet you. I'm Oliver Hynes, but my friends call me Ollie."

Red barked out, "Hear that, Kenny? That's three Newfies to one Indian now. Mind ya, it takes three of us to match one of you big fuckers, but we're gaining." He laughed.

Red weaved the truck through town as the sun peeked over the horizon and cast a faint glow over the landscape. They pulled onto the highway, heading north. Ollie peered out the window at the traffic-clogged artery. Lines of cars streamed down from the surrounding valley hills of the town, all trying to wedge into a spot on the two-lane highway. It was complete madness.

Red took the time to bring Ollie up to speed. "So, Ollie, welcome to the East Rock Disposal crew. Your cousin didn't really explain much about you, just that you're a hard-working kid. The fact that you were ready and waiting and look decently sober is a good start."

"Yes, sir, thank you, sir. I'm not sure what all you're going to have me do, but I'm a hard worker and I learn fast!"

"Sounds real good, son, but let me fill you in on what we do before you go getting too high on yourself. You ever work a disposal truck before?"

"Well, no, I've not done that, but I'll do my best!"

"Easy, kid, you'll get your chance. Anyway, we run suck trucks—big trucks with waste water tanks on the back, with pumps and hoses. Our crew's based at the Northern Lights Energy plant. We take wastewater from tanks and then pump them into the tailings ponds. Really, it's simple: hook up the hose, fill the tank, drive the truck to the pond, and dump it. There can be nasty chemicals and radioactive material in some of that waste, so you have to protect yourself—we have procedures you gots to follow. Us seasoned guys here live by the "What you don't know can't hurt you" policy. We prefer not to know. Then there's Honey here. He's on the special-ops crew. But his workload's been increasing a lot. He needs a hand, and that's where you'll fill in. Honey's in charge of draining all the septic tanks on site, a.k.a. the 'honey' tanks." Red laughed. "I think they have over a hundred of them on site, hey, Honey?"

"Hundred and three, boss—and counting." Honey winked at the boy and gave him a yellow-toothed smile.

"Ha ha, yeah, a hundred and three. He starts at one end of the plant and works to the other. Takes about a week. By the time he completes the round, he's ready to start all over. It's the most demanding position we have—the big boys on site can get mighty grumpy when they can't do their morning business."

"That's right," Honey cut in. "No better way to start the morning than with a strong cup of coffee and a good ass-chewing from some big shot caught with his pants around his ankles." He laughed hysterically, then began coughing up a well-abused lung.

Ollie grew nervous as he looked out the window at the heavy stream of traffic on the 63 highway. It was like nothing he'd seen before. As they drove up a hill that climbed from town up to the sites, Kenny explained that the legendary stretch of road known to the locals as "Super Test" had claimed countless lives, mostly in the dark, slippery winter months.

"Today'll be your trial," Red said, changing the subject. "We'll start you at twenty-five bucks an hour. Anything over eight hours is time and a half, and anything over ten hours is double time. Weekends are all double, and stat holidays are triple. What do you say, boy?"

Ollie's eyes bulged and his hand shot up to grasp the cross on his neck. The base wage alone was more than triple what he'd ever gotten in his life. He'd suck shit for that. *For you, Gran.* "Yes, sir, I won't let you down. I don't even need breaks or nothing, you'll see."

"Ha! That's a good Newfie boy for ya. Well, son, in a couple hours we'll see if you can walk your talk."

11

Early the next morning, Emma waited patiently with Albert in his office for her grandson to arrive. She hadn't seen him since last Christmas, and it brought her extreme joy to have him finally come to his senses and return home to follow in his father's footsteps.

A knock at the door, and Emma rushed to open it. She peered through first, then threw it aside and embraced him. "Oh my darling, it's so good to see you!" She held him back by the shoulders to have a full look at him. He had lost his proper military brush cut, letting it grow out to a shaggy length; this was no doubt due to the influence of that she-devil who had cast her spell over him. Emma would see to her soon enough. She and Albert would have her loving grandson shipshape and walking a straight line again in no time.

Emma turned to the desk, still holding AJ in her arms. "Albert, look who has finally come home to his roots."

She turned to look at her grandson again. His smile seemed forced.

"AJ, my boy!" Albert thundered across the office. "Welcome home, son. C'mon in and have a seat."

"Yes, my dear, have a seat." Emma guided him across the room. "Now, dear, can Grandma get you a drink, hmm? Maybe a juice or, I guess since you're an adult, maybe you prefer coffee?"

AJ rolled his eyes.

"Now, Mother, let the boy be. He's a man now. A man of industry. And this is a celebration, he deserves a man's drink." Albert winked at his son, then headed to the bar. He filled two snifters and delivered one to AJ. The two men tapped glasses and took a sip. "Welcome home, son." Albert gave a welcoming smile as he reached down and ruffled his son's hair like the old days.

Emma frowned at the early-morning drinking, but she would never question her son's judgement.

Albert turned to her. "Now, Mother, I know you're excited to see AJ, but we have business to attend to this morning. Another new recruit should be along anytime to accompany us. It wouldn't look too professional to have you here fussing over the boy, so if you'd please." He motioned toward the door.

Emma smirked. "Yes, of course. I'll leave you two boys to get some work done." She looked down at her grandson. Hardly able to contain her happiness, she leaned down and squished his cheeks between her hands, then planted a big kiss on his lips. "Oh my darling, I'm thrilled to have you back home!"

She started toward the door but then turned back. "Oh, and we are all going for supper tonight, right? Is your lady friend around the condo today? What was her name again?"

"Vicky. Victoria. But she's probably still getting comfortable, so maybe just leave her for today, Grandma. You'll get to meet her at supper tonight."

"Oh, nonsense. Nothing wrong with your dear grandma stopping by to welcome her. We'll have some time to bond—you know, girl talk." She shot him a sly wink before she closed the door behind her.

12

That morning, after a long, crowded bus ride to the plant and getting through all the security hubbub at the gate, Charlie headed up to the top floor of the administration building to fulfill his special instructions to check in at the president's office. Seemed strange to Charlie that he was to report directly to the president, but following instructions was what got him through life.

Escorted to the door by the secretary, he knocked politely and was quickly invited in by a deep yet cheerful voice on the other side.

Charlie peeked his head inside the room. The man he guessed to be the president was standing beside his desk, dressed in a dark suit. Another man stood beside him, younger and dressed in a golf shirt and khakis. Charlie cleared his throat. "Mr. Doyle, sir? I'm Charles Bidwell, reporting for work here today. I'm not sure I received the right instructions, but I was told to report to your office, sir."

"Yes, of course." The older man rushed over to shake Charlie's hand. "Charles—or do you prefer Charlie?—you got the instructions right. Come in, please, I wanted you two to meet here before I take you on a tour of the site. And please, call me Albert."

Albert led Charlie over to the desk. "This is my son, Albert Jr. He's just returned home to work side by side with his old man. If you couldn't already tell, this is an exciting day for me. Son, Charlie comes to us recommended by an old friend from one of the plants down south that recently shut down. I'm told if we have anything mechanical up here, this is the man we want working on it."

Albert Jr. shook his hand. "Call me AJ."

Albert continued, "I've recruited the two of you to work together on our newest, most exciting project, which we call 11-16." He leaned against the desk with his arms crossed beneath a boisterous smile. He turned to Charlie. "AJ here has just completed his bachelor's degree in mechanical engineering, so he has the book smarts but is still green to the industry. That's where you come in. Teach him the ways and get this thing operational with as few issues as possible. The scheduled start-up date isn't pinpointed yet, but we're looking to the spring."

The conversation paused, then Charlie said, "Well, that all sounds great... So, what is it we're putting together?"

Albert laughed and slapped a meaty paw on Charlie's shoulder. "Why don't I fill you both in on the way over to the project?"

The three men filed down to Doyle's parking spot. Charlie couldn't believe the vehicle before him belonged to a grown man, let alone a high-profile company president. The jet-black Cadillac Escalade appeared to be lifted slightly with oversized rims wrapped in low-profile rubber. The windows were fully tinted, like in a New Age gangster film.

Charlie hopped in the back row, while AJ took shotgun. Albert fired up the unit and Johnny Cash burst to life, almost blowing the windows out. He reached out quickly and turned it down. "Ah, shit! Sorry about that, guys. It's a long solo ride in the mornings." He chuckled.

Charlie sighed heavily and buckled his seat belt as they pulled out. He'd seen enough already that morning to make him contemplate calling it quits. He was at the twilight of his long career, and there he was, riding with a company president in the height of a mid-life crisis and his snot-nosed engineer son, who Charlie would no doubt be working under. These were the years when he should be relaxing and counting down the days until the end. Not babysitting some junior man he'd help catapult to the top of the corporate food chain, with no more reward than a pat on the back. He struggled to pull his wallet from his back pocket. Marge had given him a pep talk that morning before he headed out, stressing why he was doing it, and he needed another reminder. He opened the wallet and extracted a small black-and-white picture taken in a West Edmonton Mall photo booth. A picture of him with his grandson sitting on his knee.

It was taken shortly after a long bout of radiation treatment that had left

45

the child all but dead. Although the mall was Summit's most favourite place, Charlie had been reluctant to go because of the boy's condition. He was so pale, not one string of hair remained on his head, and any meat on his bones had been melted off. But Grandma and Grandpa had come to the rescue and given his parents a much-needed rest. They'd bought him some stylish new clothes and a pair of those fast-looking running shoes that lit up with every step. Then Grandpa had bought him the most specialist present: a new Edmonton Eskimos ball cap, which was the child's favourite team for no other reason than that he liked West Edmonton Mall.

Charlie couldn't take being in the hospital anymore. Watching every day as the doctors and all the educated types sucked the life out of his grandson. How did they know better than everyone else? Maybe he just needed to go outside, play ball, have some ice cream, and… just be a little boy? So as soon as the treatment ended, Charlie and Marge grabbed him and got him the hell out of there. Took him to a place where he could forget, if only for a moment. Every day they were away, Charlie watched life return in the boy. His colour came back and even some stubble began to poke through on his precious little head. Charlie was getting his grandson back.

Charlie caressed the edge of the photo capturing that moment. That moment with Summit wearing the ball cap Grandpa had bought special for him and the two of them pulling their silliest of faces. That feeling of the fragile little miracle in his strong arms and the hope that if he could hold him tight enough, maybe, just maybe, he could take on all the suffering and battle the sickness in his place.

At Summit's next checkup, the specialist regrettably announced that they were unable to get all the cancer and the boy would have to endure another round of treatment. The news all but killed Charlie.

He put the picture back in his wallet before the waterworks began and lifted his gaze to the filthy industry passing by. He'd shovel that whole fucking mine by hand for the rest of his days if that's what it took.

Focused, Charlie put the wallet in his back pocket and turned his attention to Doyle and AJ as they crossed the mammoth bridge spanning the great Athabasca River to the mining area. The area was massive, the land stripped bare of what had once been beautiful forest as far as the eye could see. In its place were deep, man-carved canyons and piles of bleach-white sand.

Arrogance boomed through Albert's voice. "Here it is, gentlemen, the mining area. Roughly one million tons of land removed to make half a million barrels of black gold, daily." He delivered a playful shot to AJ's arm. "You can smell the money!"

Thundering up over the ridge ahead came a giant yellow truck like nothing Charlie had seen before. Gargantuan… Jurassic… A key component in the mass destruction. Despite its size, the truck moved with incredible speed. "Oh god, Mr. Doyle"— Charlie reached up and grabbed Albert's shoulder—"look out!"

Albert laughed. "Yeah, they can come up on you fast." He pulled calmly to the right. "That, my friend, is the Caterpillar 797 dump truck. We have over fifty in our fleet and are looking to add another twenty next year. Each one of those things can move four hundred tons of earth per load and clip along at about sixty kilometres an hour while fully loaded."

Charlie watched, slack-jawed, as the behemoth rolled by.

"Those tires are just shy of eleven feet tall," Albert continued, "and weigh ten thousand pounds a piece! It takes thirty-four hundred horsepower to move all that. We could rip down the mountain of Mordor in a twelve-hour shift."

The likening of the raping of the land to the Lord of the Rings trilogy painted an evil image in Charlie's mind. He imagined mindless herds of disfigured orcs and giant trolls ripping at Mount Doom and filling the backs of big yellow trucks. He pictured Albert and the dark lord Sauron shaking hands over a bottle of Scotch and a couple of Cuban cigars. Then Sauron left with his suitcase full of cash to retire on his new oceanfront property in the Cayman Islands, and Albert ruled over his newly acquired demonic crew. Within a day the mountain was flattened, then the earth was sold as fuel to the highest bidder and a casino was erected in its place. The once-powerful One-ring-to-rule-them-all now found a permanent spot on Albert's office trophy wall, beside the stuffed pheasant.

Charlie leaned back and looked at AJ, who clearly had little interest in what was happening because his head was down and he was tapping away on his mobile device. But Charlie supposed that having the president for a father probably had gained him access to many a father-and-son plant tour.

As they crested the hill, a large toxic-looking body of water opened up before them—as large as any fresh body of water back home. He had no doubt what it was the minute he laid eyes on it: the toxic soup that had filled many front-page headlines for killing thousands of migrating birds every year.

Albert pointed to the sludge. "And there's the largest tailings pond in the world. It's where all the waste from our production is dumped. It's actually an old pit from one of our earlier mines, hundreds of feet deep in some areas. We had to construct the world's largest dyke to contain it. It can been seen from space—no bullshit!"

Charlie watched the noxious fumes radiate off the surface and understood what all the controversy was about.

Albert chuckled. "Even I can't sit here and sell that thing to you two. It's fucking disgusting! God knows what's floating around in there. Sometimes I drive by that thing in the winter at minus fifteen and it's frozen solid. Then I'll drive by it again the next week at minus thirty and it's fluid again. Any bird stupid enough to land in that shit deserves to die. Theory of natural selection, I say."

As they drove, the mining equipment began to disappear and the devil's bath turned back to dirt. Soon they were surrounded by the beautiful, lush forest once again.

13

Albert braked hard, causing Charlie to focus out front, where half a dozen pickup trucks were pulled off to the side of the road.

"What the fuck is it now?" Albert rolled down the window and called to a guy standing by one of the trucks.

"Some Native is blocking the road, sir. The Native relations guy is up there dealing with it."

Albert grunted. "Fuck me. All right, thank you, son." He rolled up his window and slowly moved up through traffic, honking his horn to clear the path. "Fucking Indians. Give them a billion dollars and they piss it away on smokes and booze, then a week later they're back blocking our fucking road! Waste of fucking air, they are." Reaching the obstruction, he threw the SUV into park and hopped out.

Up ahead, an Indigenous man was perched high upon a beautiful painted horse. He wore a great headdress and traditional clothing. Judging by his attire, Charlie figured him to be one of the leaders, an Elder or maybe a chieftain. Standing next to the horse, wearing slacks, a leather jacket, and a white hard hat, was the one Charlie figured to be the relations guy. As Albert marched up to them with his hands on his hips, Charlie rolled down his window, hoping to catch some of the conversation.

"What the fuck's going on here, Mark?"

He sighed. "I don't know, I thought my Indigenous dialect was pretty up to date, but this one's speaking in some ancient tongue. Best I can make out is, he's saying something about the forest speaking to him. I've tried to reason with him the best I can, but he just sits there and stares at me like I'm an idiot."

"For fuck's sake, haven't I taught you anything yet? The best way to reason with these savages is with a bottle of whiskey and a carton of smokes; don't ever leave your office without them!"

Charlie peered at AJ, who still had no interest in anything and hadn't said a word to anyone through the entire trip. Seemed as though he was going to be a fun guy to work with.

"What's the problem here, Chief?" Charlie heard Albert say.

The man sat silently on his horse, staring down at Albert.

"We've got a business to run here, Tonto. Your people got their money. This land is legally ours and you have no right to be blocking our road."

The man continued his silence.

"What?" Albert said, his tone betraying his frustration. "You don't speaka no English, eh? Move along, Little Big Horn! We have no smokes or hooch for you today."

When he received no reply, Albert stepped up right beside the steed, looked up at the man, and lowered his voice so neither Charlie nor the people now gathered around could pick up what he was saying.

***

Albert glared up at the chieftain, displeased to be in a position where he was forced to look up at anyone. He gripped the man's ankle and lowered his voice to that of a sinister threat.

"Now you listen to me, you fucking mooch! This can be a dangerous place for a man who doesn't know any better. Accidents happen here every day. I strongly suggest you move off this fucking road, or I'll make you disappear and grind that pretty pony of yours up for dog food."

Albert could tell the man understood, whether he could speak English or not. He gave the horse a hard smack on the ass, causing it to rear on its hind legs. The chieftain was quick to settle his horse while never once removing his eyes from Albert. The scene paused as Albert met the man's gaze with a menacing stare, and then he walked his horse slowly off the road. Albert smirked and waved traffic through.

Down the forest road another five kilometres, two office trailers sat in the middle of a clearing. Jutting out from the ground were several groups of pilings between piping that rose up and hung unconnected in the air.

Albert parked beside the larger of the two buildings. "All right, everybody out!"

The guys hopped out of the truck and stretched. AJ finally pocketed his phone and looked around.

Albert raised his arms out wide. "Gentlemen, the 11-16 Project."

He noted the lack of enthusiasm in each of his participants.

"I know it doesn't look like much yet, but let me explain." He walked around the lease, and the two men followed. "The 11-16 Project's part of our new SAGD facility. SAGD stands for Steam Assisted Gravity Drainage. With more of the world focusing on the oil sands industry, we're getting a bad reputation from the hippie types concerned about the so-called environmental impact the industry has on the world, and it's spreading to the general public.

"Visually, some find the mines offensive"—he smirked and slowly walked toward the buildings—"so we've been forced to evolve into a process that's less offensive. In reality, SAGD is more cost effective when it comes to harvesting the deeper deposits, but I don't give a shit how we get it, or who does or doesn't like how we get it, as long as we get it.

"Anyway, this system involves drilling a series of horizontal wells down to the depth of the oil; one set of wells will sit below the other set. Then we'll inject super-heated steam into the higher wells, which'll basically melt the oil from the sand and turn it to fluid that'll run down and get sucked out of the ground by the lower set of wells. The trick is to ensure we bleed every last drop of oil possible. So, along with the steam, we've been injecting different chemicals such as naphtha and butanes to act as additional thinning agents. Is the process actually cleaner?" He raised his eyebrows. "Fact is, we can get away with more using this system because everything happens underground. Out of sight, out of mind." He crossed his arms over his chest and smiled.

"The 11-16 Project's the next brilliant step to increasing our production. No other company in the world has tried this strategy yet and we've had to, say, skate around the truth a little. It's a stroke of genius, really. A lot of environmental committees are watching our every move. We were sure they weren't going to let us break ground with this idea with no other reason than to increase production. See, one of our production engineers decided that one way to increase our production would be to increase the pressure under the ground but still above the point where we're drawing the oil out. We have our own staff environmentalists working side by side with the government people. We wine and dine them, invite them to golf tournaments, take them on annual chartered fishing trips—you know, keep your enemies close. So, our in-house "Green Boy" informs the government representative that we've discovered a naturally existing layer of gas below the bedrock that's being extracted through our process—accidentally, of course. It looks good on us to bring something like that forward to the government, so it appears like we're working with them. The government's lacking qualified engineers, so we willingly dedicate one of our more experienced people, who comes up with the solution to send compressed air down one of our old existing wells to replace the layer of gas.

"So the environmentalists are satisfied we're correcting the issue, and voila! We have an open invitation to increase the pressure over our own wells." Albert chuckled and shook his head. "I love shit like that. Currently our SAGD facility produces two hundred and fifty thousand barrels a day. This little beauty project is expected to double production, putting us well ahead of the competition."

Albert looked to the standing structures. "These buildings are old, from the steam-injection phase. They'll be removed. Seeing as this is still experimental, we bought some used compressors from down south, and they're being packaged and delivered to the site. It's simple: take the air and push it into the ground."

Albert watched Charlie drift off toward the forest, where the only sounds were of leaves rustling in the cool breeze and the strong icy current of the mighty Athabasca flowing in the distance. He stared directly at the man until he turned around and met his eyes.

"You two have twelve months to make it happen."

14

Emma approached the door to the executive condominium suite, holding a small bouquet of flowers. A welcome offering for her granddaughter-in-law to be.

She knocked and waited. When she got no answer, she turned her hearing aid louder and picked up some obscene New Age rock-and-roll music resonating from behind the door, then snarled at the lack of respect to the building's other occupants. She drew a deep breath and replaced the snarl with her most pleasant smile, then knocked harder. Perhaps this ladylove of her grandson's was a little rough around the edges, but Emma was willing to help mould her into a proper wife. It would be fun to have someone to share some woman time with.

No answer again. She gritted her teeth and pounded on the door.

The music went silent, and within seconds, the deadbolt chunked. Emma hurried to correct her frazzled state. The door opened wide, and there stood the source of Emma's loss of control.

Victoria looked fresh from the shower, her damp hair falling just past her shoulders. Her brilliant emerald eyes peeked out from beneath the dark strands to reveal a dangerous balance of innocence and temptation.

A plain white tank top draped loosely over her, with one shoulder strap falling off to the side. Emma's eyes panned down to the next level, where the nearly transparent material left little to the imagination. Her round young breasts hung freely, the dark silhouettes of her pert nipples suggesting a chill in the air.

Emma was at a loss for words, which was rare.

Victoria looked down at the bouquet. "Oh, those are so beautiful." She flashed a smile that instantly brightened the hall. "Are they for me?"

"Well, yes, dear they—" Emma sputtered as the gift was stripped from her.

Victoria giggled and lifted the flowers to her nose. She looked at Emma with her transfixing eyes and gave a flirtatious flutter of her long lashes before turning and walking away.

Emma's gaze dropped to Victoria's bright-yellow sweat shorts. Her taut buttocks danced beneath the fabric as she crossed the room, the bottom of her cheeks teasing ever so slightly out the edge. Her gaze followed the line of her very smooth tanned and slender legs to the bright-blue butterfly tattoo on her ankle.

Victoria headed over to a mantle dividing the kitchen and living room and placed the flowers in an empty vase. When she turned back toward the door, Emma's eyes widened at the sight of the snug-fitting shorts forming a perfect outline around the treasure a woman should hold ever so sacred. Her breath halted and she placed a hand to her chest. Yes, she could see now how any man would be weak to the advances of such a tramp.

"They're perfect! Just what the room needed!" Victoria said, drawing Emma's attention back to her eyes. She held her hand out. "I'm sorry, I didn't even introduce myself yet. I'm Vicky. I don't believe we've met."

Emma lightly grasped her hand in confusion. Surely AJ had mentioned his beloved grandmother to his wife-to-be. "Yes, my dear. Well, I'm Emma."

Still no sign of recognition, so Emma continued, "Emma Doyle."

The girl continued to look at her blankly.

Emma frowned. "AJ's grandmother. Surely he has mentioned me?"

"Oh my god!" Victoria placed a hand over her lips. "I'm sorry, I don't think AJ ever mentioned anything about his grandmother. I'll have to give him shit when he comes home."

Emma cringed.

"Well, this is a little awkward," Victoria said, blocking the entrance by putting one hand on the door. "*So-o-o*... What brings you by?"

Emma squinted in displeasure, which appeared to have little effect on Victoria. The way the slut was leaning against the door jam, Emma was expecting one of her boobs to fall out at any moment. She crossed her arms over her chest. "I wanted to stop by and welcome you to the city, and to the family. Maybe I could help you freshen the place up a bit and we could get to know each other better. I play a large role in my grandson's life—I practically raised him from birth!"

Victoria bit lightly on her bottom lip and squinted back. "Jeez, it's really odd how he never mentioned you to me, at all."

Rage boiled in Emma. Obviously this girl was as stupid as she was slutty.

"Anyway, I'm sorry, Mrs. Doyle."

"It's *Ms.* Doyle, I'm not married!"

"Oh…" Victoria placed a hand over her smile. "I'm sorry, Ms. Doyle, but today isn't really a good day for me. I'm just planning on relaxing and settling in a bit. You know, new town, new place." She tilted her head to the side, fluttered her eyelashes, and shrugged her shoulders. "Maybe we can book it for another day, right?" She began to close the door, then stopped. "Oh, we have that family supper-thing tonight. Were you invited?"

"Of course I was invited, young lady! I am a very big part of AJ's life!" The opening to the room grew smaller as the door continued to close.

"Oh right, you said that. Well, great then, we'll see each other tonight. Thank you again for the flowers, they're beautiful." The door clicked shut, followed instantly by the sound of the lock latching. The music blared again.

Emma stared at the back of the door, furious. This girl would need more than just a little work. She would have to change her ways immediately if she expected to marry into the family. Little Miss Victoria Whore would bend to Emma's will or would discover just how much authority Emma had in this family.

15

Ollie was dumbstruck by the mass chaos as he and Honey got out at the site gate. Honey directed him to an hour-long site orientation at one of the surrounding work trailers, then spent another half-hour standing in line to get his site pass.

Meanwhile, Honey had occupied himself by chuffing back cigarettes and coffee while bullshitting with the others in the smoking area. He was in mid-sentence when Ollie came trudging around the corner.

"Well, holy shit, boy! I was beginning to think ya's quit already and snuck away." He grinned. "It wouldn't be the first time we lost someone before the job started."

"I'm really sorry, sir, but there's really nothing I could've done. The course is long. I just about fell asleep. But I'm ready now. I know I set us behind, so I'll make it up, sir." He snapped to attention.

Honey chuckled. "At ease, son, we'll be fine. It ain't the first time I've had to play catch-up." He swung an arm over Ollie's shoulder and led him toward the parking lot. "We'll see what kind of stuff you're made of once we get you on the end of the hose. I've seen some of the roughest, toughest men you ever did see turn into blubbering babies."

The air was heavily laden with dust from the countless number of passing vehicles. Combined with his growing nerves, Ollie found himself having to choke down every breath.

Through the dusty haze, their rig appeared. It was a big blue heavy-haul truck with a large tank on the back displaying the company logo in bold silver lettering: EAST ROCK DISPOSAL. The name hinted at the company's eastern roots, which was the case for many in the Alberta oil sands industry.

The spring-loaded passenger seat squatted and expelled a small cloud of dust as Ollie rested his weight on it. The cab was filthy; a thick layer of dust covered any spot unoccupied by garbage.

"Excuse the mess there, young fella." Honey climbed in the driver's seat. "It's been a solo mission here for a while. Well, I can't take all the credit—the Blue Dog's been with me every step." He smiled and patted the dash. "That's her name, the Blue Dog, and a fine vessel she is. Take care of her and she'll take care of us!"

Ollie forced a smile.

Honey turned the key in the ignition and the big diesel engine coughed and sputtered to life, sending a shudder through the carriage. He placed a hand on the long centre lever, shifted into gear, and released the clutch. The Blue Dog lurched forward, causing Ollie to sway violently.

"And we're off!" Honey cheered, giving a couple of quick blasts of the mighty horn.

Bouncing and bounding, they took a hard right out of the parking lot and blended into the flow of traffic. Diesel and dust stung Ollie's sinuses as they made their way down the winding road into the river valley.

Large pipelines flanked either side of the road, some crossing over it in a high pipe rack. To the left, a small freeway of racks and cable trays all ran in unison, passing over and under to create the illusion of a life-sized working microchip stretching to a large industrial city.

Ollie's heart pounded at his first look at the legendary place. *The money… the people… the power.* He smiled, confident he would find the means to get his grandmother healthy again. There was nothing to hold him back now. He looked out the passenger's window to hide his emotion from Honey.

Down through the valley the heavy truck squeaked and shuddered, leaving a cloud of fumes in its wake, then over a large arching bridge that crossed the river.

"Jeez, this sure is one heavy-duty bridge. Why such a—" He stopped mid-question as they crested the arch and a humongous truck came at them. He grabbed hold of his seat as it sped by, barely missing the Blue Dog's side mirror. He looked over at Honey. "Holy shit!"

Honey slapped his leg and let go a gut-wrenching laugh, which ended in coughing and hacking. "You should've seen the look on your face, boy! Lord Jesus, help me!" He wiped his mouth and leaned back. "That's a big ol' hauler, got hundreds of 'em. You don't wanna be messin' around those things—run ya right over and not even know it."

To the left of the bridge sat a towering cement structure with steeply sloped conveyors running into one side and a steady plume of steam billowing from the rooftop. Ollie's gaze followed the belts back to their point of origin high atop a tall cliff to an open chute. There a lineup of giant trucks sat, waiting their turn to dump thousands of tons of earth.

The plant disappeared from sight as the truck was swallowed once again by forest. Ollie was awed by the sheer size of it all. They'd been driving for a half-hour already—through the plant, across the river, past another plant, and now back into the forest. "How far we goin', Honey? How big is this place?"

"Couple more miles down the road. Our first stop's at the small station number 87. Got told this morning the shitter's plum full." He grinned. "Now we'll see what you're made of."

Just as Honey had said, the forest soon opened to a small clearing with a couple of industrial buildings. They looped around to the backside, where a large septic tank sat.

Ollie steadied his breathing. He was going to get through this for his gran. *Quick and easy. Don't think; just do.*

Every move toward the impending task jolted him: the hard brake of the truck, the reverse thrust, and each pulse of the backup alarm caused the hair on his neck to stand on end.

With the truck positioned, Honey looked at Ollie with a smile that said *"Iiiit's showtime!"* His eyes popped as he chuckled. "C'mon, boy! Shit ain't gonna suck itself." He dropped out his door and slammed it shut.

Ollie paused. *It's for you, Gran.* He took a quick, deep breath, then hopped out of the truck. He rounded the back end, where Honey was unloading a large green-ribbed hose. Ollie rushed to the other end to lend a hand.

Soon Ollie had muscled Honey politely to the side. All Honey needed do was point and shoot and Ollie took care of it all. What he lacked in experience he made up for with heart.

With the hoses all strung out and connected, it was Ollie's time to operate the business end.

"Now, you just pop the cap off the top of that tank and shove that hose inside there, son!" Honey shouted from the controls on the back of the truck.

This was it, the dreaded moment. *Don't think, just do.* He took in one last deep breath of determination and popped the cap off the tank, flinching away from the port to avoid any possible spatter.

"Good," Honey yelled, "I'm a start the pump now, and you lower the hose."

The hose surged in Ollie's hands, catching him off guard. He panicked and took a breath. The pungent stink caused his stomach to convulse; a hand shot to his lips as he gagged.

Honey howled with laughter. "Hold it in, boy! We don't need another mess to clean up!"

Ollie regrouped and began to lower the hose. Another violent surge came as the end made contact and took its first mouthful of sludge. Ollie's gag reflex triggered again and he lost his focus; the hose jumped with another large gulp, escaped his grip, and fell into the tank. With a loud bump, a projectile of spatter shot out of the portal and hit Ollie square in the face.

All went silent except the sound of the pump.

Ollie froze. Eyes closed, body motionless, breathing only enough to support life. This was the breaking point, one of the biggest fears of his life. He'd been covered from head to toe in fish blood and guts when he worked in the fisheries back home, but never ever had he been covered in another human's piss and shit. Sure it stunk, but he could wipe it off and it'd be gone. It was his pride that would bear the permanent stain. He was better than this. True, he wasn't an intellectual type, but he'd always worked hard and treated people with respect. This was his reward for all that good behaviour? Come to the land of promise to make big money by letting some spoiled, obese, lazy ass shit on him. His teeth ground together so hard his jaw hurt.

Ollie focused on his reason, his purpose, his grandmother. *Don't make this into more than it is, Ollie. It's just a mess on your face. Get cleaned up and get on with it.*

He stood straight, determination trumping pride. He pulled a rag from his back pocket and wiped at the sludge, then grabbed the hose again. The point of no return had come and gone. He'd taken it, wiped it off, and was continuing on like nothing unusual had happened. In the end he was the winner… right?

Honey grinned and cheered Ollie on. "Yeah, that's the way, son! Don't let the shit get the better of ya!"

When the tank was empty, Honey helped him wrap up the hoses and clean up the gear. He slapped Ollie on the back. "Proud of you, boy! You're gonna be just fine, welcome aboard." He chuckled.

Ollie smiled, not exactly sure how he felt about passing his initiation. In his mind this was just the beginning for him. The possibilities in a place like this were endless. But to start out, he'd have to get a little shit on him.

The rest of the day went well, and by the end, he was running the truck while Honey worked the hose. Honey entertained the crew of guys in the truck on the way back to town with stories of Ollie getting "shit-faced." The guys took him to the local pub, where the story was loudly repeated to all the patrons many times. One good thing was that Red had managed to get Ollie a room in camp, which meant he'd have his own space and free meals.

Still, with all the new excitement, Ollie found a corner seat by a window and looked outside to the darkness and passing traffic. He let his mind travel…

He missed his home, and it felt a whole world away.

16

AJ watched his father churn a large cloud of dust as he raced out of the yard. An uncomfortable silence settled as he and Charlie scanned the area. A pair of pale-yellow portable office trailers sat mounted on wooden timbers.

"Well," AJ mumbled, "guess we should go check out whatever underachievers they picked out for us."

Charlie nodded. "Yes, I guess it's time to get at it."

AJ marched ahead of Charlie, anxious to wield his instant power. He stepped up the stairs with certain stealth and wrenched open the door, attempting to catch his underlings off guard. The musty combination of cheap bathroom air freshener over mouse feces greeted him.

The sleepy three-man crew inside lifted their heads from their newspapers or card games as AJ cleared his throat.

"Gentlemen... I... this... today..." he stumbled, bringing about cocked heads and looks of confusion from his simple audience. He cleared his throat again. "All right, everyone, break time's over and the gravy train stops, effective right now."

The big blond-haired, blue-eyed man involved with the card game snorted a chuckle at AJ's attempt at authority. "Hear that, Kirb?" He slapped his cards down on the table in the direction of his opponent. "It finally gone and done it! They runs out of gravy, Lord Jesus!"

AJ felt his face grow hot and he clenched his jaw. "I'm AJ Doyle, Acting

PRICE PER BARREL

Project Manager for this facility! And this here is Charles Bidwell, second-in-command. Starting today, we have to work to get this equipment up and running by springtime. This project is of the highest priority to the company, so be prepared to work day and night, seven days a week if necessary. If you're not up to that challenge"—he paced before them, looking down with an all-powerful sneer—"then let me know now so I can have you replaced."

It was AJ's first position overseeing any type of project. In fact it was his first job outside of university. He was nervous at first, approaching a small group of unruly thugs that likely devoured small woodland creatures for breakfast. During his childhood, he'd ridden around with his father at work during the summer months. He'd seen his old man purposely belittle men twice his size, which were few and far between. *"See, son! Physical strength and ability matter none in the world of politics. Without my blessing, they'd have nothing. It's about the charisma and mental control. If you know you own them, then they'll know. Mind over matter, and some of these pathetic examples are nothing more than just that—simple matter."* His father had laughed.

Back then his father, the great president, lit up AJ's world like the sun and the moon. But later, as AJ grew, this idol was replaced by young figures with round breasts and short skirts. The warning echo of his father's voice became nothing more than annoying banter from an old man.

But he was no longer nervous. In that small office trailer, AJ found in himself what he had witnessed in his father. And he felt alive. It was a whole new exhilaration. These Neanderthals, who would normally make him cross the street in public, were his to control. Puppets on a string. He smirked at their expressions, at the verbal assault on the tip of their tongues and the testosterone swelling heavy in their clenched fists. But not one would ever dare stand up to him.

The room deadened in obedient silence. He felt taller, larger... bigger than life. The name *Doyle* ruled this country, and everyone who heard his name knew they were looking upon their future king.

AJ turned to Charlie and nodded, then crossed the room and stepped outside to investigate the other trailer.

***

Charlie cleared his throat, then began his own speech to the men in a less threatening tone.

"Yes, well, gentlemen. I'm Charlie Bidwell, or you can call me Charles, whichever you prefer. I'm going to be assuming the position of project supervisor. As Mr. Doyle already mentioned, this is a high-priority project, so there'll be a lot of people watching. We do have a deadline, so we'll need to work diligently, but above all else, guys, I just want everyone to come out of this in one piece, the same way we're going in. So let's just work safe and watch out for each other. I don't mind taking the heat for being behind schedule—that kind of stress is nothing compared to phoning a family to explain how their loved one won't be coming home. I've been in the industry for many years and have been fortunate enough not to be put in that situation, and I'm just around the corner from retirement, so I'd appreciate if you guys'd help me make it a shutout."

Charlie smiled when he felt tensions in the room lighten.

"So why don't we get started with some introductions—just names, I guess, and where you're from, and how the hell you ended up here?"

The room shared a chuckle and Charlie nodded in the direction of the very large man. "How 'bout you get us started, big guy? What's your name? Where you from?"

The man turned in his seat. "Huh? Oh, my name's Harvey Hancock, named after my granddad. I'm aware the sophistication of my accent can be hard to place, but my birthplace is The Rock—or Newfoundland to those of you's less educated." He finished with a sarcastic grin.

Charlie smiled, then nodded to the miniature version, who spoke in a monotone and with a slight roll of his eyes, as if he'd done the circuit a million times and this whole friend-share episode was just a distraction from the oversize bowl of soup he was devouring. "Yes and my name's Kirby Hancock and no we're not related—"

Harvey nudged Kirby in the arm, then leaned over and whispered loudly enough for the room to hear, "Oh shit, Kirb, I forgot to tell ya. We actually are related, since I done your sister there last week. So that makes us kin now." Harvey winked at his pint-sized companion.

Charlie watched Kirby's cheeks flush and his jaw clench, but he managed himself by keeping his eyes focused on his soup. "Oh jeez, Harv, I wasn't aware that counted. That means, then, we been brothers for years now, since your mama made a man of me. She was so sweet and gentle with me, I can remember the way she—"

Kirby caught a cuff to the back of the head by Harvey's bear paw of a hand.

PRICE PER BARREL

Then the two men grabbed on to each other like a couple of kids about to settle it out at the bike racks.

Charlie chuckled and shook his head. "Hey, hey!" He could tell he was going to have his hands full with those two.

He turned to the lengthy man leaning against the wall, chewing on a toothpick and looking out the window. His olive skin was weathered and his expression distant.

"And how about you, sir?"

There was a slight pause before the man turned, queued not by the question but by the silence engulfing the room.

"What? Oh, my name's Carl Wolfscry. I'm a native of these parts." He looked down to his two companions sitting at the table. "No relation."

Charlie looked over his crew. It was as fine a crew as he'd ever had. "Pleased to meet all of you. Looks like I have the right guys for the job—definitely not concerned about losing any of you to the beauty-pageant circuit."

Kirby released an emotional sob. "But Harv's mom said I was brilliant as a star twinkle in the night sky."

Another cuff came to the back of his head.

"You shut the hell up!"

And the two men were on each other again.

"Hey, guys!" Charlie intervened, laughing at the two oversized children. He held up his small Styrofoam cup of coffee in a toast. "Welcome to Project 11-16."

17

That evening AJ accelerated his luxury sports car out of the underground parkade and was quick to roll up the windows when the chill of the early autumn air blasted inside. The season had settled overnight, and at only 6:00 p.m., the sun had already sunk behind the treeline.

He turned to Vicky and examined, again, the ensemble she'd chosen to wear, which he felt was in poor taste for her official "welcome to the family" dinner. The form-fitting strapless black dress barely covered her bottom when standing. When sitting in the car, it rode up high enough that the pink lace of her panties shone out between her legs. It would display as such again when she took her chair at the most sought after restaurant in Fort Mac.

He grunted and stepped on the accelerator.

Vicky stopped smiling at her smartphone and turned to him. "Is there something wrong?"

He shifted uncomfortably. He'd never complained about her taste in clothing, and he hated confronting her about anything.

She crossed her arms. "What is it? What's wrong with you?"

He hesitated, anticipating the bottle of energy he was about to uncork. "I just don't see why you couldn't've picked a more respectable outfit? My fucking grandmother's going to be there!"

She shot him a look of disbelief. "My dress! You don't like it? This is the nicest dress I have! This dress that you, for whatever reason, suddenly hate cost me over five hundred dollars!"

"No, Vicky! That dress cost *me* five hundred dollars!"

"Uh!... Well, anyway, what's wrong with it? You used to love this dress. You used to love me in this dress! That's why *you* spent five hundred dollars on it!" She leaned in close to him with the bug eyes.

AJ took a second to admit her point. He'd bought that dress for her because she looked amazing in it. He regrouped, still playing the offensive but a little less aggressively. "Well, you do look great in that dress, but... I mean..."

Vicky caught it. Quick and subtle as it was, his gaze had turned down to her crotch. Her voiced turned seductive and she smiled wickedly. "What, AJ?" She put on her playful-pout. "Just tell me what's wrong, sweetie... Huh?" She ran her hand teasingly up his leg.

AJ relaxed a little. This was a game she played often. It was how she went about getting her way, and she was excellent at it. He knew she just absolutely needed to hear him say it. He rested his arm on the windowsill and stroked his chin.

She caught his downward glance again and bit teasingly on her lip.

"Honestly, sweetie, I can see... well, everyone can see your..."

"My what, sweetie? You mean my...?"

"Yes!" He quickly waved his hand toward the area in question. "Yes, exactly, your... thingy."

Vicky leaned back and clapped her hands together in a burst of laughter. "My thingy? Oooh that's good! Is that what we're calling it now?" She held one hand over her mouth until her laughter subsided, then lifted her bum and pulled her dress down enough to ensure her "thingy" was concealed. Another giggle resonated, a mere aftershock. She turned as far from him as she could, placing her full attention out the passenger window. "Well, AJ, that was very masculine. I'm not sure I can make it all the way to the restaurant. You may have to pull over and take me now, bad boy." Her voiced hardened. "One week at your new high-shit job and I have to change my whole wardrobe. Can't wait for week two."

AJ sat silent. His blood boiled beneath the calm surface. He'd lost the battle and now would have to suffer through the monologue.

"Sincerely, though, AJ, I apologize. I thought you were still the man who enjoyed having the sexiest piece of arm candy in the place. I enjoy being that. But I guess we're practically married now. I just assumed the magic would end after the honeymoon, but I suppose, why wait?" She leaned over and whispered in his ear. "And I promise to be a good, obedient girl, Daddy, and I'll make sure to lock my thingy up good and tight after tonight, so *no one!*... will ever get pleasure from it again."

AJ wanted the fuck out of the car and was thankful they were only a few short minutes away from the restaurant. A very quiet few minutes it was, the strong whirl of the engine matching the interior tension.

She was right though. Maybe that's what pissed him off the most. Last week she'd been wearing less than that dress, and he'd been loving it.

Finally, they pulled up in front of the Royal Oak. With its dark brick exterior and two gas torches flanking either side of the entrance, it had the façade of medieval times, of an establishment frequented by nobles.

AJ got out and took a deep draw of the crisp air. It was just a small fight, they'd had them before. *Don't sweat the small stuff.* But he could see Vicky wasn't through with him yet. She was waiting patiently for him to come around and open her door. He had lost and she'd make him pay. He opened her door and stood off to the side so she could make a graceful exit.

She smiled as she straightened, then turned and lightly patted him on the cheek. "Thank you, dear." She grinned and continued toward the door.

AJ followed his fiancée like an obedient puppy, lengthening his stride so he could open the restaurant door for her.

***

Inside the reserved banquet room, the rest of the Doyle family waited in their usual uncomfortable silence around a large rectangular table made from a thick slab of granite. Albert and his mother sat at the head positions and his wife, Patricia, sat at his side. She was always one to wear a pleasant smile, even in the most awkward of situations. Albert knew his mother couldn't stand her, such a meek and fragile woman. To start any type of conversation with the two would result in his mother cursing out Patricia for what she saw as a failed marriage.

Patricia had been a big part of AJ's life, a long time ago. Playing hide-and-seek in the park, or caring for him when he was sick. But she was a sheep surrounded by wolves. Over time, she'd been pushed to the side, dissolving to little more than a heavily medicated mute.

Albert watched as his mother sat in her in her high-back chair constructed of tarnished steel and faded leather and pretended to marvel at the décor he knew she'd seen many times. It was the best, and she insisted on the best for her family… for her boys.

Her arms were crossed and she was tapping a finger on her bicep—the signal that she disapproved of something. Albert guessed it was because AJ and Vicky were fifteen minutes late. To some it would be fashionable, but to his mother, it was complete disrespect.

He felt the seconds tick by on his wristwatch, up his arm and right into his brain. Finally, the door pushed open and AJ escorted his young trophy into the room.

Albert sat up in his chair as he took in the sight his son had brought home. Vicky's hair lay flat to border her finely defined cheeks and complement her beautiful big green eyes. Down his gaze panted over her firm young body, held passionately by a very tight and incredibly short designer dress. As she turned slightly to either side to include the whole room, an electric-blue butterfly tattoo on her ankle hinted at innocence. A flirtatious smile and flutter of lashes triggered Albert's most primal instinct as he picked up her scent from across the room. He collected his napkin from the table and dabbed lightly at his lips.

She was to be admired. Albert had played with women of her nature when he was young himself. A stimulating banquet for the unbridled hormones of the young male. A notch on the bedpost, a trophy for the case that would instigate many bragging sessions to his friends. But for a wife?… No.

He looked to his mother. She sat silently as the happy new couple approached the middle of the table. Her jaw tightened and one of her hands clenched the armrest as the other aggressively fondled her cloth napkin.

Vicky stood beside the table with AJ, his arm placed properly around her hip. She flashed a starlit smile. "Oh my! How beautiful and"—she glanced at the wall sconces providing the dim room's only light—"dark and… yes, very nice!" Her expression never faltered, but the air stunk of sarcasm.

AJ took his cue to officially introduce Vicky to his family, motioning toward his parents. "On this side is my mother, Patricia, and my—"

Vicky squealed softly and opened her arms wide as she scurried to the end of the table and reached across to grasp Patricia's hand. "Oh, Mrs. Doyle, it's so wonderful to finally meet you! AJ speaks of you all the time, and this is just so wonderful." She stretched her lithe body to muster as much of a hug as she could from the strained distance.

MARC GREGORY

Albert's eye's bulged. Vicky's effort had placed her ass right in front of his face, and her already-short dress was slinking ever so slightly and teasingly up her buttocks.

He felt she was either very naïve, or a precision instrument.

Grandma Emma missed nothing; Albert heard her teeth grind and saw her napkin begin to fray. She grew flush at the bullshit display of affection.

Both men focused their gaze at the same point while life in the room paused. When their visual lines crossed paths, they turned away quickly.

Albert coughed softly into his napkin and AJ maneuvered his body to block the display from his grandmother, placing his hand on Vicky's shoulder to signal that it was time to move on.

"Oh, yes, how silly of me." She straightened and tugged down her dress.

"Victoria, this here is my father, Mr. Albert Doyle… Senior."

With impassioned theatrics, Vicky's hand shot to her mouth. "Oh my goodness, Mr. Doyle, it's such an honour to meet a man of your stature." She shook his hand frantically, then bent at the waist and wrapped her arms around him.

Albert felt the warmth of her skin and breathed in the light dusting of her perfume. His heart beat sped and his pupils dilated. His brain sent a command to his hands to clutch, but what small amount of intellect that remained shut down the order. It took all he had to dilute any unholy thoughts of his future daughter-in-law. Flashes of what he could make of that little bitch if the room were empty and the door were locked tickled his primitive masculinity.

As Vicky bent over Albert, her dress lifted again. But this time the view was aimed directly at Grandma.

AJ was quick to intervene.

He cleared his throat and said, "Yeah, and over here, sweetie, is my grandmother, who I guess you met earlier today.

"Oh yes, of course." Vicky sprung to Emma to perform the same illusion. She held her tightly, fully—a little too much so.

AJ must've noticed his grandmother's disapproval because he pulled out a chair for Vicky and invited her to join him at their places at the table.

The conversation was light over drinks and appetizers. Albert and AJ dominated mostly with shoptalk. Patricia and Emma kept silent, fussing with their blouses or brushing at the tablecloth. Vicky contributed the occasional wisecrack, which caused a brief pause in the discussion and drew modest grins from the men.

Emma cleared her throat loudly.

As if on cue, Vicky leaned in closer to the men in an obvious attempt to convince Emma she was very involved at the moment.

Emma cleared her throat again, a little more loudly this time. "So, Victoria!" She put down her glass and dabbed her lips with her napkin, then smiled pleasantly. "You must be very excited with the new engagement and the big wedding to plan. Have you two set a date yet?" She tilted her head slightly, the sweet smile never wavering.

The question caught Albert's interest, and he stopped the other conversation.

Vicky leaned back stiffly in her chair, looked up at the roof, and took a breath.

Using the moment to formulate an escape from the widow's web, Albert thought.

Then she leaned forward with an award-winning smile that instantly captivated Albert. She looked sweet Granny straight in the eye and laughed lightly. "Oh no, Miss Doyle, my heavens." With a fingertip, she elegantly brushed her hair away from her eyes and tucked it behind her ear. "I'm not the kind of woman that gets off on all that fancy material stuff." She accented her innocent smile and puppy eyes with a dainty shrug of her shoulders, then reached over to place her hand on AJ's lap. "Just simply having my man acknowledge his love for me before the universe is all I ever need." She leaned toward AJ with a look of endearment and rubbed the tip of her nose on his cheek, then followed up with a tender kiss before turning back to the room.

"I'm picturing, perhaps, a wedding inside a honeymoon?" She rolled her eyes to the roof and tapped a finger to her chin. "Yes, AJ!" She smiled. "Doesn't that sound wonderful? Travel to some distant, exotic place and maybe climb to some ancient ruin or to the top of a fabulous waterfall in the deep jungle. Somewhere sacred, to confess our love for each other."

She reached across the table, her dazzling green eyes wild with emotion. She daringly rubbed Emma's hand. "Doesn't that sound just so… romantic, Miss Doyle?"

Emma tugged her hand back instantly, rubbing at it as if it had been burnt by acid.

Albert chuckled at Vicky's eagerness to win over his mother. He smiled at his son, placed a large hand on his shoulder, and gave him a fatherly shake. The two men settled back into their previous conversation at a low murmur, with Vicky leaning in as if Emma's questions had been answered.

But Emma wasn't done. She reached back across the table and placed her hand on Vicky's.

This time it was Vicky who flinched.

"My dear, that does sound very wild and romantic. I think it's a wonderful idea. Although it doesn't sound like there will be room for anyone else on this incredible journey." She looked over at her son with doleful eyes. "But that is no matter. This is not about us, after all. It's about you two. So yes, go and see the world, celebrate your love. Then when you return, you'll be ready to settle down and start a family. That is, if you didn't already start one on your little journey here." Emma let out a joyful shriek and placed a caring hand to Vicky's cheek.

Vicky's smile fluttered and the confidence drained from her eyes as she turned from Emma. "Um, oh… well, we haven't really discussed…"

"You haven't what, my dear?" Emma leaned toward Vicky and pulled her hand closer. "Surely you and AJ have discussed the plans for children? Tell me, how many are you wanting?"

"No, Grandma," AJ cut in, "we haven't discussed having children yet."

Emma released Vicky's hand and gasped. "Oh my, you haven't? Well, AJ, Victoria… my dears, this is definitely something that should be seriously discussed before you join in marriage. AJ, honey, you know how important it is to the family that the Doyle name be passed on."

This topic drew Albert's full attention. He didn't want to pry too much, but if his mother wanted to shed light on the subject, he was more than willing to listen.

"Grandma, please," AJ said. "Now isn't the time, or place."

"Oh, but, my darling," Emma pushed on, "I really think this should be addressed sooner than later. More complications can arise the longer you wait. You must get started on this while she's still young and fertile."

Vicky choked on her food. She fanned at her mouth and managed a muffled "excuse me" as she pushed back her chair and rushed from the room.

Emma turned to her grandson. "You haven't discussed children with her? Do you not want—"

"Yes, of course I want children, Grandma!" AJ's voice was hushed, but stern.

"She wants children, too, just give her time. Let her get settled. All women want children eventually."

"Oh, my dear, you can't just assume that." Emma looked to her son. "Albert, don't you have anything to add?"

"Yes, son, I have to agree with your grandmother on this. You really should discuss this with Vicky before you get married. It's not an issue to be taken lightly. Carrying on the Doyle name is of utmost importance. You're the last male, and if you don't have a son, the name will be buried with you. I know you two are still young, and maybe now isn't the time either of you are wanting to jump into parenthood." He placed his hand upon AJ's shoulder and looked him in the eye. "You're an incredible young man. You are my son. I love you and I trust your judgement regarding whomever you decide to marry. I just hope carrying on the family name is as important to you as it is to the rest of us?"

AJ yielded to his father's honesty. "Yes, Father, it is a priority for me, for us. We'll have children and the name will not be buried, I promise."

Albert patted his shoulder and smiled. "Good, then." He looked across the table to his mother. "Now, that's enough talk of children and raising families. I'm afraid we've upset Vicky. If she's going to be a part of this family, I want her to feel welcome. So, no more trivial shit tonight!" He shot his mother a stern look.

Emma dropped her eyes to the table and nodded obediently.

Vicky returned from the ladies' room looking quite ill. She stood beside AJ, leaned in, and whispered something in his ear.

AJ put down his fork and wiped up, then stood and announced they had to go as Vicky was feeling under the weather.

Albert stood and hugged them both, thanking them for coming and wishing Vicky a quick recovery. The couple made their way around and hugged Patricia goodbye. As they passed by Emma, AJ reached around from behind and gave her a big hug and kiss on the cheek. Vicky slipped right passed and out the door without so much as a goodbye.

18

By the time Ollie was done his shift at the week's end, the sun was all but set. He jumped in the crew truck after another exhausting day, but on this day he had something to celebrate. It would be the first night in his own personal place—his room at camp. There were a couple of different camps, but his boss had some pull and was able to secure him a room in the newest and most-sought-after camp, The Aurora.

Red took a right after the plant gate, down a dark road, then around a corner to a welcoming yard and a vast parking lot lit up brightly by numerous streetlights. They crept through the lot, braking for vehicles backing out of their stalls and for dirty and tired pedestrians weaving through the rows of parked cars with their lunch pails and duffel bags in hand.

The drive led into a crescent before the entrance to the camp foyer. Ollie's gaze was glued to the window. The camp consisted of multiple construction trailers stacked three stories high and with multiple wings. It was rumoured to house ten thousand workers. Supper was ready every night, breakfast every morning, and many supplies were available to pack a proper lunch. For most, this was a just a camp—a place to keep the rain off your head while you were away at work. But for a young man thousands of miles from home who had never stayed at a hotel or resort in his life, it was a palace of wonder. Ollie felt special that a large company would see enough value in him to provide him with such accommodations.

The camp was just outside the plant security gate, so he could be home within a minute. No more long drive back to town, listening to everyone bitch and moan about their day. He'd be showered and have his belly full before they even got back to town. Things were looking up. He thanked the guys and waved goodbye, then entered his new home.

The huge lobby was brighter and cleaner than he expected, with the ceiling reaching up to the full height of the building. Everyone had to remove their footwear and place it on the boot rack in the entranceway. Straight ahead was a large concession. To the left was an internet sitting area filled with couches and tables and people tapping away at their doodads and whatzits. To the right was the entrance to the dining area, where a line of people waited for the person ahead to scan their ID card to gain access. Right beside the door he first came through sat the security window.

Ollie walked up to the window to find a very large black lady on the other side, who rolled her eyes away from her computer screen and up to him in a manner suggesting she was not impressed with the day, her job, life in general, and him.

She smacked her gum loudly and raised an eyebrow.

"Oh, yes, ma'am," Ollie stammered. "I'm workin' for Rock Disposal." He fumbled to pull out the now-crumbled-up paper Red had told him to hand over to the person at the security desk. "I'm supposed to be checkin' in here tonight… ma'am." He smiled innocently.

"Uuuuuh huh." She looked back down at her monitor while striking the keyboard lazily. Without looking up from her screen, she asked in a heavy, unfamiliar accent, "How long you work here now, boy?"

Ollie corrected his posture and smiled proudly. "It's my first week, ma'am. I come all the way from The Rock— er, Newfoundland, *way* out east, on the Atlantic,"

She paused with the typing and gum-smacking long enough to raise one eye up to him with an expression that said she was not impressed. "Uuuuuuh huh." She turned back to the monitor. "Well y'ain't bin here long 'nuff to stay at Aurora. Newbies stay at Muskeg camp—just there"—she shot a thumb out over her shoulder—"'cross the parking lot."

Fear gripped Ollie even though Red warned him he'd be told this. He'd heard the stories about life in the Muskeg camp, and wanted nothing to do with it. All kinds of nasty things happened there. The walls were paper and provided no shelter from the elements or the crude neighbours. The bathroom facilities were way down at the end of the halls in a group area: *"Keep your soap on a rope!"* he could hear Honey say with a laugh. *"And if you do drop it, best you just let it go, ah ha ha ha!"* Booze, drugs, rape, dead bodies, vampires, werewolves, and all-around poorly mannered people. Ollie would much rather return to town than stay in that hell. But Red had assured him he had a spot at Aurora.

"No, please, ma'am. Here"—he pointed frantically at the paper he had handed her—"my boss wrote a message on the back for you to read if there was a problem. Please!"

She humoured Ollie and turned the paper over slowly, seeming to enjoy watching him squirm.

On the flip side Red had written instructions that in the case there were any problems or concerns with admitting the boy to the Aurora facility, the guard was to call her superior, or rather her superior's superior—a name rarely heard or spoken—complete with a contact phone number.

She chewed her lip, picked up the phone receiver, and hovered her finger over the buttons. Then she hung it up and tapped her finger madly on the countertop as she scanned the letter again. She looked Ollie up and down before doing up the paperwork, then got Ollie to sign on the lines and handed him his key card. But not without one final threat…

"All right, boy," she sneered. "I let you in 'cause I'm tired and you caught me on a good day. But don't you dare go telling no one I let you go by or I kick you skinny white ass down to Muskeg. They need some fresh meat down there."

"Yes, ma'am." Ollie breathed again, and a large smile grew on his face. "Thank you very much!"

"Down to the left hall, then up the stairs to the right. Now git before I change my mind. I don't wanna look at your skinny ass no more!" she growled.

Ollie fled toward the hall, fumbling not to hit anyone with his heavy duffel bag, apologizing to anyone who seemed the slightest bit disturbed by his presence. He followed the signs to the staircase and made his way up to the third floor, then up and down the maze of halls until he found the number to his room: 321.

He searched frantically for his key, forgetting where he'd put it and fearing he'd lost it and would have to return to the security lady. But there it was, in his pocket, confused with his bankcard.

He examined the fancy device above the door handle, which had no instructions, then swiped his card through in what he supposed was the proper manner.

Bzzz

It hissed back at him and flashed an angry red light. He cursed it silently and swiped again.

Bzzz

He cleaned off the card on his shirt and tried yet again.

Bzzz

So close! He was so close to all the peace and quiet he had yearned for now for weeks. A space to call his very own lay just on the other side of this... *Stupid, stupid door! And this fucking plastic card!*

Bzzzz

Fuuuuck! Please just let me in! I'm right here, if we can just work together... What's wrong with the old metal keys? At least they worked! Fucking computer shit... Ain't there no one decent who can help me or show me?

Bzzz

Fuuuuuck!!!

Ollie raked a hand through his hair and looked up in pleading desperation for anyone who could help him get the door open.

***

Mary-Ann was serving her one weekly evening up at the Aurora camp to do an inventory check in all the storage rooms. At first she'd taken the assignment as an insult. But after the unmentionable happening with Mr. Doyle, she appreciated the distance. It'd been several weeks since the incident. For some while after, she'd had a hell of a time dealing with it. Asking herself what she had done to deserve such a thing, the scene—the sounds—playing repeatedly over in her mind. She knew things like that happened all the time to women; it was all over the media. So... let it take you down, or use it to be stronger. But she couldn't help questioning what was happening on the other end. Was he now scheming to get rid of her, fearing she would talk? Would she lose her job? The idea that she herself was concerned about the consequences stirred her anger. Thinking about it in any manner would never let her heal.

She shook her head to rid her brain of any such nonsense, then continued her counting of toilet paper in the final storage closet of the day, way up on the top floor. As time had passed, she'd begun to appreciate taking inventory as an easy job. With no superior to look over her shoulder, she took her time and enjoyed the peace. But she didn't like all the men staring at her. The male-to-female ratio was in extreme favour of the woman—or perhaps dis-favour.

Having written down her total, she double-checked to ensure she hadn't missed anything, then backed her way out into the hall.

Bzzz

She looked toward the familiar sound of a failed swipe card. A slender young man, about the same age as her, was running his hand through his shaggy blond hair. He lacked the usual air of ignorance or arrogance, as most men by that point would've started screaming bloody murder down the hall, demanding this and that from any staff who happened by.

Bzzz

She smirked, wondering how he figured it should work better than the last try. Then he lifted his head and looked down the hall, straight at her.

It was the first full look she got of his face. His eyes were a beautiful blue, complemented by a dimple-flanked scowl.

Their eyes met for a second, then they both blushed and turned away.

Mary-Ann's heart fluttered. She stood frozen, like a rabbit in headlights.

Not hearing any movement from his direction, she twisted her head ever so slightly toward the boy. He was standing erect, back toward her, with a large duffel bag at his feet. Absolutely motionless. But then his arm slowly reached out, without moving any other muscle, to swipe the card again.

Bzzz

Mary-Ann snickered at his awkwardness, and when she tried to hold it back, a snort forced its way out, loud enough for him to hear.

She covered her mouth and listened again for movement, hoping she hadn't insulted him. She'd normally never offer to help any man in camp, but this young man wasn't the average, egotistical male. In fact he seemed more scared of her than she was of him.

She cleared her throat and found herself nervous about approaching him. She took a quick breath…

"Are you having trouble?"

There was no response. The boy held strong to his position. He appeared to have stopped breathing.

"Excuse me, um, sir?"

PRICE PER BARREL

There was a slight twitch before he turned slowly. He looked back in her direction, and flinched as if surprised.

Mary-Ann watched him, and the longer she watched, the more she realized how handsome he was. Tall, but not too tall; slender, but with a bit of muscle; broad shoulders; blond hair; those blue eyes; and very definitely not a player. He must be new—the all-high-and-mighty of a six-figure paycheque hadn't had a chance to swell his head.

***

"Oh, uh." Ollie wasn't good in the presence of girls when he was freshly showered and dressed in his best clothes, never mind when he'd just finished a twelve-hour shift of sucking out shit tanks. And this stranger at the end of the hall was one of the prettiest girls to ever talk to him.

His knees quivered and a layer of sweat developed on his forehead. She was so pretty—too pretty for him to be looking at.

He struggled to find a casual pose. First he shoved his left-hand thumb behind his belt and let the rest of the hand dangle. But then his right arm was just hanging with nothing to do. He quickly stuffed his right hand and the key card in the pocket of his jeans, then reassessed the left-hand situation, with all its cool-guy, thumb-in-the-belt— wait, why not just use the pocket like he had with the right hand? Ollie was sure to change facial expressions with every new pose, and he expected at any time now to hear the young lady blasting away on her safety whistle.

Stop! Stop it Oliver! he shouted in his head. With both hands still in their pockets, he leaned his shoulder against the wall at a geometrically impossible angle and came to an awkward rest. *Breathe, stupid. Don't forget to breathe!* "Oh… yes, h-hel— hey, hi, I mean, yes, hey." He decided to just stop talking, hoping that raising his brow mysteriously would be enough.

"Are you having some trouble?" the girl asked. "Would you like some help?"

As pretty as he truly found her to be, Ollie wished so very much to continue this conversation at a better time and place. "Guushhh… well, it's nothing, really." He smiled and waved it off casually.

She moved toward him and he panicked as her beautiful smile drew closer. He whipped back around to face the door, ramming his shoulder into it and wrenching on the handle, but it didn't budge. "I think I have it." He fumbled in his pocket until he found the card key, then swiped again.

78

MARC GREGORY

Bzzzz

He softly bunted his head against the door. *Fuck.*

He became aware of her presence right beside him. He jumped back and stood dead straight with his hands at his side, sure to keep a full arm's length between them. "Uh, yes, well, I was just gonna, I mean…" Exhausted, he breathed in deeply and exhaled out. With the fall of his chest, so collapsed his whole offensive line.

His eyes dropped to the floor and he launched into a speech, all stuttering put aside.

"Truth is, I'm new. Only been here a week and just got moved into this camp here 'cause my boss knows some big people. It'd be my own place as I been livin' in buddy's garage till now. The guard lady was gonna send me to the Muskeg camp, which I heard's real bad. But I got by, and now I'm here, but my key don't work. I don't wanna go back to the security 'cause if I upset the guard, she'll for sure send me to the other camp." His frame softened and his shoulders sunk. There was no hiding who he was, and someone like her wouldn't be interested in a stinky ol' nobody from Newfoundland. Just by the look of her, he figured she could have her pick of any man.

The girl's eyes widened and she was quiet, and then she smiled politely and held out her hand.

Ollie's jaw dropped. He frantically tried to wipe his hands on any clean patch on his clothes but could find none. "Oh, uh, no, miss, you shouldn't. I mean, my hands are really dir—"

She giggled. "Your card, silly, not your hand."

"Oh." His whole face turned red hot. "Right, sorry." He handed the card to her.

She grabbed it by its tip, and as she did, she looked up into his eyes. For a moment, they both held tight to opposite ends of the little plastic card. He looked down into her beautiful large eyes, and she smiled, her upper teeth pressing down softly on her bottom lip. To Ollie, she was a centrefold model out of one of those classy men's magazines. He'd never been so close to a woman like her before. His heart sped and certain masculine parts found some spring.

***

As she was held in his hypnotic blue gaze, Mary-Ann, for the first time possibly ever, didn't feel intimidated by a man. He came across as real—just a simple, hard-working guy by the looks of him… and the smell. Despite the smell, she found him attractive. Her heart sped, and for once in a very long time, she felt hope for something normal, something real, but…

She broke from the trance and her smile disappeared. "Yes, thank you." She turned to the door. She was just a simple cleaning girl. Even if they were to get together, he'd someday find out—find out she was… used, tarnished, soiled past the point where she would be acceptable to a fine, upstanding gentleman.

"So, what are you doing out here?" she asked.

"Well, I came out here from *way* out east—Newfoundland."

She snorted. "Yes, I already guessed that. You're not the first Newfie to come this way to find his fortune. Be stranger if you were actually from Alberta." She realized her tone was a bit harsh and hadn't meant to come down on him. He seemed nice, and nothing about her situation was any fault of his. She cleaned the magnetic stripe on the card and swiped it through the scanner.

Bzzz

"Yes, well, I ain't actually out here to get rich, miss."

Mary-Ann looked back up at him. "No? Well, why in the heck would you move out here, then?"

"It's my gran, back home. She's all I got left for family and she's very ill. She needs special care, and it's the only way I could think of to make enough money so she can get better."

If that was a pick-up line, Mary-Ann had never heard it before, and now her heart raced. She had a sudden, instinctual urge to grab him, kiss him, and hold him close. A picture flashed through her mind of them together: a beautiful house and the perfect young family, far from Fort Mac and its filth. She had to remind herself it was not a possibility.

"I'm sorry," she said. "I didn't mean to assume you were just out here to get the big dollars."

"It's all right, ma'am. I actually am out here for the big dollars, for now. But as soon as my gran gets better, I'm going back to be with her. I like it back home better anyway. I miss working the fishin' docks. The money isn't as good, but things are just… better. I can't really explain it."

Mary-Ann nodded and flipped over the small paper sleeve the card had come in, then placed one hand on her hip and looked up to him. "Well, uhhh, Mister…?"

"Oh yes, ma'am, my name's Oliver, Oliver Hynes." He stood tall and pulled back his shoulders. "But people call me Ollie for short." He smiled sweetly.

"Oh, Mary-Ann, Mary-Ann Kibbnok. And I think I've figured out your problem, Mr. Hynes— Ollie." She grinned. "This room here is room number 321." She pointed out the number on the door. "The number on your card"—she held it close before his eyes—"is 312."

Ollie bit down on his lip, closed his eyes, and raised his head to the ceiling.

"Fffff…kkkk" he hissed, then lowered his red expression back to her. "So, did you hear the one about the smart boy from Newfoundland?"

"…No."

He said nothing, just raised his eyebrows and grinned.

Mary-Ann laughed, and Ollie's grin grew wider.

"C'mon, Newfie boy, I'll show you where this key is meant to go."

He picked up his bag and walked beside her. "So, *Kibbnok*, that sounds a little Newfie?"

"Yes, well, you're right about that. My parents are from Newfoundland, but not me. Been here all my life—never actually seen the ocean on either side."

Ollie looked stunned. "Oh, you must go some time. I'd love to take you and show you the ocean for the first t—" He stopped short and blushed.

"So what kind of work are you doing here?"

"Oh… I, uh, drive… I drive truck, the big trucks with the tanks on the back. The big trucks with the tanks."

"Oh, right! So what do you move with the big tanks?"

"Yes, well, I move stuff—liquid things, I guess. Not really all that sure yet, haven't been overly involved in the filling of the tanks yet, I'm just driving right now."

"Well, here's 312." She swiped the key card through the scanner.

Beep beep

The green light flashed, and Mary-Ann pressed down on the handle and pushed the door open. "Home sweet home." She smiled.

"Oh wow! That works much better. So… well… thank you, I s'pose."

There was an uncomfortable pause before Ollie reached over to take control of the door.

Mary-Ann backed away. "You're very welcome. It was nice meeting you, Mister— well, Ollie." She smiled again. "Have a good evening, and enjoy your stay at Aurora." She turned and walked back toward the storage room.

"Wait, Miss… Ann, Kibbnok?" He shook his head. "Miss Mary-Ann, please."

She stopped and looked back.

"Listen, I know this isn't the best… Well, I mean I just wish… Well, I wish I could at least've had a shower but… this is all I have to work with and usually… I mean, I never… before this…"

Mary-Ann figured she knew what Ollie was about to ask and her heart was torn. She knew it couldn't be. But if it could have been, she felt she would've liked it to have been with a guy like him.

Ollie continued to ramble. "Well, I mean, I'm gonna be staying here for a while, and you come here sometimes I guess, too, so if we were to be… y'know, maybe we could just go to the cafeteria and… I mean, it wouldn't be a—"

She stopped him there. "Yes, Ollie." She smiled. "I'd really enjoy having dinner in the cafeteria with you some night."

He gasped and clasped his hands in front of him, rocking on his feet with the biggest, happiest little-boy smile ever produced by a grown man. "Okay, then, Miss— well, Mary-Ann. It's… dinner, sometime… at the cafeteria?"

His excitement made her blush again, reminding her of unspoiled innocence. Something she once had. "Goodnight, Ollie." She waved goodbye, then turned the corner.

***

Elated, Ollie stepped in his room and closed the door. It was arguably the greatest day in his life. He was always a coward when it came to women and so couldn't figure where he'd gotten the courage to ask her out. It hadn't been sexy, but he'd gone for it. Maybe because he had nothing to lose… but something incredible to gain. And now he had his own room and dinner with a girl—the most beautiful girl ever. She'd agreed to go out with him! And she'd called it dinner! And that is really like a date!

He came back down to earth and scanned his room. It was small with a single bed, a simple desk with chair that doubled as a nightstand, and a closet. He had his own sink but the bathroom, consisting of a toilet and shower, was shared with his neighbour. The guys called it a "Jack and Jill suite"; the bathroom door could be locked from the inside to prevent anyone from entering while occupied.

It wasn't a penthouse, but it was his and he would make it home. After showering and arranging his things, he placed the most important item on his nightstand beside his bed: a picture of his gran. He crawled in bed, then kissed his fingers and touched them to the picture. He turned off the lamp and turned over to go to sleep.

"I bet Gran and Mary-Ann would get along real good." He smiled as he drifted off.

19

Emma had hardly slept after having to tolerate that skank over dinner, and she was still fuming when she arrived at work later that week.

The nerve of her. She challenged me right in public… in front of the whole family! No! It can't happen! I can't allow it.

Her mind scraped for a way to make AJ see Victoria wasn't right for him—and not for the future Doyles. Nothing good could come of them being together, and if no one else was bold enough to stand up to the challenge, she would. But how could she break them apart without her grandson turning against her?

Some movement down the hall caught her attention. She turned to see Mary-Ann arrive, early as usual. Emma smiled at her good, sweet Mary-Ann; so innocent, so beautiful, so hard-working, and loyal to the bone.

Now there is a woman worthy of a Doyle man. Why can't AJ meet someone like— Well now…

She couldn't force it to happen, but she had the power to influence it. It would be wonderful to have that strong Newfoundland girl to carry on the family. Emma marched down the hall toward her immediately.

Mary-Ann was smiling and humming a tune as she dusted off some picture frames in the hall, apparently oblivious to Emma's presence.

Emma cleared her throat, and Mary-Ann jumped and turned to look at her.

"Oh, Ms. Doyle!" She put a hand to her chest. "I'm sorry, I was just… I didn't hear you coming."

Emma chuckled. "Oh, I am sorry, dear, that is my fault. I never meant any harm. In fact, I am bringing you some good news." She took the young lady's hand lightly. "You see, I've been in kind of a bind as all these new project buildings keep popping up all over the place and we are already short on staff. I know you've been putting in some time helping out at the camp, and I appreciate it very much. You're so good to the company, and don't think it's going unnoticed. There is this new project way across the river—the 11-16 Project, I believe it's called. There are just a couple small trailers as of now, but they can't be ignored, and I can't afford to send multiple staff members over there because they're needed here. I need someone I can trust." She looked at Mary-Ann pleadingly. "My dear, you are the only one I can really, truly send over there to take care of the place properly." Emma couldn't have her plan fail, so she sweetened the pot to a point where Mary-Ann wouldn't be able to refuse. "Um, my dear, can you drive? What I mean is, do you have a proper driver's licence?"

"Oh yes, Ms. Doyle, I do. I don't have my own vehicle, but I do have a licence." She smiled.

Emma smiled back. "Oh good, good. Well, I can let you off your duties at the camp and—"

"Oh, no... No, Ms. Doyle. The camp needs me up there. I have my own little system for inventory, and it'd be too hard to train someone else because... you know, the high employee turnover and all." She chewed on her lip. "No, Emma— or, I'm so sorry, Ms. Doyle. I can manage them both... all. I can do the camp and the new place across the river... uh, 11-16?"

Emma found the young lady's dedication nothing short of admirable. She didn't want to upset her, so she grasped both of the girl's hands in hers and squeezed tightly as she searched her mind for a solution. "Okay, Mary-Ann, here's what I can propose. You continue to clean Mr. Doyle's office and perform your camp duties, as well as take on the 11-16 Project. You are relieved of all other tasks, just focus on those three. And since they are so far apart, I will get you a company vehicle."

Mary-Ann gasped. "A... company...?"

"Yes, my dear, you'll be driving clear from one end of site to the other. The plant bus just isn't going to be efficient enough for you to get everything done. Besides, I'm sure it doesn't even go out to the 11-16 yet. I will get a company vehicle assigned to you and only you. And you will be able to drive it home."

PRICE PER BARREL

Emma smiled and patted Mary-Ann's hand.

Mary-Ann's jaw fell open. "Ms. Doyle… oh! Are you sure?"

"Yes, my dear, it is the only way it can be done. I trust you, my sweet, but this is a responsibility that has never been entrusted to someone from our department before, so I am counting on you not to let me down."

"Oh, Ms. Doyle, thank you! Yes, ma'am, I won't let you down. Thank you, thank you!"

Emma smiled at her own genius and the girl's happiness. "Yes, all right now, dear, it's settled, then."

They nodded together.

"Good, but there is still work to be done, so get along with your tasks and I will arrange everything. Check in with me toward the end of the day, before you head up to camp, and I will have a vehicle ready for you."

"Oh, thank you, Ms. Doyle!" She flung her arms around Emma and gave her a big hug.

Emma squeezed her back just as hard. She would be a fine granddaughter, one Emma could be proud of.

She watched as Mary-Ann scurried off down the hall and out of sight.

As Emma admired Mary-Ann's innocence, her mind drifted…

Stephan had been insatiable with their love. He was so cute, the way he begged, but she was more than happy to satisfy the needs of her man.

One night in the park, a half-drunk Stephan was sitting with his back against a tree and she was on her hands and knees pleasing him when she felt her dress lift lightly in the back. She thought it was the breeze until she felt hands grab firmly onto her bottom. Startled, she looked back to see Andrew smiling and unzipping his pants.

Stephan placed a hand on her cheek. "It's all right, baby. He's our friend— we're all friends—no one'll know." He shot her his twinkling smirk and tucked a stray lock of her hair behind her ear. Then he placed his hand behind her head and pressed her back down.

Her heart raced. She didn't understand how Stephen could not be jealous. But then she felt the warm, hard press of Andrew in behind her and a gentle, reassuring caress on her head, and she accepted the situation and even became aroused, and the night played out as a wonderful, erotic adventure.

She kissed each of her boys good night and made her way home beneath the starlit sky. Her uncertainty had vanished and she flushed with excitement. Now instead of having only one of her true loves, her chances for escape had doubled.

Afterward, some nights she'd meet up with Stephan, some with Andrew, but mostly they were all together, laughing, drinking, doing drugs, and enjoying one another. The boys were always talking about which teams they wanted to sign with and all the places they would see. Emma would relate her fantasies of visiting big cities like New York or possibly moving to California, and the boys would chuckle.

The chuckling faded in Emma's mind as she returned to the plant, and her plan for Mary-Ann and AJ.

Then another light went off in her head: *Why not have a backup, hit it from all angles?* She marched back to her office and got on her computer to check the local listings.

20

With the seasonal battle of warm versus cold well underway, Charlie arrived at the 11-16 site on the day of equipment delivery to find it cloaked in a heavy fog. It felt as if snow were suspended in mid-air.

For the morning journey over from the main site, he'd chosen to jump in the crew van. He'd explained to AJ that it was a strategic move, that he liked listening to the guys' morning banter as a good way to see where their heads were at and douse any of the negativity that could grow over time on such high-priority projects. But in reality, Charlie just didn't want to ride over with the asshole.

It's the last stretch, the last run to retirement, he constantly reminded himself. As soon as Summit was better, he'd leave the industry, forever, to spend time with his grandson.

He exited the van, and the area stood in absolute stillness. He took a second to breathe in the peace, which was suddenly broken by the annoying repetition of a vehicle's backup alarm.

Making his way through the fog, he followed the noise until a pair of headlights peeked through just down the slope from the trailer. The big semi was stationed beside the support piles, where the first equipment skid was to sit. The rest of the crew drew up beside Charlie to watch. It was the first major piece of work they had to do, and they all seemed a little confused as to what their role was.

Charlie looked around and found that AJ was late, in his usual fashion. He'd honestly prefer the boy not show up at all. "Well, c'mon, kids, time to get to work. Go get your gear on."

"The huh?" Kirby responded, still a little drowsy.

"Our gear," Harvey said and lightly slapped Kirby upside his head. "The stuff we brought with us, in the corner there in the backroom. Them blue coverall-thingies and the boots with the hard toes… like your head."

Kirby rubbed his head. "Oooh… that's a long time ago. Not sure anything'll fit anymore."

"Well, you just tell me if your boots don't fit your feet, and I'll kick 'em up your arse for ya. Technically that's still wearing 'em."

"Pretty certain that'd downgrade the safety rating, Harv."

"That's actually a really good point. I'll just kick 'em up there for shits and giggles, then."

Carl and Charlie watched on in stunned silence, then Charlie nudged Carl in the arm and nodded toward the truck. "Let's go see if we can have a look at what we got."

Charlie greeted the driver with a smile as he climbed out of the truck's cab. "Good morning, boss, what you got here for us? You sure it goes on this spot? I understand we have three of these skids coming?"

"Yes, sir," the driver answered. "The other two are about another hour behind. But the crane should be here any time. This one goes on these piles, best I can tell from the print."

Charlie frowned. "The print?" He'd been asking AJ for prints for over a month but never got anything—nothing on the equipment or the site. "Where'd you get a print from? I don't even have a print!"

The driver reached behind the driver's seat and pulled out a schematic. "This is all I got from my boss, sir. I'm not sure why you don't have one?"

Charlie cleared a spot on the trailer bed and opened up the print. He shook his head. "Well, thank you for this. Mind if I steal it and scan a copy quick?"

"Be my guest."

Charlie headed toward the job trailer just as Harvey and Kirby came out and stumbled down the steps, swatting and ranting at each other. Then the loud hiss of pneumatic brakes let go up by the yard entrance, and Charlie turned as a crane came to a stop.

He looked back over to the twins. "Can you two quit sharing the love long enough to get that crane over and place that skid for me?"

Their bickering stopped as they looked over at Charlie. "Oh, sure, Chuck, we'll get on it first thing."

Chuck? Charlie stalled, then decided if that was the extent of disrespect he received from those two, he was lucky.

He went into the trailer and placed the print on the scanner, wondering where Carl had disappeared to. When the machine had finished, he gave the copy a quick glance, then stepped out to survey the site.

The fog had lifted enough for him to make out the silhouettes of the truck and crane in the distance. He listened to the Hancocks holler at each other while slinging up the load.

"You gonna double wrap that over there, Harv?"

"What for? It's a skid, Kirb, not your sister."

But there was another sound in the background—low and unfamiliar, a humming or groaning. Charlie strained his old ears for a direction.

He skirted the trailer's perimeter, stepping softly around back. He continued off into the fog, to an area with some more support pilings and an old wellhead. The sound grew louder and an outline began to form in the murk. A person, a man... Carl.

As Charlie pulled up quietly beside him, Carl continued to look straight ahead, slowly lifting a lit cigarette to his mouth and taking a deep draw. He then pointed to the ceremony taking place in front of him.

Charlie squinted, and there he was, a spirit in the mist: the old chieftain who'd blocked the road. He was scantily dressed in ceremonial garb, his body covered in tribal paint. He was hunched over and turning around slowly in circles, hopping on one foot, then the other. His left hand stretched out to the side, palm up to the heavens. In his right hand he held a wooden stick, with a wooden ball dangling from a piece of twine tied to its end. Smoke billowed in large plumes from the ball, and the air stunk heavily of burning moss.

Charlie had respect for all cultures. But this happening, at this time, caused an uneasy feeling he couldn't understand.

"Carl," he whispered, "what's he doing? Can he do it somewhere else? Or maybe after working hours?"

"I'm not really sure," Carl responded, keeping his eyes trained on the spectacle. "This kind of thing isn't very common these days. It looks a lot like a war dance."

Charlie's eyes bulged. "A what? War? We can't have this—not war, not now! When is it happening? Is he calling in a group of guys, or how does this work? Talk to him, Carl, please."

"No, that's the part that's strange to me. He isn't preparing for battle."

"Okay, then, what? Honestly, this is scaring the shit out of me. We can't let AJ see this, or there *is* going to be a war. So, if he's not preparing himself for battle, then what?"

Carl lifted his cigarette for another drag. "I think… it seems like he's preparing the land? *Pfft*"—he shook his head—"doesn't make sense. I never could interpret that shit." He dropped his smoke on the ground, stomped it out, and headed back.

21

It'd been a couple of weeks since Ollie met that beautiful young woman. Mary-Ann was her name, and he'd never forgotten it once. She'd been the focus in all of his dreams. True, he didn't know much about her. He just sensed she was one of the good ones. Her sweet smile and warm eyes.

In the life he'd lived growing up back home—school, work, looking after things around the house for his gran—Ollie had never met a woman for him. Never held hands, never a kiss… nothing. He'd had a look at a friend's dirty magazine once, but the girls in there seemed a little too aggressive for his liking. He wanted a sweet girl; a loyal, honest wife to him; and the best of mothers to their children, A good woman he could proudly take back home to his gran.

Ollie's head began to spin, and he rested it against the window of the bus en route to camp. His eyes glazed as he travelled back thousands of miles, and forward many years…

A small house stood alone on an acreage on the high field, overlooking the ocean. Mary-Ann prepared a Thanksgiving feast while their children played in the yard, running toward the cliffs. But they knew not to get too close, as Mom and Dad always said. They were good kids—twins, one boy and one girl.

Mary-Ann smiled as she looked out the window above the kitchen sink, watching the children doing their best to get a kite in the air. Ollie crept quietly up behind her and pushed the tips of his fingers lightly to her tickle spots, just enough to get her attention, before wrapping his arms snugly around her and whispering in her ear.

"You're the most beautiful woman in the world, Mary-Ann. You've made me the happiest a man could ever be. I love you."

He would tell her every day. Swear on his gran's grave...

The bus screeched to a halt in front of the camp. As the dozens of men stood and gathered their belongings, Ollie stayed seated. He found himself in the same embarrassing situation that had plagued him for the last few weeks. He cursed it, but at the same time, he welcomed the new emotion and all the wonderful sensations it stirred. Except for when time demanded he stand... erect, in public.

Think bad thoughts, think bad thoughts... Work! Think about work, yes. Big nasty truck... Honey, sucking out the shit tanks. It didn't take long to erase the romance and retreat to normal.

Thinking about his work status reminded him of the fact that he and Mary-Ann would never be more than a dream. He was what he was: an undereducated underachiever from Newfoundland. The only job he could get in the great land of promise was running the shit end of a sucker hose.

She was a beautiful diamond. It was only a matter of time before some man of great wealth would discover her and take her away, into the sunset. It was just best he didn't get involved. There'd be a girl for him someday—not a Mary-Ann, but a good woman nonetheless.

It was nothing to get down about. He really didn't have time to entertain romance anywat. It would only interfere with his mission. Get the work done and the money in the bank, and get back home. He kicked his boots off and placed them on the rack, then headed to the dining area—the same routine he'd followed every day since he got his own place.

***

Mary-Ann raced up to camp after finishing her duties at the main office. She marched rapidly through the lobby and down the wing, then took the stairs two at a time to the supply closet on the third floor, just down from Ollie's room—the same thing she'd done every day since they met. She looked at her watch; she was on time, the same time she'd found him there. Yet, once again, there was no Ollie. She opened the closet door and counted the rations. Not that she needed to—she was required to count them only once a week, and this was the fourth day in a row.

She decided to stay in the room and leave the door open a crack so she could

nothing bad would ever come. He was that kind of man—she'd known it

sh

hear if anyone was coming. She leaned against the wall, laid her head back, closed her eyes, and breathed a deep sigh.

It was foolish. Her silly schoolgirl dreams of she and Ollie and their little house and family by the ocean, the kids playing in the yard as she greeted him at the door when he returned home from work. The house would be clean, and a good dinner would be ready. He would smile and scoop her up in his arms, then look deep into her eyes, kiss her passionately, and tell her how beautiful she was and how happy he was with the life they'd made together.

She wasn't a girl who needed much for materials—a roof overhead, clothes on their backs, food on the table. Safe in his strong arms, he'd protect them so nothing bad would ever come. He was that kind of man—she'd known it immediately when she looked into his eyes.

But he wasn't coming. For all she knew he'd left and gone on to something bigger and better. He was beautiful, and strong, and kind. He deserved a woman the same. A beautiful girl... beautiful and clean.

She was not that. She was just a maid. She mopped mud and cleaned toilets. She was soiled.

Her chin quivered on exhale, and tears ran down her cheeks.

It was no use getting all worked up. There'd be a man for her, sometime, somewhere—not an Ollie but... someone. She dabbed her eyes, but the tears continued to run. Head down, she entered the empty hall, locking the door behind her. She kept her head down and her pace up as she retraced her steps, but not so fast as to draw attention. In her peripheral vision, she saw the security counter coming. She was just about out the front door...

WHAM!

Mary-Ann spun a full three-sixty, then braced herself on a lounge chair. She watched the opposing party fly face first into the corner of the security counter, then down to the ground.

Her hand shot to her mouth.

He moved, slightly at first, then slowly pushed up to his feet and turned to her with those familiar baby-blue eyes.

"O-Ollie?" She wiped her wet cheeks.

His eyes widened and blood began to seep from a cut over his eye. "Mary-Ann?"

They shot toward each other, closing the gap instantly. He wiped at one of her tears with his thumb at the same time that her hand rose to his cut.

"Mary-Ann! What's wrong? Did something happen? Did someone hurt you?"

He looked furious, ready to strike. She knew then that he was her knight, and she welcomed his caring touch—strong, yet kind... with that bit of a funky smell.

"Ollie." She giggled through new tears of joy. "You're bleeding!"

They paused with eyes locked. The moment tense with excitement, she felt his pulse sending waves through the space between them.

Slowly, the background noise returned, along with the reality of where they were and the many people watching. They broke apart, back to their insecurity. But the blushing grins remained.

Mary-Ann pulled a handkerchief from her pocket and pressed it to the wound over Ollie's eye. "I'm really very sorry. I feel so clumsy, I should watch where I'm going."

Ollie took control of the cloth, the boyish smile never fading, his twinkling eyes never leaving her.

"Wha...? Oh, no, it's nothing. It was my fault, I'm always running into things. Well, I mean..." He looked toward the cafeteria. "I was... I know it's not much, and people complain about the food, but, well... we kinda said that... So, now...?"

Mary-Ann's heart was about to break through her chest, his lack of speech being the biggest compliment she'd ever received. She glowed and tingled like never before.

"I'd love to join you for dinner."

His smile was like the sun that brought existence to her world.

He gestured toward the dinner area. "After you, Miss Mary-Ann."

22

Vicky woke early so she could have coffee with AJ before he left for work. She watched as he chomped away on his cereal while tapping and scrolling on his annoyance of a smartphone—or, as she liked to refer to it, "stupid piece of shit."

There she sat, wearing a very short and very revealing nightgown that draped perfectly over her body, silhouetting her perfectness. Her hair was messed slightly in that sexy, casual way that used to drive him crazy. Victoria Secret would sign her on to seven figures if they saw her in that thong—she was hot…

So what the fuck's wrong with this guy? He used to skip class if I let a fart go in the morning.

She thought back to the days they spent in the parks, smoking grass and making love. She smiled at the memory. Then she looked across to what he'd become: wearing a tie over his dress shirt, head down, eating fibre cereal and doing shit on his phone. He didn't even know she was there. Was this it? Was she really looking at the future?

She leaned over and let the neck of her gown fall open, then reached her foot out beneath the table and began playfully digging her way up his pant leg.

He paused his eating in mid-crunch and turned his attention to her, looking anything but amused.

She rolled her tongue playfully around her lips, putting a glint of trouble in her eyes. "C'mon, AJ, your daddy's the big guy on the ladder. Call in sick and take advantage of me." She slithered her hand across the table and wrapped his tie around her wrist. "We could think of a more useful purpose for this tie—play 'Naughty Girl.'"

AJ grabbed her arm. "Vicky." His tone was sympathetic, as if he was aware he'd been neglectful toward her. "Right now I have to concentrate on my job. It's the best thing for both of us." He pushed her hand away, then reached up and straightened his tie before taking his bowl to the sink. "I've been handed this important position and have to prove I can handle it."

Vicky retreated into her seat like a child who'd been placed in the corner for a time out. She drew the neck of her gown together tightly, then crossed her arms and stared at a single spot on the floor in a pout. She'd never have guessed the day would come when a man would turn down the opportunity to spend the day naked with her. Especially in favour of a filthy, stinking, fucking oil sands plant!

She listened to his stupid "I am the all-mighty" speech. *"Blah, blah, blah…"* The rage of rejection grew inside to her boiling point, then her whistle blew.

She giggled loudly and with enough authority to let Mr. I'm-All-That! know his speech was over. "Oh listen to you, gonna get in there and roll up your sleeves, prove it to the world!" She stood, keeping one hand clasped tightly to her neckline just to ensure he was aware the offer was officially closed. She pushed her chair in, then leaned back against the wall and looked at him with eyes cold as ice.

"Is that the plan, AJ? You gonna go out there and change their world? Put it all on the line? No cost too great?… Let me clue you in a little, sweetie, 'cause the obvious is hard to see when your asshole is wrapped around your head." She took a couple of light, taunting steps toward him. "You are where you are in life 'cause of your father. You're nothing more than Albert Doyle's boy. You know what, AJ? Maybe you are all that. Maybe you are the fucking Jesus Christ of the oil sands. I could be sitting here telling off the biggest fucking genius on the face of the earth. Reality is, you could live, sleep, eat, and shit that plant—you could increase the profitability a thousand percent and literally walk on fucking water—but it doesn't matter, 'cause in the eyes of the people in this town, and in this industry, you are Albert Doyle's son. And you got to where you are for no other reason but that. And everyone will credit any achievement you ever accomplish—no matter how much honest effort you put in—to that single fact. Albert Doyle's son, little AJ Doyle."

She'd pushed him hard on other occasions but had never seen him move in that way. She couldn't recall even seeing him cross the room—she blinked, and when her eyes re-opened, he was on her. One hand gripped her neck, pinning her to the wall, and his free hand cocked back in a clenched fist. Gasping for air, she held hard to his wrist, trying to push him off. She felt the trembling in his body and saw the look of pure madness in his eyes.

But she didn't back down, the look in her eyes daring him.

He dropped his hands. She immediately bent over, gulping in air.

He grabbed his coat from the back of the chair and walked out, slamming the door behind him.

***

AJ raced out of the parking garage and onto the main highway.

She's right.

She knew it… he knew it. All his life he had lived in the shelter, the Albert Doyle shelter. How could he ever prove himself? Why bother trying?"

Keeping his foot heavy on the pedal, AJ popped the lid open on the centre console, reached inside, and grabbed his flask.

23

Mary-Ann pulled up to the security gate and swiped her card to raise the pivot arm, then smiled and waved good morning to the guard, who smiled and waved back.

Although winter was in the air and the temperature was well below zero, Mary-Ann's mouth was fixed in a permanent grin. Down through the valley and over the bridge she drove, on course to her first day over at the 11-16 Project, singing and bobbing her head along with whatever song was playing on the radio. It didn't matter whether she liked the song or not. Perhaps what she was really moving to was the rhythm of the fluttering heart of a young woman in love.

So distracted with how wonderful and beautiful life and everything in the universe was, she almost missed the turn and ended up skidding to a halt when she saw the very small sign indicating the site.

All was quiet in the yard as she parked. Hopefully she'd gotten there before the crew and could get her business done before they arrived. She hopped out of the cab, grabbed her cleaning supplies from the back, and struggled up the stairs and through the door of the trailer. As she went to step inside, she caught her foot on the step and stumbled, sending her gear crashing to a cheap linoleum floor caked in mud.

She looked around to figure out the best place to get started. It was a standard portable office. To her left was a common area furnished with a couple of foldable tables and chairs. Straight ahead was the doorway to an office; ninety degrees to that was another door she guessed led to the utility-*slash*-bathroom; and to her immediate right was a doorway leading to yet another office.

She'd get her chores done as quickly as possible without compromising any of her professional quality. She had her work cut out for her, though. The workers had been left to deal with their own filth for a while, she guessed. She filled her bucket with warm, soapy water, then put her head down and got to work. What was different about that day—what had been missing in the past—was the sweet girlish grin she wore as her mind trailed off to her Ollie. She even caught herself humming a tune at times.

How lucky could a girl be to find such a diamond in this rough? Life hadn't been overly kind to her in the romance department, but she'd kept confidence in her heart until, finally, he came... her knight. From best she could tell, he felt the same for her. There were still the lingering, natural insecurities: would he like her when things became more intimate—her kiss, her body, her breasts, and her? When she thought about their first time together, she sometimes grew angry. Would he know? Would he be able to tell? What would he think? Would he stand up and walk out? Was he expecting a sweet, pure young woman with all her innocence intact?

It's not my fault, she'd told herself repeatedly after reading up on some of the psychology of rape victims. It was hard, though, having no one to confide in. Her mind was sometimes a very dark and lonely place to be.

She stood, took a breath, and changed the direction of her thoughts. *Ollie, Oliver, Mrs. Mary-Ann Hynes.* She repeated her new mantra as she scrubbed.

She grew nervous after almost an hour had passed; she wasn't really in the mood to meet a whole new crew of workers, usually consisting only of lonely, greasy men. There was always at least one who'd make a sexist comment. Sexual harassment was taken very seriously by the company, but more often than not, a complaint limited one's chance of advancement, so most women just took it with a friendly smile. Hopefully the crew had been held up with some permit or safety meeting.

Finally ready for her usual finishing touches, she wiped down the desk in the far end office and organized the things on the desk in her own tidy fashion, and then she marched across the trailer and did the same in the other office. When she pulled the office door closed behind her, a brief flash of light from the brass nameplate on the door caught her attention and she read the name. Her heart stopped and her chest grew tight as her breath stalled. The name struck fear in her soul. AJ DOYLE.

Doyle?... AJ?...

She was not decorated with a high-end diploma, but she could take an educated guess at what the *AJ* represented. She'd heard rumours that the prized son had returned.

Why?!... Why send me of all people here to clean up after this... son of a pig!

No one knew what had taken place behind closed doors...

Or did they?

Paranoia set in as she listened for approaching vehicles. She decided she'd done enough and it was time to pack up. Just as she reached for her bucket, a familiar screech came from the yard. She peered carefully out the window. A group of men were exiting a large crew van.

She clumsily gathered her things in one poorly planned load, buckets bouncing off her knees and poles sticking in all directions as she rushed to the door. She shifted her cargo left and right to free a hand to operate the knob and then pressed her weight against the door. It flew open and sent her stumbling onto the steel grating, spilling everything to the ground.

There was an awkward silence as she looked down upon the onlookers.

The older gentleman in the lead was the first to break the silence. "Well." He smiled.

His eyes were just like her grandfather's.

"Good morning, young lady," he said. "I'm guessing you were sent to clean up after us?"

She held still and surveyed the crowd for the son of the man who'd stolen from her something that could never be returned. But none of them vaguely resembled Doyle spawn. The tension in her body eased. "Yes... yes, sir."

The man stepped closer and offered his hand. "I'm Charlie, Charlie Bidwell." He smiled gently.

Mary-Ann accepted his greeting. "Mary-Ann Kibbnok, sir."

"Well, Mary-Ann, it sure is nice to have a young lady visit and brighten up the place for us. I apologize for the disaster the boys and I left in there. If I'd got word they were sending you, I would've at least cleaned up a bit so your initiation day wouldn't be so... well... disgusting." He blushed. "I'll make sure and keep the guys in line from now on—as much as you can line these guys up anyway. Try to make things a little easier on you. Thank you, Mary-Ann, it's a pleasure to meet you, and welcome aboard."

"Yes, sir. Only doing my job, sir."

"The name's Charlie, Mary-Ann. Or you can call me Charles, or Chuck. No need for formalities."

"Yes, of course, si—" She smiled, catching herself. "Charlie… Thank you, Charlie. I'm done for today, and now you all can have a fresh start."

She began gathering her stuff again, and the boys were quick to lend a hand and load everything into her truck. She climbed in and started the engine, then waved to the group of men, who stood side by side, waving back.

She breathed out and turned the truck around. As she approached the lease exit, another vehicle turned in. It slowed to a creep as it passed by. The driver looked out the side window and straight into her eyes… those eyes… that familiar, cold, demeaning stare. A shiver crawled up her spine. There was no doubt who she was looking at.

Mary-Ann quickly turned her gaze back to the road ahead and punched the throttle, leaving the yard in a small puff of dust.

24

KNOCK KNOCK KNOCK

Vicky barely caught the sound over the roar of her blow dryer. She switched it off and waited.

KNOCK KNOCK KNOCK

"Well, now, who in the fuck would that be at this time?" she muttered as she wrapped her hair up in a towel and balanced the wet mass on top of her head.

The knocking continued and she called out, "Just a second… coming!"

She grabbed the pair of sweat shorts draped over the side of the laundry hamper and hastily slid them on as she rushed to the door, then peeked through the peephole. The most she could tell was that the body on the other side was male.

She did one last check of herself: braless under a white tank top and damp from the shower. She crossed her arms over her chest. As soon as she opened the door, she wished she'd had more time to prepare.

She took in the man head to toe, doing her best not to be obvious about it. He stood about six feet tall, with short, wavy dark-brown hair. She estimated about a grand spent between suit and shoes.

Vicky possessed a skill to accurately judge character almost instantaneously. Despite the man's clean-cut appearance—every hair and thread in its assigned position, flawless smile, twinkling eyes, and perfect posture—he was not to be trusted. Knew what he wanted, and would sell his own mother to get it. He was a bad boy. Not the bald, tattooed, smash-a-beer-can-on-his-head kind of bad boy. This was the political bad boy, the type who could screw you over hard and have you smiling through the whole thing, as if he were doing you a favour.

The Wall Street stud cleared his throat. "Excuse me, miss." He flashed a slick smile. "I didn't mean to disrupt you while you— maybe I should've called? I was just excited to get over here and introduce myself after the company contacted me."

Vicky raised her brow.

"Oh, sorry." He reached into his pocket and produced a shiny metal cardholder, then handed a business card to her. "I'm Justin McGillivray, Real Estate Agent for Northern Gold Real Estate." He held out his hand.

Vicky grinned. *Real estate agent... yes, that fits perfectly.* "Oh." She hesitated to uncross her arms so she could accept his hand. *What the hell—not like it'll be the first set of tits this playboy has seen.* She let her arms fall and accepted his hand with a playful smile.

His grasp was light, but masculine. Their eyes met; neither one flinched. It seemed an even match. They grinned, then broke.

He cleared his throat. "Yes, well, the company sent me your contact information and told me to make you my top priority. If I came at a bad time, you could just..."

Vicky finally caught the hint. "Oh, well, I guess, if you don't mind waiting for me to get ready? Would you like to come in? I have a fresh pot of coffee on. It won't take me long."

"If it's not a problem? I hope I'm not interrupting any of your plans?"

She held the door open and motioned him to pass. "*Pfft,*" she snorted as he walked by. "Plans? What plans would I have? My fiancé goes to work at the plant for fourteen hours a day. Dark when he leaves and dark when he comes home." She walked past Justin into the kitchen, where she pulled a coffee mug out of the cupboard by the sink and poured a cup.

She looked at him, standing obediently by the door. "Well, you may as well kick off your shoes and come in for a seat."

He walked in the kitchen and accepted the cup from her hand, looking confidently into her eyes. "Thank you, miss."

"Oh, call me Vicky. Yes, so he takes off to work all day and I don't know anyone up here, and really, this place doesn't exactly give off the feeling that a lady can walk around safely by herself. There's a lot of sketchy-looking people out there—bums or addicts or drunken Natives. The last time I went to get groceries, I came out to two men fighting on the hood of my car."

Justin smiled. "Well, I'm not going to try to sugar-coat things for you. This is the great wide wilderness up here. Then you get these big companies starting up and spreading their wealth around to the chosen few. In all honesty, every Native up here—man, woman, and child—should be a millionaire a couple times over by now. Shitty thing is, a couple powerful families run all these tribes, and the ones who aren't in that precious circle don't see a cent. It can be— or rather, it very much *is* a dog-eat-dog world up here. All these people travelling from all around to come work, seeking their riches, and most end up living in shanties down by the river. Shanty towns may work down in Mexico, but try living in one when it's forty below."

Vicky retreated to the bedroom, yelling back about her thoughts on the town so far as she made herself more presentable. "So, what are you planning to do with me today, Mr. McGillivray?" She peeked her head around the corner.

He grinned. "Well, if you're bored, I could treat you to lunch. You can tell me a few specifics on what you're looking for in a place, and I'll see if we can get in to look at a few."

She came out wearing a pair of form-fitting jeans and a complementary turtleneck sweater. Her smile lit up the room as she watched him scan her up and down with an approving grin. "A lunch date? This'll be nice." She walked to the closet by the door and pulled out her winter coat and scarf, grabbed her purse, then looped her arm through his. "Shall we go, Mr. McGillivray?"

He seemed insecure with her forwardness. It was just the way she liked them.

"Justin, call me Justin." He shot her a sly smile.

25

Charlie and his men scattered when AJ pulled into the yard at the 11-16 site. Charlie retreated to his office just as the young manager entered.

He sat in his chair, breath held as he listened for the telltale footsteps on the hollow floor. Normally, AJ's visits to the site were short, his involvement minimal. Winter had set in, snow was on the ground, and daytime temperatures could range anywhere from five above to forty below, so progress on the site had been slow. But it was only a matter of time before political pressures caused the dam to burst.

He heard a couple short steps to the coffee pot. After the heavy clank of the pot being placed back on its base, the footsteps came in a flurry, straight to Charlie. He straightened in his chair and braced for the confrontation.

AJ marched through the door.

Charlie was sure to start on a friendly note. "AJ, good morning, how are you?"

AJ did not look impressed. He stared at Charlie with an air of authority before saying, "What's the status on this project?"

Charlie saw a man who was attempting to play dictator but was incredibly unsure of himself. The kind of conditions Charlie most hated working in. He squinted. "The status?"

"Yes, the status! Where are we… progress-wise? What kind of timeline until completion?"

"Well, AJ, it's pretty early in the game for me to be giving you any type of accurate completion date." He turned to a table behind him and shuffled through the pile of drawings littered there. "We just got the packages properly aligned, levelled, and welded into position. But the weather's gotten cold and we have no lighting or temporary heaters for the buildings, so the guys have to take more breaks to warm up. I asked you about getting instrument and electrical crews over here for us as soon as possible, but so far no one's come." He pulled out some drawings and held them out to AJ, who was pacing the room and chewing his nails as he listened. "Look at these prints. All this equipment is used; some of it hasn't run in years. None of this stuff's designed to work in sequence with each other. The pressures, the logic—it all has to be calculated and tested. They really gave us little to work with."

AJ stopped pacing and slammed his fist down on the desk. "Listen, I just got out of a meeting with my fa— the president and some other higher-ups, and they want this thing going as soon as possible! They've bumped the start-up date to June! We brought you on this project to make this stuff work! So I strongly suggest you and your crew of... fucking... stooges get off your asses and start making shit happen!"

Charlie didn't like to play yell-and-scream, but this wasn't his first showdown. "You know, AJ, I want this mess to go away just as much as the next guy— actually, more than the next guy. The only way this project's going to go away is if we finish it. For this to be finished, we are all going to have to do the jobs assigned to us. So you're going to have to get a lot more involved than driving around in your company vehicle, sipping from that fucking flask you got stashed. Don't think I haven't been smelling that shit on your breath. You know what? I'm gonna make this adventure as easy on you as possible, 'cause quite frankly, no one here likes you. But I do need you to get us resources. So I'm gonna write you down a list." He ripped a sheet of paper from his notebook and began to scribble. "We need heaters, lights, and I want no less than a four-man electrical crew, two instrument techs, and a goddamn good programmer! These are the things we need to progress. The longer it takes you to supply these resources, the longer me and my crew of stooges sit on our asses! Got it?" He leaned back in his chair, crossed his arms, and gave AJ a point-blank look. "I know why I was brought here and I will get this done as soon as possible. Because no matter what delusion you have rolling around in your head, I'm not here 'cause I'm having a lot of fun."

AJ was the first to flinch in the stare down when he grabbed the list. He took a sip of his coffee, then turned to walk out the door.

"Hey, AJ," Charlie called.

AJ stopped and looked back.

"I'll do what I can to get this done on time, and make it run," Charlie said. "Just a heads-up though. I've never seen anything like this done before. I'm not sure anyone has. So the odds are against us."

AJ just continued on his way.

Charlie listened to his heavy steps make their way down the length of the trailer, then the slam of the front door. He exhaled.

26

Justin McGillivray escorted Vicky to one of his favourite lunch spots. As they took their seats, Vicky was quick to start the conversation.

"So, *Justin*"—she smiled—"you're here, living in the land where the streets are paved with gold. Why aren't you heading out to the plants with all the other Johnny Lunchpails?"

He grinned. "Well, you see, I don't really have any connections at the plants. No uncles or brothers. So, in order for me to get out to the plants, I'd have to start at the bottom… and that means"—he gave a shiver—"manual labour."

"Oooh!" Vicky's hand shot to her mouth. "You poor baby! But that would mean you might get dirty, or chip a nail!" She laughed and picked up her glass of water.

"I'd really rather not talk about it. The thought is just too overwhelming. I might not sleep now." He grinned. "I considered going out to the plants after high school. There's lots of courses to get students introduced to the trade and engineering programs, or whatnot. But then you watch all those people heading out every day in their cars or buses and coming back all dirty after spending the day out in the cold. And there's a lot of unhealthy shit out there. Honestly, it's just not how I roll. So I got into the real estate gig. There's a lot of commission to be made when the average price is a half-mill. And I get to dress nice and treat all the lovely young women to lunch."

Vicky always appreciated a game of kiss-and-tell.

PRICE PER BARREL

Their waitress came by with an ice bucket and a bottle of their finest red, pouring each a glass.

"Well," Vicky said, "look at you figuring it all out. So, while the Johnny Punch-clocks are out busting their asses in the cold and filth, with pictures of their beautiful wives folded in their wallets for that little bit of extra encouragement, you're seducing those wives over lunch, then banging the asses off them in the master bedrooms of some of the swankiest mansions in town? And making a commission? A home wrecker disguised as a real estate agent?"

Justin choked on his wine. "Miss Bellham, please, you make it sound so dirty. I'm providing a selfless service. The men going out to these plants and working such long hours, breathing in those nasty poisons—it's tiring, and depleting on their sex drive. They'd think even less of themselves if they came home to an eager wife pleading for physical fulfillment that they couldn't satisfy. They should be left to relax, crack a beer, and watch the game on their big 3D televisions. He's happy, she's happy, the marriage is healthy and strong." He smirked.

"Oh, I see. Well, when you put it that way, it seems very, um, charitable of you."

"Yes, charitable! That's what it is!" He tipped his glass to her, between smiling eyes.

"So, then, Mr. McGillivray, is this your way of suggesting I am your next charitable donation?" She batted her eyelashes with a slight purse of her lips.

"Indeed not, you're a member of the Doyle Empire. It's a well-known name in this town, and not one that would be wise to cross. It could be very bad for my business, not to mention my physical well-being. I've been given strict orders to treat you with my fullest respect. So, until your real estate needs are met to your full satisfaction, consider me at your beck and call, day… or night." He smirked again.

"Oh, well, that'll be so handy. So, for example, it's midnight and my hard-working husband's putting in some overtime at the plant when suddenly I get this urge to… look at a house. I call you and you come right over?"

Justin leaned in and looked directly at her. "I'll be there so fast, you'll have every reason to suspect I was waiting right outside your door." He oozed with confidence.

She laughed as she sat back in her chair and tossed her hair over her shoulder. AJ had become obsessed with his work and she'd been locked up in

110

that condominium many months. A long time since she'd been let out to play. This guy was no knight in shining armour, by any means—more like a weasel in a nice suit—but he knew how to treat a lady, and he could hold his own in a conversation… Perhaps she should drag this out a while?

Justin raised his glass. "Here's to charity!"

Vicky raised her glass and they shared a laugh.

27

The number of daylight hours grew smaller. On the day of winter solstice, the sun barely rose above the southern treeline, and the residents of Fort McMurray enjoyed less than seven hours of long shadows streaked with sunlight.

The Christmas season had arrived. Half the town's population decorated their trees, hung the stockings, and curled up by the fire with their loved ones. For the other half of the population—the transients who'd left behind the ones they love to seek fortune for their own personal reasons—Christmas was nothing more than an opportunity to make overtime cash by covering for those who were enjoying the festive season.

The push for the 11-16 Project was on through the holidays, and all of Charlie's crew had reluctantly agreed to work. After they had left for the night, Charlie stayed behind to try to make sense of some of the prints and put together a game plan to move forward. AJ had finally followed through on supplying the equipment and labour Charlie had requested, but even with the added resources, they were having trouble gaining traction, like bald tires on an icy hill.

He took off his reading glasses and rubbed his eyes, stretched his arms over his head, then rested back in his chair and let go a large yawn. He needed to take a break. He wheeled his chair across the room to his computer. Refreshing his email, he found a new message from his son. It was a video message labelled *Merry Christmas Grandpa*.

He smiled softly and a tear began to form. He clicked on the tab and watched the loading symbol circle for a few seconds before an image appeared. Summit was sitting in a chair with his favourite ball cap on, the one Charlie had bought him. His mother and father were squatting beside him in the background, smiling happily.

Charlie chuckled at the merry holiday portrait. He and Marge had planned to head out West and see them for the holidays, if only for a couple days, but work had gotten in the way, as it had many times before. Times like this made Charlie despise his job. But looking down at the healthy glow in his grandson's face right now made it all worthwhile.

Summit smiled and waved, then began to speak. "Merry Christmas, Grandpa and Grandma. I'm sorry we couldn't come and see you this Christmas. I miss you. But it's fun because we can do this video for you and then we'll kinda be there with you. Mommy and Daddy told me to tell you that the doctor says I'm doing really good, and I'm getting stronger." The proud young boy curled his arms out to the side and flexed his muscles. "I'm racing with the other kids at school now—I even beat one of the other boys!"

His smile sent Charlie into a full stream of tears. Charlie's son and daughter-in-law broke into tears themselves, stealing a quick hug with each other behind Summit and wiping their eyes with their sleeves before facing the camera again.

"And guess what else!" Summit said. He reached up slowly, grabbed the brim of his cap, and whipped it off.

Charlie chuckled at the sight of his full head of hair, his bangs even reaching down to cover some of his forehead.

"I have hair now! Lots of it! I use shampoo in the shower, and I brush it every day. Daddy even bought me my own special brush, it's pretty cool. I can brush it into a Mohawk if I use some of Mommy's hair stuff, and then she got me some green stuff and I went to school with green spikes! The other kids thought it was super cool, and that's the day they let me race with them!"

Charlie wanted to grab the boy and squeeze him so tight as he swung him around in his arms!

"So, I guess that's it for now. We're all doing really good, but we miss you guys, lots! I hope we can be together soon, and I can show you all the stuff I can do now at the playground. Thank you for doing so much to help us, Grandpa and Grandma. We love you lots and lots!"

In unison, they all said "Merry Christmas!" and blew kisses, and then the screen fell black.

Charlie grabbed a couple tissues from a box on his desk, blew his nose and wiped his eyes, then exhaled heavily. *This, this is cause for celebration.*

He kicked his chair back from his desk and marched across the trailer to AJ's desk, then rummaged through the drawers until he found the bottle of whiskey. He snagged a Styrofoam cup from beside the coffee maker and headed outside.

The sky was clear and the stars shone brilliantly as he stood on the landing and enjoyed a deep breath of the brisk night air. The temperature had warmed to minus ten and all was very still; this was the north in winter hibernation. Light snow fell, but it was like no other snow Charlie had ever seen before. The flakes were lighter, larger, and more crystalline, like so many depictions in children's Christmas books. It was what he'd heard the guys refer to as "Northern Lights snow." They claimed it only fell around the industrial plants, created by the massive plumes of process steam hanging over the mines.

He sat on the top step, and the hollow sound of crunching snow beneath his boots echoed over the frozen tundra. He poured a shot of whiskey and tipped it back. "Ahhh," he breathed, and smiled. His boy was winning races. He wiped the remainder of a tear from his lip.

Charlie froze at the sound of a small whinny and snort. He scanned the winter darkness beyond the bright glow of the yard lights. Then, from the entrance, came the sound of heavy hooves crunching through the snow. Then plumes of exhaust puffing from a horse's nose. The chieftain he had seen before sat tall upon its back.

The two men looked at each other. Charlie was not scared or intimidated by the man. Although the language barrier prevented them from having any type of in-depth conversation, they were both men... elders of men. Charlie felt they would find more in common than not.

Charlie raised his hand in greeting. "Hello." Then he motioned to the sky. "Beautiful night, isn't it?"

There was no response.

Charlie motioned him forward. "Why don't you c'mon over? No one else is here, they've all gone home."

The man remained still. Then, to Charlie's surprise, he dismounted and led his horse over until they stood within a few feet of him.

Charlie gave a welcoming smile. The man stood silent and still, planted like the great trees of the forest, the wrinkles on his face like the age lines on a fallen spruce. He stared deep into Charlie's eyes—so deep it was almost intrusive.

Charlie held his position. He had nothing to hide. If they both searched deep enough, they would find common ground. He, too, had walked his piece of earth.

Charlie broke the silence. "Aw, c'mon, Chief, no need for a standoff tonight. I'm not planning on chopping anything down." He poured another shot of whiskey and held it up. "It's Christmas, time for peace." He had no clue what the man understood of the English language, but his gift broke the probing trance.

The chieftain reached for the cup, raised it to his nose for a sniff, then relaxed and cracked a smile. He took his spot on the stairs beside his new comrade.

Charlie chuckled. "There ya go." He raised the bottle to the man. "To the ones we love! God bless them this Christmas."

He grinned at Charlie, then, with a stuttered motion, raised his cup to the bottle.

"Cheers!" Charlie said.

Each man took a swig, the chieftain from his cup and Charlie straight from the bottle.

"Ha, well, your visit tonight was unexpected, but a pleasant surprise." Charlie reached around and patted the chieftain on the back.

"Ay-Hay," the man replied.

"You know, Chief," Charlie started, then paused. "I, uh, is that all right if I call you *Chief?*"

His new friend did little more than raise a curious eyebrow.

"With all the commotion since I've been here, I've never really had the time to sit down like this and just… take it all in. Really beautiful country up here. I can understand why you give us Whities such a hard time about ripping it up." He took another pull from the bottle. The drink was smooth and warm, instantly relaxing. Combined with the promising message from his grandson, he felt a joy he hadn't in some time. He looked up peacefully toward the top of the treeline.

The chieftain launched into a speech in his native tongue. What he was saying, god only knew. But for Charlie, it fit the moment.

The man dug into a pocket on his hide jacket, then pulled out a lengthy wooden pipe and a tobacco pouch, his speech taking on the form of a chant or song. He packed the pipe full, set it ablaze, and took a long draw, exhaling a large plume of white smoke that drifted for a supernatural time before it dissipated slowly into the cool night air. Then he passed it to Charlie with a smile and nod.

Charlie wasn't much of a smoker, but this was a night for celebration, and he supposed it would be rude to turn it down. He accepted and took a long, steady pull, then slowly exhaled a thin stream that stretched through the air like a jetliner trail. As he watched the smoke float away, his head flooded with a giddy disorientation.

This can't be straight tobacco.

Wide-eyed, he looked on as the man's head distorted in and out of focus while he continued his chant. Charlie turned back to the forest and felt his face flush. His eyes squinted and his gut clenched as he succumbed to a short bout of uncontrolled laughter. He pulled himself together, only to succumb again. The chorus of the chant heightened as other voices joined in and the echo of a distant drum began and grew suddenly closer. Combined with the smell of whiskey and smoke, Charlie's every sense was hyper-excited.

The trip took a turn and the laughing stopped. Charlie regained control of his motor skills and sat in calm wonder, taking in his new surroundings. The trees seemed to shift and move from one spot to another. The verse and the drumbeat grew to a climax as an explosive orange hue drew his attention to the treetops. His mind opened with awe as his gaze rose up to the sky above.

The song stopped instantly as the sky burst into flame. Violent waves of colour in bright yellow, red, blue, and green shimmered and flickered. The earth stood silent but for a faint crackling in the distance.

They're alive... I can... hear them!

Charlie froze in place; he couldn't even blink: the Aurora Borealis, like he'd never thought possible. He understood how people in ancient times could interpret it as angry gods or a coming apocalypse.

He listened closely; hidden within the crackling white noise of the furious night sky, he heard the familiar sounds of his loved ones. Within the racing colours, a faint, shimmering outline appeared. Then he made out her kind and gentle face, the one he'd fallen in love with the moment they met. Her precious head was resting on her pillow, and her warm eyes were staring into his heart. He remained dumbfounded, not wanting to blink and risk losing that split second of enchantment.

"I love you, Charles Bidwell." A colourful streaming hand reached down from the sky and caressed his cheek; he could feel her passion. "You're a good man."

The face faded, the colours swirled, and new sounds emerged faintly from the static: that of a laughing boy… a sacred place in his heart.

"Over here, Grandpa! Pass it to me!"

The colours took shape, lending visual theatrics to sound, and there was young Summit running around in the field, looking back for his grandfather to pass him the football. Whispers of happiness filled the background, along with random scenes of the boy's parents running around in modest attempts to block the young child. A spiralling football came shooting into the picture, leaving a whirlpool of shimmering rainbow colours in its wake. With a short burst of speed, Summit stretched out his arms as long as he could, then he made a dive for the ball and… he caught it! Jumping up in ecstasy, he held up the ball. "Woo hoo! Look! I caught it! I caught the ball, Grandpa! I actually caught it, and I dived— did you see me, Grandpa? Did you see me dive!"

Young Summit's excitement was so real, so contagious as he sprinted toward Charlie, who sat dead stiff on the stoop. He raised his arms as the boy grew closer… and closer, his smile so close…

Charlie let out a shout of joy. "Ha ha! That's my boy!"

As suddenly as the vision appeared, it faded. Reality pushed a lone tear down the side of his face. He remained still, arms raised, then let them slowly fall back to his side.

The chieftain looked at him with a wise grin.

Charlie searched the sky, hypnotized by the crackling lights, hoping for another shot at catching Summit.

Softly, the old wise man started into song. The song felt peaceful. Maybe it was a song about a man who'd passed through the storm and now, on the other side, had seen the first ray of light in the darkness. The peaking waves of sound smoothed over Charlie like a gentle hand reaching down to calm him with its soothing touch.

The story began to roll, one chorus straight after the other. Mystical voices filtered softly through the trees.

The chieftain stood and gathered the reins of his horse, never missing a verse. He mounted the steed and nodded a goodbye to Charlie, who paid him little attention. Still singing, he turned his horse away into the darkness. Charlie's gaze dropped from the sky just in time to see the pair disappear in a wisp of mist as soon as they hit the treeline. The fire in the sky extinguished the moment the song stopped. No more lights, no more song, no more visions, no more Chief.

Charlie's intoxication lifted and he took a deep breath of the fresh forest air. *Where was I? Did that just really happen?* He looked down at the whiskey bottle sitting beside him. "I think it's time for me to put you back where I found you," he muttered.

He pressed himself up from the stoop, bent over and grabbed the bottle, then paused… A man and his horse. Fresh snow on the ground and not one track, neither foot nor hoof. His heart skipped and he raised his gaze to the treeline.

He smiled. Whether it had been Alzheimer's or a visit from a spirit, it was a much-needed adventure.

"Goodnight, my friend." Charlie waved to the trees, then turned and went back inside.

28

Ollie had signed up to work through the holidays. It was great money, and he hoped it would help take his mind off the festivities he was missing back home.

It was late Christmas Eve and he had just returned to his room after a sixteen-hour shift in the frigid cold. All day he'd wished for his shift to end, but now, alone in his room, he wished to be back at work.

He lifted the picture of his grandmother from the nightstand. He'd looked at it every night during the depressing days of the Northern winter. A reminder of why he was there. She would've suffered the same for him.

As he looked upon her smile, tears built in his eyes. At this time back home, friends and neighbours would be gathered around the bonfire at the park in the centre of town. In the past Ollie would get the engine started on the old truck to give the cab some time to warm up, then he'd pack up all the baking his gran had done. Something she did every year. All of the children and many of the parents praised her for her baking; some even declared it was the best part of the holidays. She always brushed it off as nothing, but Ollie knew the time she spent on it. It was arguably her most favourite event of the year.

Ollie would drive her to the park and set her up with her favourite lawn chair and quilt, then lay out all the pastries. It was always so perfect: kids would run from their snow forts and the skating rink to meet them, all the trees would be decorated with sparkling lights, Gran would receive greetings and hugs from people she loved.

But this year she'd be unable to attend due to her condition. He imagined what the festival would be without her, and his mood slumped a little more.

***

Mary-Ann scurried down the hall of the camp. Not too fast, in fear of upsetting the goodies in her basket, but she had to get to Ollie's room before they grew cold. She had texted with him casually throughout the day, pretending she had some family event to attend that evening, but she was really planning on surprising him. They'd been spending more and more time together, and although he was very slow to advance the relationship in any physical way, they were both very happy together.

Her work at the plant had been lightened over the holidays as staff had been cut back to little more than a skeleton crew. She'd finished up her chores by early afternoon and then rushed over to the camp, stopping to ask the security guard at the front counter to let her know when Ollie arrived before she headed to the kitchen. The kitchen staff had been kind enough to let her use their facility to work on some of the special delights Ollie had mentioned his grandmother liked to make for the holidays. Thankfully Ollie ended up working late because she had messed up a couple of times.

She stopped at his door, smoothed down her new red dress—nothing overly erotic as she didn't want to make him feel pressured, but a girl has to look good—then reached into her basket to add her final Christmas touch: her Santa hat. It was an accent she hoped would bring a little extra sex appeal. Then, lightly and nervously, she knocked.

Muffled through the door, she heard his voice. "Hello, who is it?"

She didn't reply, not wanting to give herself away. She knocked again, a little firmer this time. As soon as the door opened the slightest of cracks, she yelled excitedly, "Merry Christmas! Surprise!"

Judging by the look of him, it was a very unexpected surprise.

Still dressed in his grubby work clothes, tears were streaming down his soiled face, red and burnt from the frigid wind.

Mary-Ann suddenly didn't feel like her surprise was so welcome.

"Oh, Ollie," she said and bowed her head. "I'm so sorry, I didn't mean to catch you at a bad—"

"No!" Ollie interrupted. "No, Mary-Ann, please." He reached for her but then pulled back and hid his grungy hands behind his back.

"I just wasn't expecting… I'm such a mess. You, well…"

Their eyes met, and even beneath all the grime and windburn, she could see him blush. She was so close, all she wanted was for him to grab her, hold her, kiss her, love her… She just wanted to be his everything.

"You look very beautiful tonight, Mary-Ann."

She blushed right back at him.

"I, I mean, you look beautiful every night… and the day too. All the time, you look beautiful all the time."

She couldn't help giggling, then held up her basket. "Merry Christmas, Ollie. I remembered the stories you told about your grandma's Christmas baking, so I thought I'd try. Well, I'm sure they're nowhere near as good, but—"

"Mary-Ann, please, just… Thank you, thank you very much. So, I… well, I mean, if you wanted, you could come in."

She smiled up at him and he stood aside, holding the door open as she passed.

He let the door close behind her, and within a minute, the pungent stench of his workday filled the room. Combined with her baking, it smelled of Christmas cookies that just passed right through ya.

"I should probably shower. Sorry, I just really wasn't expecting… I'll be quick, I promise."

"Ollie, it's fine, I'll be fine." She giggled again. "Go, I'll be here waiting."

He smiled. "Okay, I'll be quick. Please have a seat on the bed. Or the chair, if that's more comfort—"

"Ollie!"

"Yes, right, going. I'll be fast, don't leave." He disappeared into the bathroom.

Mary-Ann sat on the bed, trying her best not to wrinkle her dress. She heard the shower turn on and took that moment to check out Ollie's living quarters.

She'd been in the camp rooms before to help change the linen and mop the floors. The workers left most rooms in a state of disaster—soiled clothing thrown everywhere, muddy floors, and some awful clogged toilets. But not her Ollie. His room was tidy, with everything in its place. She walked over to his sink to find it sparkling—no gobs of toothpaste or globs of… *bluh*. A shiver rose up her back. *Cleanliness is next to godliness.* She smiled.

She sat back down and looked down at the drawer of his nightstand. She chewed her lip as a slight bout of guilt passed. But the need to know overpowered her. She opened it just enough for a quick reveal of any dark fetishes and found just a ruffed up paperback and a pair of nail clippers. Closing the drawer shook a picture frame sitting on top. Closer inspection found the smiling face of a cute elderly woman.

Her heart gasped. *What a sweetheart, he keeps a picture of her by his bed.* She felt tears building and squeezed them back before they ruined her makeup.

The proverbial cloud Mary-Ann had been floating on began to grow into a dark, sinister fog, choking her lungs and burning her eyes as her mind wandered from Ollie's clean and proper camp room to her sordid past.

It had been some time since… since that… that pig had his maleficent way with her. He'd requested that she come to office a few times, but she'd ignored the command. Such a filthy, awful man! Dirty and just such— Why, why her? Why'd he have to choose her? To stain with his disgusting filth! Forever!

She stared blankly at the floor, trembling.

Stained in ways that could never be hidden, not from the one who could've been her true love. That chance had been taken from her, taken from them. Stains and dirt—no amount of lipstick or a pretty red dresses could ever cover them up.

The pipes in the wall thumped. Mary-Ann blinked and sat up straight. All was silent except for the slight sniffle she made as she looked down and brushed the wrinkles from her dress. Ollie would surely come out and ask her to leave after seeing the state she was in. How was it that a grown lady could go from Christmas cheer to suicidal tendencies in the time it took him to have a shower? Obvious signs of the crazies. No matter—she could never let it go further anyway. No matter how much she wanted it—him… them—she could never let him find out.

Ollie walked out of the bathroom and locked the door, then turned to Mary-Ann, who looked up at him with a tear-streaked face that she was sure said, *"Here I am, me and all my crazy."*

"Mary-Ann! What happened, are you all right? Did I do something to upset you?"

She wasn't expecting that reaction. Now she thought she might actually prefer him asking her to leave rather than having to explain her state.

"No, Ollie, no. I'm sorry."

He rushed to the sink, pulled a handful of tissues from a box sitting on its edge, and handed them to her. "Well, what's wrong? I showered, and packed my work clothes up tight in a garbage bag. Does it still smell really bad?"

She couldn't help breaking into a smile while dabbing at her eyes. "No, Ollie. You're so sweet. I... well, it's kind of silly, really. I saw the picture of your grandma on your nightstand and it... it brought back a lot of old Christmas memories from when I was young. So then I got thinking of you and you're being so far away from home, and her. I just felt so sad for you."

He sat down beside her and leaned forward, resting his elbows on his knees. His eyes dropped to the floor and he took a deep breath. "Well," he mumbled, rolling his clammy hands together. He swallowed audibly. Then he took another deep breath, sat up straight, and looked her in the eye.

Mary-Ann's breathing stopped, and so, she swore, did her heart, caught off guard as she was by this man who stared so purposefully at her. A man transformed into one of great will and determination who filled her with both fear and lust.

"When I first came out here, I— well, I had nothing but the shoes on my feet and the shirt on my back. I'd never been where I was going, and I knew nothing about what I was getting into. But that's how I was raised, and there ain't nothing I won't do for the ones I love. But..." He searched for the words. "But you're crazy, Mary-Ann, crazy and silly."

Her breathing intensified. Was he building her up just to slam her down? Tears streamed heavily as she waited. Then she felt his hand come to rest with intention on her lap.

"You're crazy! 'Cause there ain't not one soul on this earth would feel sorry for me right now, in this lonely camp, far away from my home, because I'm sitting beside you. The most beautiful... and smartest..." he stumbled, clearly searching for a word. "The most genuine and special woman I've ever met."

She watched tears well in his eyes as he maintained focus on hers.

"I'm so grateful for meeting you! I'm trying to tell you how much you mean to me, but I'm, I'm just not getting it like I want to, so badly! Maybe if..." He slid his hand from her lap and reached around her waist, wrapping it firmly. At that moment there was no distance, no wall, no army that could keep their lips apart.

Hearts thundered like a stampede across a barren plain. A tidal wave of endorphins flushed away all the dark memories of the past. Like two people teetering on the edge of a high mountain ledge, there was nothing before, or after—there was only now.

Mary-Ann felt a rush of yearning and she turned to face Ollie, her hunger clearly fuelling his own lust as she wrapped her arms around his neck and pulled herself to him. Their youthful innocence beat down primal need, the tender touch of passion surging in to fill the cavernous void that had burdened them both for far too long.

She pulled, Ollie pushed until they found themselves lying beside each other, their hands groping and fingers clutching like the claws of caged animals.

***

He grew large and stiff, to a point he had never known, and Grandma's Christmas baking fell to a distant second place on his list of holiday favourites.

His mouth watered and his head spun, dizzy with primal urge. Ollie the gentleman surrendered to Ollie the hunter as he slid her dress up until it rested on her hips. He reached around to caress her young firm bum, a fruit he'd guiltily admired from afar since the first time he saw her. She was wearing a pair of the thong panties like he'd seen in porn magazines. He couldn't hold himself back and pulled forcefully at the string. Mary-Ann let out a slight moan that set him on fire.

She grabbed him firmly and forced him onto his back. Climbing on top, she looked down on him with the intensity of a woman who knew what she wanted, and by fuck she was coming to get it! She slowly pushed the straps of her dress from her shoulders, never once taking her eyes from him. Then she reached behind herself and released the clasp on her bra, and with timid suspense, she let the restraint slide from her breasts…

Ollie's blinking reflex had completely shut off. He didn't want to miss a second of what was happening. He lay there in a rigor mortis–like state until he became aware that Mary-Ann was waiting with an insecure look on her face.

He broke from his death trance, sat up, and placed his hands caringly on either side of her face, then kissed her passionately. Craving the warmth of her body, he reached down and pulled his shirt off, then wrapped his arms around her and pulled her close. He kissed her lips sensually, then began a soft, tender trail down her neck to her chest and on to her erect nipples, taking his time to explore and excite them. The awkwardness had passed and it was all coming together so naturally, so beautifully.

She was the perfect woman. He had no doubt that what was happening between them was more than just meaningless sex or mindless lust. He wanted her—fully, completely—not just for that night, but for always. Her touch felt of home and tender caring. Something he had not felt for far too long. Something he never realized he missed so much.

124

He slid his hands to her shoulders and pushed her onto her back. He kneeled beside her and took hold of the crumpled dress around her waist. She lifted her bum slightly, and he slid it over her hips, then lightly traced over the fine contours of her slender legs and tossed it to the floor. He lay beside her and pulled the blankets over them, then removed his own constraints. He turned to her and their lips met again, kissing and suckling. She reached down and took him in her hand, softly at first, then with torrid aggression in response to his rock-stiff acceptance of her.

He slid his hand into her panties and she spread herself wide, assuring him she was there for his taking. His exploration found her trimmed, warm, and dripping with want. No longer able to wait, he relieved her of the lace inconvenience and took his turn on top. He looked deep into her loving eyes, then gently wrapped his hand around the back of her neck. All he wanted was her pleasure: the sound, the smell, the taste of her all around him. The lust, the passion—everything was so new to him but long overdue, as though his body had been ready for his mind to catch up and everything had come together then and there. He wanted to show her everything he could be, wanted to raise her up higher than she'd ever climbed before. It would take a man to provide this for her, so a man he became.

Staring into each other's eyes, he leaned in until his swollen tip caressed her lips, warm and welcoming. He backed away and prepared for the grand entrance, the life-changing moment. His time to show her. His time to shine. He pressed forward again, fully.

As she engulfed him, she let loose a sensuous groan.

His body quaked and he grabbed hard to her squeezing... The sensation was—

"*Fu-u-u-ck!*"

He rolled off to the side, breathing fast and heavy. It had passed; whatever it was had passed. His breathing slowed and the intoxicating sexual cloud fogging his mind cleared.

Mary-Ann was looking at him in an unblinking stare.

He looked down at her stomach, the covers having been thrown back during his seizure.

"Oh!" He had just, indeed, shown her all the man he could be. His cheeks went hot. "Mary-Ann, I'm— oh my gosh!" He jumped out of bed and scrambled for a towel, then rushed back to her side and began wiping what amounted to more than twenty years of sitting on the bench. "I'm really, I'm so…" He couldn't look her in the eye.

As he dabbed at her, trying to mop up the filth he'd covered her with, he felt the warm, tender touch of her fingers running through his hair. He looked up to see her smiling sweetly at him. Sweetly, like the young woman who sat across from him in the cafeteria. Sweetly, like the girl in the pretty red dress and the Santa hat who brought him baked goods for Christmas. She was still there, she was still smiling sweetly.

She placed her hand on his cheek and motioned him toward her. He obeyed and crawled up to rest beside her. She sat up and put her arms around him, bringing him back down to the warmth of her naked body. She kissed him tenderly, then laid her head back on the pillow and stared at him as she bit softly on her lip. "Oliver Hynes, you sure know how to make a woman feel special."

He paused for a beat, puzzling over her riddle, then grinned. "You're welcome."

She snuggled in closer to him. "I'm right here, and I'm not going anywhere. I promise we'll have many more chances to get this all figured out." She giggled, kissed him softly, then reached over and turned off the lamp.

"…Well… how 'bout now?" he asked.

29

Boxing Day: time for the traditional Doyle family dinner at sweet Granny Emma's house.

Having never visited the place before, Vicky was quite surprised at the grandness of the old woman's place. The Christmas angel ornaments and twinkling white lights dawned a scene of subtle elegance.

"Hmph, not bad for a cranky old bitch," she sneered as she got out of the car. Over the last few months, her disposition toward her wicked witch of an in-law had grown hostile, and she made no attempt to keep it secret.

"Vicky, please!" AJ spread his arms out. "Can you just suck it up and get through this night? It's just one night, for fuck's sake!"

She paused at his sudden outburst, then stuck her tongue out at him.

As they walked the path through the shovelled banks of snow, the Christmas spirit surrounding them had little effect on Vicky's humbug mood. They passed through the white archway preceding the front door, then AJ grabbed the lion-head knocker and rapped.

Vicky stood pouting at the ground, scuffing the walkway with her high heel. "Smile!" AJ demanded.

She flipped her spoiled-bitch aura to a happy bride-to-be façade: radiant smile and eyes warm with love.

The sound of footsteps approaching made the couple straighten themselves for the greet. The door opened sudden and wide, with Emma Doyle standing in wait, dressed in a fine blue evening gown complemented by large shimmering diamond earrings and a pearl necklace. She dressed like a woman of sophistication, but her smile was that of a loving grandmother.

"AJ, how wonderful to see you! We were all wondering what was taking you so long?"

AJ accepted his grandmother's embrace and Vicky looked past her, to his parents standing in the foyer. Dressed up as they always were.

"And Victoria! Oh, my dear, you look so lovely tonight, as always."

Emma gave off no scent of ill feelings and hugged her tenderly, but Vicky wouldn't be surprised if the old bat had a knife ready to stick in her back. She gave out a giddy squeal as she reached out to the old woman with arms wide, and with a smile that would send Disney characters worldwide into a fit of envy, and hugged her with such exuberance that she practically lifted her of her feet. After the moment of sentiment, Vicky turned and stepped through the entrance with another smile that brightened the room.

"Oh my god, Emma!" she said as she hugged the rest of the clan and marvelled at the splendour of the house. "Look at this place! It's *so* beautiful, I just— wow!" She clutched both hands over her heart. "I can't believe it's taken so long for me to see this. But, well, I guess I was never really invited."

But the back-and-forth game with Emma wouldn't end so easily.

"Well, yes, Victoria, I've been meaning to ask you over. But with your being so busy running around with your realtor friend— oh, and how is the house hunting going so far, my dear? Dragging on some, hmm?"

The reference to her newfound friend suggested the old girl had a hand in setting it all up. But Vicky was always in for a good game of cat and mouse. Besides, she felt a little jealousy was good for AJ. She shrugged off the question. "Still looking, nothing's really caught my eye yet." She maintained her flawless smile and continued on her self-guided tour.

After sitting everyone down in the living room for a drink and some idle chitchat, Emma announced that dinner was ready and carried herself with a strong sense of arrogance as they moved to the dining room. The room was tastefully decorated with old wood furnishings, glass door cabinets, and expensive fine china. The food was abundant. A large golden brown turkey was set in the middle of the long oak table, surrounded by traditional holiday fixings.

"So, AJ," Albert began the conversation while working on a mouthful of stuffing, "how's the project coming along? There's only a little over five months left until the scheduled start-up."

Vicky suppressed a smile. Of course it was a subject AJ would've avoided during dinner. One, because he didn't feel the project was going as good as it should, and two, because he really hadn't a fucking clue. He was honestly working on nothing more than crossed fingers. The stink of booze on his breath every night confirmed he was in over his head, definitely in no position to begin answering questions about completion deadlines, which she knew plagued him with guilt.

"Good, it's coming along good," he said, face down to his plate, through a mouth full of potatoes.

"Good?" Albert replied. His tone suggested he was unsatisfied with the simple response. "What exactly does 'good' mean? Have the electricians started yet? Have the mechanics looked things over?"

AJ mumbled something incoherent.

"What? What was that, son?"

"Yes!" AJ snapped back. "I, I think so." He grabbed for his glass of wine and took a large gulp.

Vicky's eyes widened as she felt the tension build. They was gonna have an old-fashioned shootout right there at Christmas dinner. From *O holy night* to *Oh, holy shit!*

"You *think* so?" Albert put down his shovel, wiped his mouth, and focused purely on his son. "What exactly does that mean? How is that an acceptable answer from the project manager?"

AJ stopped chewing. He leaned back in his chair, closed his eyes, and took a deep breath. Then he took another sip of wine in what she guessed was a bid for time to conjure what he hoped would be a suitable answer, enough to get through the dinner. "All the equipment and buildings are in place and the guys are working on it." He lifted his eyes and scanned his audience. Emma picked lightly at her food, feigning ignorance to everything and smiling to herself. His mother, as always, sat with her face down to her food. His father remained silent, both fists clenched like two hammers on either side of his plate.

Vicky watched the man in her peripheral vision. For a moment she thought he might do the proper thing and let the conversation slide. But this was AJ's father, the head of the fucking beast. She'd learned passiveness was never his strong point; passiveness was never a consideration.

PRICE PER BARREL

"The equipment! The buildings!" The air began to tremor. "That shit's been in place for months, AJ. Don't feed me that fucking bullshit!"

Vicky kept watching Albert; she could see the internal battle. It was a frontline project and he needed answers—had any other manager given him bullshit answers like AJ just dished, Albert would have him hanging from a tree. But this fuck-up manager was his own son, placed in the position by his own hand. Business or family, which would win? With a proud man like Albert, the real surprise to her was that he didn't walk around with his dick in his hand.

"Have they figured out how to get the logic to communicate between the equipment?" he continued.

"Yes!" AJ snapped back. "I'm pretty sure..."

Albert chuckled. "You're pretty sure? Well, that's solid. That's something I can take to the board in the new year. My son, the PM, is pretty sure something is happening! I think they'll be satisfied with that!" He threw his napkin down. "Tell me, son, do you even show up at the site? Or are you too busy driving around the plant drinking in your company fucking vehicle! Or better yet—do you even remember where the fucking project is!"

Silence filled the room.

"I put my neck on the line—my reputation—to place you in that position! Handed to you on a silver fucking platter! I gave you top-quality support—this should be a goddamn cakewalk for you! And I can't believe you're just going to completely fuck it up!" Albert thrust back his chair, slammed his hands on the table, and glared at his son.

AJ stared blankly at the wall, numb to his environment.

Like a sudden gunshot, Albert picked up his plate of food and sent it hurling across the room. It smashed against the wall, shrapnel of Christmas dinner and fine china spattering the guests. Everyone jumped in their seats but were quick to settle again.

AJ still gave no response.

Albert slammed his fist on the table again with a loud snort, causing the dinnerware to quake. He stood, nostrils flared and face beet red, and thundered, "GODDAMMIT, BOY! YOU FUCKING ANSWER ME WHEN I'M TALKING TO YOU!" The big man scooped up a handful of mashed potatoes from his wife's plate and lobbed it at AJ, hitting him smack in the side of the head with a loud *WHOP!*

130

The assault earned a reaction. AJ sprang to his feet, wiping gobs of potato from his face and hair and slopping them down on the table. For once in their lives, the family saw the fatherly traits had been handed down as AJ shook with rage. He pointed to his father and stared straight into his eyes.

"YOU!" he yelled back, rabid, foaming spit spattering from his mouth. "YOU! THIS WAS *YOUR* FUCKING DREAM!" He paused, his chest heaving as he gathered fuel for his next attack. "THIS IS YOU! YOUR DREAM. NOT MINE! NOT EVER!" Done with his speech, AJ reached for a clean napkin and scrubbed his face. Then he stormed out of the dining room.

Vicky held her napkin over her mouth as her gaze darted from person to person. All heads were down. She lowered the napkin slowly and set it calmly on the table. "Well, dinner was really… lovely, Emma. Thank you for having us. Let's do it again sometime." She stood, gathered her belongings, and went in search of her lesser half.

She stepped out into the cold night air to see AJ sitting in the car, tipping his flask away from his mouth. White plumes of exhaust billowed out the Porsche's pipes into the still frost of the winter night. She got in the car and slammed the door as he tucked the flask in his inside jacket pocket.

She smiled. "Well, that was really nice. Do you think she made that stuffing from scratch?" She laughed while she buckled her belt.

AJ punched the accelerator, the tires spinning wild as the ass-end of the car fishtailed away from the curb and down the snow-laden road until they disappeared from under the streetlamp.

"Shut the fuck up, Vicky."

30

With the Christmas season in the past, the days turned from growing progressively shorter to consistently longer. The beginning of spring was only a couple months away, and for Ollie Hynes, love was in the air.

Ollie and Mary-Ann had spent as much time together over the holidays as work would allow. With reports that his grandmother's condition was stable, Ollie was able to focus all his energy on Mary-Ann, and he let himself be swept away in a current of passion.

On his adventure in Fort Mac, he'd expected to find the days of winter cold, the hours of work endless, the dirt on his clothes and beneath his fingernails thick. But he'd never expected to find a fairy tale like Mary-Ann. Beneath all the filth and the long, dark nights, he'd found tender lips, soft skin, and the most beautiful smell he'd ever tasted. His delirious smile could not be erased.

For some people, this radiance of positivity is addictive and contagious, spreading warmth and happiness to whoever's present.

But to others, well…

Ollie met up with Honey early on the first workday of the new year.

The morning was still pitch-black and another bitter cold spell had moved in. With the wind chill factored in, it felt like minus forty. A frosty gust of wind stirred the dry snow on the ground beneath Ollie as he practically skipped across the parking lot toward Honey.

"Well, well, look at you," Honey said as Ollie jumped in the passenger's seat with a smile uncommon for someone about to start a twelve-hour shift pumping frozen shit. "What's gotten into you? Been drinking already?" He chuckled.

Ollie blushed as he stuffed his lunch sack behind his seat. "No."

Honey waited for his apprentice to continue, then gave up and asked, "Well, then what? Don't tell me walking across a freezing-ass parking lot's got you excited about your day. So what is it? Spill it, junior."

"I just enjoyed… having a couple days off." Ollie smirked.

"Drop the bullshit, boy, what's her name, and how far d'ya get?"

His cover blown, Ollie decided to give up some information. Not too much, though, out of respect for Mary-Ann. If word got around, she could get some hassle from the guys in the plant.

"She's just this girl I met, a while back."

"You met a girl? Where? In town? She good? What's she charge to make me smile all stupid like you? Hahahaha!"

Ollie suddenly wanted to punch him in the face. But he knew Honey was just being Honey, so he managed to brush it off. "No, no, it's not… she's not that… she works out here."

"Here? Out here in the camp? There's thousands of guys in that camp and, like, ten women. Never heard of anyone falling in love with any of them. Is it one of the cooks? Cleaning staff? Those little pygmy girls they dig out of the jungle? Watch your step with them, boy, they got some shit to spread that ain't yet been discovered by us. Might end up having to hack your winkie off, if it doesn't fall off on its own. Shit, I heard tell of a guy one time, he got to fooling with some of them foreign girls and his shit just burst into flames. Combustion-somethin', they called it." He cackled himself into a violent hack, then rolled down the window and spit some mucous into the swirling chill. Wind carried small shards of ice into the cab, ruffling papers and feathering through his hair.

"No, she's not from the jungle. She doesn't work in the kitchen."

"Really? You mean to tell me you found some sort of respectable white girl, in camp?"

"Well, yeah. She's from The Rock, back home."

"Oh! A good old Newfie girl, eh? Well, watch yourself, don't get too attached. There's a lot of men around here that'll line up for their shot at a good woman. Men with a lot more going for them than runnin' a shit truck. If she's all that, she won't stick with you long. But what the hell, man, enjoy it while you can.

PRICE PER BARREL

Any time a guy can come to work up here, stay in camp, and find a decent girl to dump a regular load in—well, that sort of set up don't come 'round much, if ever." Honey shifted the truck into gear and headed off through security, then down to the plant.

Other than the growling of the rig engine and the squeaking and groaning of the truck interior, the cab remained silent as they made their rounds from site to site. Ollie looked at all the guys in a way he never had before. Hundreds, thousands, and some looked right around the same age as him and seemed to be running some of the jobs, ordering guys around. Not a speck of dirt or grime on them. Decent-looking guys, too—some of them anyway—as good-looking as himself for sure. They could easily take Mary-Ann from him. All it would take was for one of them to notice her. They probably had their own houses in town. Or at least something better than a camp room.

He stood on top of the septic tank he'd just finished hooking up. The loud whine from the truck began, and people turned their heads to him, one by one, as the sound ricocheted across the yard. Their glances only lasted a fraction of a second before they returned to their business. Nobody cares about the shit-truck guy. Ollie's jaw clenched, and he felt the dried-out filth on his cheeks tighten and crack. The sensation was repeated when he clenched his fists. He hated dirt on his hands. Sometimes the rough feeling of it gave him the same irritating sensation as running his teeth along a wooden Popsicle stick.

The cold wind blew shivers up his spine as he dismounted his perch. He jumped in the passenger's seat of the truck just as Honey finished up his end of the shift update to the boss. He cranked the rig's heater fan and placed his chapped hands over one of the vents. The rushing air delivered a pleasantly warm, yet stinging sensation.

After a couple minutes of *uh huh*s and *sure thing*s, Honey hung up the phone, then rested an elbow on the steering wheel. "Well, that was the boss. Sounds like we're 'bout to start into a busy season of sorts. He says with all the new projects on the go, they've been told to expect demand to increase at least fifty percent till the summer. So in order to keep up, he's looking for one crew to volunteer for night shift, which pays five dollars an hour more, and having only one crew means that crew will always have work and make a shit pile of OT. So, I volunteered us." He looked over at Ollie.

"Listen, kid, I'm guessing you've never worked night shift before. It's way

134

better. There's only a skeleton crew on nights, through the whole plant. And they never expect as much work. So our workload should be, like, half of what it is now. The only real bad thing is that it's at night. It takes a couple shifts to get used to it. But once you're past that, you'll never want to go back to days."

Ollie tried to compute everything Honey was telling him. It sounded like a pretty straightforward decision. More money, less work—no-brainer. He could talk to Mary-Ann, and maybe she'd get more work up at the camp so he'd see more of her during the day. This could actually work out for the better.

"Okay." He shrugged. "When do we start?"

Honey slipped him a wink. "You go home right now, stay up as late as you can, and sleep as much of the day as you can tomorrow. Then meet me at the usual spot at 7:00 p.m. Don't worry about being too sharp for tomorrow night. They cut us slack for a couple days.

"Get ready to make some money now, boy."

31

For the 11-16 Project, the new year meant turning over a new leaf for AJ.

The first Monday after the holidays, Charlie pulled into the yard and was not-so-pleasantly surprised to see AJ's truck at the site bright and early.

When he stepped in the trailer, he was surprised again to find the young manager clean-shaven and dressed in his coveralls, eyes wide and de-glazed, not even the slightest hint of booze on him. It was true that up to that point, Charlie never liked AJ. But he'd learned over time to never say a person can't change, as rare as it may be.

"Good morning, Charlie"—AJ held a very professional expression as he reached out to shake Charlie's hand—"and Happy New Year to you."

Charlie accepted the hand and returned a pleasant smile. "Yes, AJ, thank you, and a Happy New Year to you as well."

AJ motioned toward his office door. "Could I have a moment of your time, please?"

"Oh… Yes, of course." Charlie smiled and walked past him, into the office.

When both men were seated, AJ said, "All right, I know I haven't been too involved in this project. You might say I've been suffering from… well, a lack of interest, I guess."

Embarrassed for him, Charlie found it hard to make eye contact.

"So, what I'm looking to do here now is to maybe… start over again? I understand if your opinion of me is lacking, but I hope maybe we can actually work together, going forward. I understand now that you're a very valuable resource. I'd like to learn from you and help you out in any way I can." He stood and smiled sincerely at Charlie as he held out his hand again. "What do you say? To a new year, and a new beginning?"

Charlie stood and shook his hand with a smile. "Sounds like a great idea to me, AJ, thank you."

"No, Charlie, it's me who owes you a thank-you for putting up with me."

Charlie nodded subtly. "Agreed." He grinned.

They shared in a laugh and returned to their seats.

"Well, then," AJ continued, "how 'bout we take some time for you to bring me up to speed—"

The sudden squealing of brakes came from outside.

A white plume of snow billowed up past the window and both men jumped up to see what was going on. A black Cadillac SUV was parking in a cloud of snow and engine exhaust. Even before the weight of the vehicle settled, Albert Doyle Sr. was jumping out of the driver's seat. The big man stomped through the ankle-deep drift, then marched up the steps and took a second to stamp off the loose snow.

AJ quickly returned to his chair with a look of suspense.

There was some thudding up and down the trailer before a light rapping came at the door.

"Yeah," AJ responded.

Albert opened the door and did a double take of the two sitting together. He looked directly down at Charlie. "Do you have a minute?" he said, not acknowledging his son at all. "I'd like to have a word in my truck." He motioned toward the door.

Charlie grasped the armrests of his chair and began to lift his weight. "Oh, yes, of co—" He paused and looked over to AJ.

AJ shrugged with a tense smile. They both knew who held the higher hand, and the decision to be made was neither of theirs.

Charlie continued to his feet. "Sorry, AJ, if you could just excuse me for a second?"

AJ nodded. "Of course, I'll be here when you're done."

Charlie followed Albert out of the office, then they slid on their winter gear before heading out into the cold. Both men entered the running vehicle simultaneously and slammed the doors.

Albert cranked up the heater fan, then unravelled his scarf and removed his toque and tossed them to the back seat. He took a minute to adjust his mass before he looked at Charlie. "So, first off, what the fuck was my son doing dressed in coveralls? You ever seen him dressed like that before?"

Clearly father and son were no longer a happy couple. And if Charlie didn't pay attention, he'd likely wind up in the middle of it. "Well," he replied, "I believe he was wearing coveralls the day we went on our tour?"

"Yeah, four fucking months ago!" Albert rubbed his face. "Anyway, since he's here and he likely knows what this is about, I'll try to make it quick." He turned to Charlie and began using animated hand gestures. "I know that you know— well, everyone around here has fucking realized, I'm sure, that AJ hasn't been much involved. Listen, we both know you have the brains and the experience to run this job blindfolded. I can't say enough how much I appreciate your agreeing to join this project, even with my awarding the PM title to AJ—a decision I now regret, and am truthfully quite embarrassed about. So I'd like to make you an offer. I'd like to raise your pay another twenty percent. In return, I'd like you to take control, but do your best not to step over AJ. It'll be sort of an undercover project manager role, and you report directly to me from now on. I'll want weekly updates."

Charlie stared straight out the window for a moment, then he looked over at Albert. "Listen, I'll admit AJ's dropped the ball on all this. And yes, I'm comfortable assuming the role of PM as long as we can keep this between us, about the raise and everything. I'm just not interested in getting caught up in a big emotional, political power struggle. I can do up weekly reports and email them to you, no problem, but please, let's just keep this discreet."

Albert let out an audible sigh. "You read my mind to a T, old friend. I'll agree to whichever terms you demand. I just need this project to get up and running as smooth as possible. Any help or support you need, don't bother filtering it through AJ anymore. Just contact me directly and I'll get you the required attention." He held out his hand. "Thank you, Charlie."

Charlie accepted his hand.

Albert put one hand on the steering wheel and the other on the gear shift. "There's just one other thing I need you to do. Tell AJ you now have orders to report directly to me. It'll let him know he's off the hook for any further responsibility, and he'll likely just stay out of your hair. I feel it's necessary for the project to continue with minimal hassle."

Charlie's shoulders tensed. AJ wasn't going to like this. It would benefit himself and the project, but he didn't want to have to deliver the unwanted news. He was also curious about AJ's turn in attitude, and what it might have led to. But they couldn't take any more chances in lost production time.

He donned his toque and stepped out of the vehicle. He entered the trailer, hung up his coat again, then kicked off his boots and placed them to the side, all the while practising his approach with AJ.

He walked into the boy's office and closed the door behind him. He chose to stay standing, his hands behind his back, clutching the knob as he leaned back.

AJ looked up immediately. "Well, what did he say?"

Charlie cleared his throat. "Not much, really. He wants me to report directly to him. He didn't explain why or anything, but—"

"Thanks." With a long sigh, AJ turned to his computer and clicked on the mouse. "Thanks, Charlie, no need for an explanation." He glanced up and nodded toward the door. "Please close the door behind you."

As Charlie passed through the lunchroom on the way to his office, he noticed the small crew of guys were watching him with dumbfounded expressions.

Charlie looked at his watch. "Time to get at it, guys; in fact, it's past time. Dress warm, it's cold out there." He smiled.

***

Behind his closed door, AJ sat in a silent fit, grinding his teeth and clenching his fists. What he would say—what he would do—if his father were there, in the room with him? His father hadn't even given him a chance to redeem himself, not in the slightest. There was really nothing for him to do now. He could read the writing on the wall: *Stay the fuck out of the way*.

He smirked. Getting paid to stay away actually sounded like a pretty good gig. He stretched his leg out and toed open his bottom drawer. There sat a half-full bottle of something he could do with the rest of his time.

***

Albert waited a minute after Charlie entered the trailer to make sure he didn't have to intercept any physical assault. But everything seemed peaceful. He threw the Caddy in reverse and pulled out of the slot, then shifted into drive and headed out to the main road. He slowed at the intersection and turned on his left blinker, then checked right for any oncoming traffic.

There, in the middle of the road, somewhat camouflaged against the brown and white forest backdrop, sat the old chieftain upon his horse. He was completely motionless, other than the white clouds of breath. Right there, in the middle of the road.

I should just run that motherfucker down right now.

But there was a time and place for everything, and this was neither. So Albert shot up his middle finger and completed his turn in the opposite direction, spinning tires down the snowy gravel road.

32

Vicky straightened her hair in front of the mirror. The holidays had brought many new surprises within her family-to-be, and the new year had already managed to fracture some proclaimed resolutions. One being AJ's declaration to become more involved in his project at work—*"take the bull by the horns"* was how he'd put it.

That promise failed on the first day. When he'd gotten up that morning, she sensed a new determination about him, like a man who had just accepted his meaning in life. Then he'd come home red-eyed with defeat and stinking of booze. He never did mention how his day had gone. But it was simple to assume it hadn't gone as planned.

There was a role she was expected to play in such circumstances. But her motto was more of the "Everyone for herself" type.

So the last week had been one of tense air and few words around the junior Doyle residence. It was getting quite unbearable for her. So she was happy to accept the invite from her newfound friend that morning to meet for a nice lunch and discuss some new listings.

Aware of the winter conditions, she went outside wearing a short skirt and a stylish, puffy white winter coat, which hung lower than her skirt, to wait for him to pick her up.

It wasn't that she was dressing to impress Justin. He was decent-looking, and somewhat charming, but she was dressing to impress every man within eyesight.

PRICE PER BARREL

Since arriving up North she'd found little time to be out and about, and she was a women energized by attention. It was so easy for her, squeaking her toys in front of the dogs.

She found Justin waiting for her in his high-end Land Rover Sport. He actually jumped out to open the passenger door for her. He was a true go-getter, and she deserved such treatment.

Off they went to the local Earls, which was one of the finest establishments in town, staffed by sexy waitresses who worked hard for tips, and they usually made out quite well, considering the service had never been anything more than mediocre in her experience.

***

What Victoria failed to see was Miss Emma Doyle sitting across the street in her running vehicle. Emma had placed a call to Justin the night before, suggesting he get back to work. She had set up the reservations for them and everything, insisting of course, that he keep everything hush-hush.

She gave the two a couple of minutes to get seated comfortably, and then she parked her car and made her way inside.

"Can I help you, ma'am?" asked the beautiful, young, and trashily dressed hostess.

Emma dusted the snow from her boots and removed her coat, draping it over her arm. "Well, I'm meeting someone here, but I'm not sure if I'm too early." She fidgeted around uncomfortably.

"Would you like to have a look inside to see if they're here?"

"Well, yes, if that's all right?" She poked her head in the doorway. She knew where to look, and how to make herself casually visible to the party.

"Emma?... Ms. Doyle?" Justin rose slowly from his chair.

She turned nonchalantly toward his voice. As she did, Justin rose fully, with hands out and a welcoming smile.

"Oh... ho, ho," Emma responded with her sweet, motherly voice and a saint-like smile. "Justin, my boy, how are you?" She placed a tender hand to his cheek.

He smiled. "I'm good."

She rested her arms on his, as though they were a bit more comfortable than acquaintances.

"Well, actually"—he gestured toward Victoria— "I'm here with what I understand, or rather *who*, is your future daughter-in-law."

She laughed and slapped him playfully on the shoulder. "Don't think I'm not wise to your charms. You know very well that she will be my granddaughter."

"I assure you it was an honest mistake." He winked and chuckled. "Why don't you join us? Please, we have room."

"Wait, Justin." Victoria smiled and raised a calm hand to the couple. "I'm sure she's meeting someone here already, isn't that right, Emma? Otherwise, why would you be here?"

"Oh, of course, how ignorant of me." Justin clapped his hands together, waiting curiously for her response.

"Well, yes, my dear"—Emma reached down and placed her hand lightly in Victoria's—"that was the plan, but I received a text from her, just now." She turned back to Justin. "It's Stella, dear, Stella Burschand. You know her, don't you, Justin, dear?"

"Oh right. She works in the bakery up in Thickwood, that Stella?"

"Yes, of course, dear." She turned back to Victoria and grasped her hand again. "She's a good friend. We play bridge together once a week, but lately, with the holidays and such, we've been having such difficulty finding the time." She laughed pleasantly. "So we had agreed to meet down here for lunch, but she says she won't be able to join me; something has come up, apparently. She never mentioned exactly what it was, but I don't like to nag, you understand, none of my business." She tilted her head with a casual shrug and a squinting smile.

"Oh, well, that's perfect, then!" Justin retrieved her coat and guided her around the table, pulling out a chair out between him and Victoria.

***

For the first part of the meal, Vicky sat with as subtle a pout as she could manage while picking, unsatisfied, at a plate of calamari. The other two caught up on town events and whatever—*Blah, blah, there goes my fun afternoon.*

She was getting quite tired of her soon-to-be grand-pain-in-the-ass. One small part of her would just like to call a truce with the old bat, but that would be admitting defeat. She straightened herself and leaned into the conversation.

The two blah-blahs paused at her surge of bright, smiling interest.

"So"—Emma's gaze darted between the two—"what is it that you two are doing here together?"

"Oh, Emma." Vicky smirked. "Justin is our—mine and AJ's—realtor. You know that. I believe you were the one who told him to contact us." She stared the old woman straight in the eyes and bit down on a piece of calamari, slicing it clean in two with her flawless white teeth.

"Oh, ho, ho, that's right." Emma reached across the table and grasped Vicky's hand again, shaking it playfully. "Silly old me, my mind must be slipping a bit at my age."

"Oh, Emma." Vicky leaned back to avoid any further contact. "You seem very much aware to me." She shoved the other half of the squid in her mouth.

Justin cut in. "I invited Vicky to lunch so I could show her some of the new properties that have come up." He reached for his briefcase "Is it all right to go through them now, with the two of you here? Maybe you can bounce some ideas off of each other?"

"Well, yes!" Emma responded immediately. "Yes, Justin, that's a lovely idea, don't you think, Victoria, dear?" She looked over with a courteous grin.

Vicky watched—barely—while the other two flipped, then pointed, then chattered, then flipped; the occasional "uh huh" being the highest interest she could muster.

Dinner wasn't the end of it either. Justin and Emma found three properties of interest, and he arranged to see them all after lunch.

After the meal, Vicky climbed in Justin's SUV and they followed Emma up to her place. The old bat had insisted she drop her vehicle off and then ride with them; that way, they could all be in on the discussions and she could familiarize Vicky with the different neighbourhoods.

"What a coincidence, running into Emma at the restaurant." Justin smiled.

"Uh huh," Vicky replied with a drop of sour as she looked out the passenger's side window.

There was a deep, awkward silence before Justin continued as if he were an idiot to it. "It's really nice of her to come along with us and help out. It's always good to have another opinion on such a big decision, especially an experienced one." His smile never twitched.

Vicky took a notable breath, brushing her hands lightly on her lap. "Yep, she's a peach."

Emma jumped in the back seat of the Rover and took the horse by the reins. She insisted they start at the place farthest from hers and then work their way back to drop her off. On their way to the first place, she said, "So, how is AJ doing these days, my dear?"

Vicky smirked and returned her gaze out the side window. "Well, he seems a little off since the festive family dinner. It looked like things may change for the better for an hour there, on his first day back. Then he came home smelling like a drunk, puked in his mouth, and passed out on the couch."

She caught a reflection of the old woman in the window. Her jaw was clenched and she was adjusting herself in her seat.

"Yes, well, that's why it is important for him to have the love and support of a good woman at home," she said matter-of-factly. Then she raised her chin and applied a layer of arrogance to her tone. "You know the saying, 'Behind every great man is an even greater woman.'" She smiled.

"Yes, I've heard that before, and I'd like to be that for him." She turned to her audience and nodded with sincerity, then turned back to the front. "I'm just planning my strategy. Now that I have you here, Emma, maybe I could tap your knowledge a bit. I'm having trouble deciding whether to kick his ass or suck his—"

"Here's the first house!" Justin interrupted. "Just coming up here on the right," he added with an awkward laugh.

They went through the first two houses fairly quickly, with lots of talking on Emma's part as she puttered ahead, nitpicking at the curtains and flooring, while Vicky and Justin followed behind, making quizzical expressions at some of the old woman's critiques, then giggling.

By the end of the second house, Vicky began to wonder how they'd ever made the short list. Neither were anything of interest to her, and by the way Emma picked them apart, it was obvious she never intended to give them a chance.

At the final house, she understood why Emma meant for them to work their way back to drop her off. The large home stood on the edge of a hill sloping to downtown and had a great view overlooking the city.

"Now, this place is in a great location, and just around the corner from mine. So I could be there for you, Victoria, when the pitter-patter of little feet arrives," Emma said as she exited the vehicle. "And put together by the best builder in town, isn't that right, Justin?"

"Yes, Tundra Construction is the most-sought-after builder in the area."

The moment she got out of the vehicle, Vicky could tell this place kicked the shit out of the others. It was like comparing a limousine to a shopping cart.

Inside the marble-tiled grand foyer, the group removed their shoes and looked up at the towering twenty-foot ceilings. Dark hardwood stretched out from the entrance toward a ten-foot-high rock wall encasing a triple-sided gas fireplace, which separated the living room from the open kitchen.

Emma led Vicky and Justin around the main floor, explaining the house's features with an almost psychic insight.

Just as they began the tour upstairs, Emma looked down at the screen of her phone. "Oh!" she exclaimed, placing a hand to her chest. "You two must excuse me, I have to get somewhere a bit more private to return a call. Don't wait for me, continue on, I'll catch up!" she sang as she shuffled down the hall to the staircase.

As the old bird disappeared, Justin leaned over and rested his forehead heavily on Vicky's shoulder. "My god," he exhaled. "I'm sorry, I hate to speak ill of your in-laws, but thank fuck she's gone." He lifted his head and met Vicky's smile, then placed his hand on the small of her back and gently pressed her in the opposite direction of the staircase.

He walked her to the two spare rooms, each decked out strategically with staging furniture to mimic children's quarters. She passed by with an unenthusiastic grin, the wheels in her mind churning up potential alternatives for the spaces.

"Well, if that doesn't interest you, fear not. I always save the best for last." He slid his arm fully around her waist and pulled her unmistakably closer, tighter, and looked down with a perverse smile, as if he had just invited her up for coffee.

She batted her long eyelashes; she never liked to turn down a good coffee.

Back down the hall and past the staircase, the lights in the other wing sensed their motion and came on, soft at first, then growing to a full glow by the time they reached the dead end, secured by a set of powdered-glass French doors.

Justin bent over dramatically and grabbed both handles. He paused before the climax, looking back to his curious client, who bounced slightly on her heels and bit lightly on her lip as she waited.

He turned the handles with a *chunk* and paused again. "This is why I make the big bucks," he said, then gracefully flung the doors wide. He spread his arms, looked to the ceiling, and spun into the room. "Welcome to your Eden!" he announced. "Your oasis! Your place in the universe." He walked over to another three-sided rock fireplace, which divide the main room from the master bath. He grabbed a remote control off the mantle above, then continued with smooth confidence. "Your place, where you can come in, close the door…" He motioned for her to shut the door, and she trotted across the room in her heels, giddy with excitement. "…you close the door"—he gave her the thumbs-up—"kick on a fire"—he held the controller up with one hand and hit a button, and a sudden *WOOF!* of flame popped in the fireplace—"dim the lights"—he stroked his thumb around a dial mounted on the magic wand, and the room fell eerily black—"or"—his voice broke the dark silence—"let in some sun!" A soft buzzing entered the room, and slivers of snow-white light broke the shadows and grew slowly, until the whole wall opened in floor-to-ceiling windows.

Vicky walked toward the breathtaking view as it was revealed. The house overlooked the entire downtown, which was backdropped by endless forest and rivers. Cars rushed down the highway far below, red taillights creating a red stream of energy.

With the room fully lit, she explored what could potentially be her new personal space. The bathroom hosted a double-sink vanity, a full-length mirror, a soaker tub built for two, and a separate room for the toilet.

"Kick on some music!" Justin's command echoed, and the room filled with concert-hall-quality opera from strategically placed hidden sources.

Vicky was thrilled by the sound quality, but she wrinkled her nose at the music choice.

"No?" Justin examined the controller. He hit another button and Cracker started playing "Low."

"Yeah!" She raised her hands in the air and swayed to the music, dipping and swinging as though she were the main attraction on a bar top.

She danced her way over to Justin, then turned her back to him, grinding up and down. Spinning around to the other side of the room, she threw her arms to the air and dropped down on the bed. "Woo hoo!" She clapped her hands together. "This is what I'm fucking talkin' 'bout!" She bobbed her head to the music, her hair tossing messily and seductively, then looked at him and laughed wildly.

"Yeah!" He met her eyes, then danced over to her with his hips gyrating. "Then!" he announced as he drew within arm's length. "After the party, you settle down into your plush king bed for a little whoop-whoop!" He grinned mischievously.

Catching him off guard, Vicky grabbed his tie with both hands, then yanked him down close to her.

He braced himself so that only their foreheads touched.

Vicky looked him dead in his eyes with hunger. "So, tell me, Mr. McGillivray." She spoke with hushed intent. "You think you got what it takes?"

Justin stood between her spread legs, stunned. "I, uh, I..."

A startled sound came from the entrance. "Oh! Um, uh-hum!"

The two innocent acquaintances froze in position and turned their heads toward Emma, who looked frazzled.

"Emma!" Justin forced Vicky to release his tie, then straightened himself. "Emma, we were... I was just showing, and, and explaining to Vicky about the Egyptian sheets. The thread count is... lots! It's up there." He disappeared into the bathroom.

Vicky looked over at Emma with an innocent grin.

33

Ollie was just over a week into his first night-shift experience. The flip side to the dimension he was raised to know and accept as how people lived.

People were darker at night. Void of emotion and expression, pale, lost, dehydrated of life. The whole environment walked a drunken line between conscious thought and dream, occasionally stumbling off to one side or the other.

The day when they made the switch, Honey had instructed him to stay up as long as he could that night, then sleep all day and meet him back for their shift at 7:00 p.m. the next evening.

It had sounded simple enough: sleep during the day and work all night. There wasn't much daylight to miss at that time of the year anyway. Dark when you get up and dark when you come home.

It sounded better, actually: he'd actually be free in the daytime. He could head out for walks on nice days. And he could spend the weekend days with Mary-Ann.

He pictured sitting and talking with her over lunch, her smiling face, the way she blushed—so beautiful. He smiled to himself and he felt his body warm. This whole night-shift thing could be for the better. It was a sign they were meant to be together.

Back in his room that first night, he'd had a long, cleansing shower, then towelled off and tried to think of what the hell he was going to do all night. He dressed and went down to the games room, where he found a shelf full of used books. He searched the options until one caught his eye, then returned to his room.

He woke up at 2:30 a.m., face up on his bed, fully clothed, with the book lying on his chest open to page 5. He breathed a sigh of relief; he'd only slept a few hours at best. He went back down to the kitchen, where the night crew always kept a pot of coffee brewed and some snacks placed out. He topped up a cup of black, grabbed a couple of sugar-laden pastries, and headed back to his room.

Sitting on his bed, he took a large sip of coffee and a couple bites of a cinnamon roll, then relaxed back and attempted to read again. He was extra cautious this time to get up and move around when he felt the slightest hint of sleepiness.

Ollie figured he could just stay up most of the day and maybe grab a nap in the early afternoon. It should be no problem—by that time he'd surely be exhausted.

And when the time came, he was exhausted, but sleep eluded him. He lay down in bed a few times, but he couldn't get it done. Doubt would build and he'd tell himself to relax or try to shift his focus by counting—everything, anything. But still, no sleep.

Honey had mentioned that the first night is usually the worst because many newbies can't sleep during the day. All you can do is tough it out, he said, stay busy at work that night and then get home and pass out. Then the schedule is set.

Ollie had been hoping to avoid the rough initiation, but it would be what it would. So, he suffered through that first night, letting Honey sit in the warm truck cab while he tackled exhaustion head-on, working in excessively sub-zero temperatures to wrestle frozen steel fittings in the beam of truck headlamps while wearing soaking-wet gloves.

After the shift, he'd gone back to camp, stumbling down the hallway, dirty and frozen but wearing a sweet grin.

Pillow.

He'd jumped in the shower and imagined the cool, plush sheeted surface resting against his showered cheek, then slowly easing him down, conforming to every contour of his face, his body wrapped tightly in his warm blanket. He took a long, hot shower, then jumped out, shiny and fresh, and hopped straight into bed, pulling the covers over and flicking off the lamp.

But sleep hadn't come. Again. He'd lain down for hours, thinking it'd have no choice but to come. *It has to come! It has to happen! Sleep has to happen…?*

Now, sitting in the warm cab of the truck while Honey went to bullshit with some operator-friends, he realized sleep didn't have to happen. It wasn't a law, or a right; it was a privilege—an ever-so-euphoric privilege. He'd been sure he'd get a couple hours in—he'd lain down pretty much all day except to go to the bathroom or grab some eats—but he'd never woken up wondering what had happened to the last two hours, or even the last half-hour.

He was alive and awake enough to perform all basic motor skills, but his mind? The thought process had a glitch. He was sometimes unsure of what he'd seen, what he'd heard, or what he'd spoken—if at all. Something was bent or twisted. Somewhere… he wasn't sure. In this new dimension, Ollie found that up was sometimes down and left sometimes wrong. His appetite had been downgraded to carrying around a full thermos of coffee. He couldn't remember the last time he'd taken a shit; he wasn't sure if it was something that could happen at three in the morning.

There was one lighted candle in his darkness. The weekend was coming. Mary-Ann had been unable to meet with him during that week because they were short-staffed, but she was heading out first thing Saturday morning to greet him when he got to his room, and she was going to try to bring some good home cooking with her. Ollie had to work all weekend, but she would stay so they could spend time together. As long as they were together, she'd said. Which had made his heart pound.

He stirred from his groggy state, watching Honey and his buddies in the poorly lit bus stop–*slash*–smoke shack. Ollie rubbed his eyes to ensure what he was seeing was accurate. It appeared as if they were passing around a pipe. The lighter flickered around the circle multiple times, making two or three rounds before it was returned to Honey, who waved, then exited the shack and began his trip back to the truck. Ollie sat back quickly in his chair.

Honey hopped in and paused for a minute, looking at Ollie and then out to the smoke shack. He grinned and buckled up, then backed the rig out of its spot. On the road to the gate, all was silent until Honey grunted and broke the darkness.

"You know, night shift's a lot different than day shift. It's a little bit trickier to handle, and it's hard to find good guys that can handle it. After you work it for a bit, you learn certain tricks to help keep your sanity. So, when companies find a good night-shift crew, they realize it's worth not asking questions." He paused again and looked out his side window, sucking in his cheeks and smacking his lips. "Sometimes some of us guys get together for a little pick-me-up." He turned to look at Ollie.

Ollie stayed facing forward, wide-eyed but neutral. He gave a simple nod.

Honey reached over and gave him a light jab. "Right on! I knew you'd get it." He laughed. "You know, you had a good first week. You gave 'er, bud, but you're looking a little rough." He squinted. "Well, if you're ever interested in that pick-me-up, just let me know, and I'll let you in on it."

34

Emma made it to work extra early to make sure she didn't miss Mary-Ann. She approached the young woman as soon as she came through the door.

"Mary-Ann, dear." She grasped the girl's arm lightly and guided her down to the supply closet. "Please hurry and grab your supplies, we're heading straight over to the 11-16 Project to clean there first."

Mary-Ann's expression communicated her confusion.

"Oh no, my girl, it is nothing of panic. I just need to speak with my grandson. He's the manager, you know." She smiled and patted the sweet girl's hand. "I have something important to speak to him about, and I just hate driving across this place in broad daylight, let alone in the dark. It's always nice for a lady to have some company."

"Oh!" Mary-Ann smiled. "Oh yes, I completely understand, Ms. Doyle. Just let me go and get my stuff and I'll meet you by the exit."

In the truck, Emma started with casual chitchat, blabbering around as she searched for her best segue into the day's mission.

"Yes, well, I am having a bit of a tough time with the family lately," she blurted. "A bit of a spat broke out over the holidays, I'm afraid—during the Christmas dinner at my place, to be exact. What a waste, all that good food." She shook her head. "I just don't know what to do, young love." She smiled and touched Mary-Ann's arm. "Then, I was out with my future granddaughter-in-law." She huffed. "We were with the realtor. Handsome fellow, I suppose." She huffed again. "We were at one of the new units up on the hill, overlooking the city, you know? It's a beautiful place, expensive, but, well, my grandson gets paid very well." She winked and patted Mary-Ann's arm again to make sure she was paying attention. "And it's right over by my place. I suggested it would be good as I could help out when the children begin to come." She shot a beaming smile. "Because I know my grandson is a true family man, I think he'll want a fair-sized family, maybe four children." She glowed. "I just— well, I feel so bad even saying it…"

Mary-Ann came to a stop at an intersection and looked over to her troubled boss. "It's fine, Ms. Doyle, it's just me and you here." She lifted a gentle hand to the woman's shoulder.

"I just don't know about her. *Victoria* is her name. I just don't think she's the right one for my AJ. I— well, I left her and the realtor alone, but only for a couple of minutes because I had an important phone call to make." Tears began to build in her eyes.

"Yes, go on." Mary-Ann handed her a tissue she pulled from the door cubby.

"Well, I went downstairs to get some privacy. When I returned upstairs, I…" She paused, bearing down as if to hold back a swell of emotion. "I found them in the master bedroom, and they were in, in… I suppose… a suspicious position on the bed." She let go of a pressured sob and blew into the tissue.

"Oh my, that's just horrible! Well, what kind of a woman would do such a thing? She has it all: a handsome man, wealth, the support of a loving family. Women like that just make me so mad! No appreciation for what they've been given. I know a hundred women that would gratefully trade for her opportunity. Sheesh!" Mary-Ann finished her two cents, then checked the abandoned intersection once more before continuing on.

It was exactly the kind of response Emma was hoping for. She watched Mary-Ann in her peripheral vision as they drove. Such a naturally pretty girl, brought up with proper family values and deserving of her grandson.

As they drove along, Emma fell silent, watching the scenery pass beyond the window…

Stephan had finally fulfilled yet another one of Emma's fantasies one morning at school by inviting her to be his date to the team's year-end awards banquet and the after-party.

All week, Emma had been on top of the world. At long last, she would be presented before her world on the arm of her man. Such an opportunity required a step up in wardrobe. So late one night, at the risk of a severe beating from her passed-out father, she snuck into the secret stash of money he kept hidden in a jar in his dresser drawer. The next morning, she skipped her first-period English class, rushed down to Adele's Fashion Boutique, and bought the dress she had been admiring, straight from the window display: a faint-yellow sundress that perfectly displayed her finest assets. She was beaming as she twirled in the mirror. Because taking the dress home was not an option, she had the merchant hang onto it until she could return for it.

After school, she returned to Adele's with her makeup bag and spent over an hour preparing for the gala. Ready to go, Emma checked the time: half an hour until she was set to meet Stephan in front of the coffee shop. She'd been hoping he would invite her to his house beforehand to meet his parents, but she would surely have time to win them over during the banquet...

Emma snapped back to the present when they pulled in the yard and found the lot was empty. It was still early for the crews to start arriving. Still, Emma was holding out hope that AJ would come in early and show some effort.

They sat in the truck and waited. Slowly, workers began pulling in, parking, and unloading into the trailers. The ladies remained in their vehicle, waiting for AJ. It was a half-hour past start time when he finally rolled in.

Emma jumped out as soon as she saw him.

He looked over. "Grand— Emma? What are you doing here?" He looked passed her to young Mary-Ann collecting her supplies from the truck.

Emma tapped a finger to her wristwatch. "Mr. Doyle!"

"Yes, I know. There must've been an accident on the highway, traffic was backed up." He looked confused. "What are you doing here?"

"I need a moment of your time, in private, dear. It'll only take a moment, and then Mary-Ann and I will clean the facilities and be on our way." She attached herself to his arm. "Can we use your office?"

The workers had already cleared out of the trailer, so they had the place to themselves.

After they had kicked off their boots at the door, Emma turned to Mary-Ann. "Just busy yourself out here, dear, while I have a minute with AJ in his office."

"Yes, of course." Mary-Ann wheeled her mop and bucket to the washroom.

Emma closed the door and was on her grandson as he took his seat. "Oh, look at yourself, love, you're a bit of a mess, aren't you?" She brushed his hair to the side, wiped something from the corner of his bloodshot eye, then straightened his tie. "Smells like you had a bit of a party last night."

"No, Grandma, it wasn't a party, just a couple drinks to unwind after work."

"Uh huh." She smirked. "How was Victoria this morning, was she up to make you breakfast?"

"No, you know she doesn't do that."

Emma's jaw clenched. "Yes, she's not into that type of thing, but she is into… things, isn't she?" The way she punctuated the question lent a sense of direction to the conversation.

An expression of discontent settled on AJ's face. "I understand you don't like Victoria; I get it, all right? Now, whatever this is about, can we just lay it on the table and get on with our day? I'm very busy."

"W-well…" Emma stuttered, taken back by his insistence. "If that's what you prefer." She paced the floor slowly, building courage. "I was out with your fiancée and the realtor, Justin. You and Justin went to school together, right? You know his reputation?"

He looked down at the desk, picked up a pen, and twirled it between his fingers, his confidence clearly broken by the scene she was painting. "Yes."

"I found them by fluke. I went to meet a friend for lunch, but she fell ill and didn't text me till I was waiting in the restaurant. I saw them there together. Justin invited me to join them, and he showed us a binder full of houses—well, me mostly, Victoria oddly didn't show much interest. Anyway, one thing led to another, and we went to go view some places." She sat down and reached across the desk and grasped his hand firmly. "At the last house, I left them for a moment to make a call. When I found them again, they were in the master bedroom. They weren't—well, you know—but it definitely wasn't something I would refer to as innocent."

His face turned red and he stopped twirling the pen. She watched his mind convulse as his grip on the pen tightened.

"I'm sorry, honey. I didn't ever want to have to approach you with news like this." She dabbed lightly at her eyes.

He rapped the pen on the table several times, then threw it down and leaned back heavily. He ran both hands up his face and through his hair, then clasped them together behind his head and let out a trapped breath. "Well, I'm sure it's nothing. I'll question her about it tonight, that's all I can really do." He widened his eyes and smiled through a clenched jaw.

"Yes." She gave a hopeful smile. "Yes, talk to her. You're likely right, I don't know what's acceptable these days." She stood. "Well, I'll let you get back to it. Sorry to disturb you, sweetie." She backed out the door. "I'll get Mary-Ann in here right away to give your office a quick clean, then we'll get out of your way."

She scurried over to Mary-Ann, who was busy mopping the lunchroom floor. "Mary-Ann"—she grabbed the girl and straightened her up, wiped some excess mascara from around her eye, and made some light adjustments to her hair—"I need you to stop this, dear, and go quickly to clean up my grandson's office. She whispered, "He's a bit troubled right now,"and guided her to the door.

"Oh! Yes, oka—" was all the girl could get out before Emma shoved her through the doorway and closed the door behind her.

***

A young woman stood against AJ's door, clutching a mop handle.

He was still leaning back in his chair, feeling as shocked as she looked. He studied her. She was definitely cute, even in her cleaning gear. Not too skinny or too plump, a good-size rack, and a pretty face. She'd be a trophy for any average Joe looking to stuff a bun in the oven. Currently, all he was interested in stuffing was a shot down his throat. He didn't need to be a genius, or sober, to see what his sweet granny was up to.

He felt sorry for the cleaner, likely fucking clueless as to what mess she was in the middle of. He stood with a polite smile and reached out his hand. "Sorry, Miss… Mary-Ann, is it?"

"Y-yes, Mary-Ann Kibbnok, sir." She accepted his hand timidly. "I work for your grand— Emma… Ms. Doyle."

He chuckled and smiled kindly. "Yes, my sweet grandmother."

"Yes." She returned a smile.

"Well, I'll make this easy on you. I'm not really concerned with anything today, other than the bit of mud on the floor. You've been doing a hell of a job; I'll put in a good word for you with the boss." He winked, then moved out from behind the desk so she could start.

He walked around to get a more complete view of the girl. He couldn't help admiring her while she bent over to mop. *She's definitely easy to take in. Invest some money in a dress, and she could be something.*

PRICE PER BARREL

"So, how do you like working for the old bird?" He grinned. "She treating you well?"

"Oh my, yes! She's the best boss I've had, treats me like gold."

AJ responded with a smug frown. "Hmph, good to hear, I guess."

She made her way around to the far side of the desk and started mopping back toward him, clearly unaware of the invitation her cleavage had just sent to his lurking eye.

He grinned. *Maybe Grandma isn't so bad after all.*

35

Saturday!

Mary-Ann drove out to camp early the next morning, exhilarated about finally seeing Ollie. They had shared texts and a couple short calls throughout the week, and her poor man sounded so... beat up. He needed her. She smiled and pressed harder on the gas pedal.

She was waiting at the gate as promised when he got dropped off.

As soon as he jumped in her truck, she let out a soft squeal and an explosive smile. She threw her arms around him and pulled him across the cab, kissing him lustfully. Forgetting what he did for a living.

With her assault complete, she faced forward and saw a scrappy-looking older gentleman walk past the headlights on his way through the parking lot. His eyes turned from irritated to pleasant as soon as he noticed that she'd noticed. Then he waved.

"Ollie, who's that?"

"Huh? Oh, that's my boss, or lead, or... whatever."

"He seems interesting," she said with a sarcastic look.

"Yeah, he's a little different, but he keeps us working. Let's get back and get me showered, sexy." He leaned over and kissed her on the cheek.

***

Back in his room, Ollie chuckled as he closed the door behind them. He and Mary-Ann had come in during rush hour for the dayshift.

PRICE PER BARREL

"What?" She smiled and slapped him lightly.

"It's nothing." He laughed. "I just bet it's the first time any of have seen a sexy girl pull her big wheelie suitcase down the hall."

"Well, none of them's as good as you." She stretched up and gave him a peck on the lips. "Now get that sexy butt in the shower!"

Ollie let the warm water pour over him. He closed his eyes and lifted his face to the stream. Smiling. He was smiling again. It had faded, somewhere, in all the commotion... Lost, in the darkness.

She was back, and she'd brought his smile with her. It was right, what Gran had told him once when he was young...

He'd been sitting across from her at a picnic table outside the seasonal ice cream hut. The day had been bright and hot, but the ocean breeze had been blowing just enough to keep one comfortable. A young couple had walked by, smiling and laughing, holding hands.

"How do you know, Gran? How do you know when you got the right one?" He took his ice cream cone away from his tongue just long enough to motion to the lovers, and then got right back to work.

She licked at the drips making a break down the side of her cone, then huffed at his curiosity and smiled. "Heaven's sake, child"—she reached over and ruffled his hair—"you don't you go worrin' about none of that at your age." She sat back and laughed. "Go fly a kite, or catch a fish, why don't you?"

"Oh, come on, Gran. How do you know? No jokin'!"

"Well..." She gave him a serious look. "She'll become your sun."

"Oh, come on!" He rolled his eyes, got up and walked around the table, and stood in front of her. "Tell me, Gran!"

"It's the truth. She'll be like a beautiful ball of energy that shines a special light just for you." She winked.

He cocked his head. "Really?"

"Yep." She poked her head up and looked down the street, down the valley, to the rocky shores below. "Just like that lighthouse there," she said and pointed. "It sends out a special light for all the passing ships so they don't get lost. So they can always find home." She smiled. "She'll have a special light for you and you'll be naturally drawn to her. She'll give her energy to you and you'll want to return it. She'll give you reason."

"Well, if I need one of 'em, who's my sun now?"

She had responded so quickly she must've been waiting for that exact question. "Your gran!" She had smiled and pulled him in for a big, cold, ice cream kiss.

"*Awe*, Gran!" He had wiped at his mouth and the two had laughed together… She was his sun…

The shower was thick with steam, and he felt beautifully nauseous. He finally made the effort to turn it off and get out, knowing that what lay on the other side of the door would make him feel even better.

He dried off and slipped on the pyjamas he had hanging on the hook, then towelled his hair as he exited in a cloud of fog. "Oh, does that feel beaut—"

There, laid out on the bed, was a traditional picnic blanket and basket. Mary-Ann sat off to the side, leaning back against the wall and looking absolutely radiant.

His jaw dropped. "Mary-Ann, what did you do?"

"You like?" His dumbstruck reaction clearly pleased her. "I told you I was going to bring you some home cooking."

She opened the basket to reveal a back-home classic: Jiggs dinner. Complete with blueberry pudding.

"Oh, Mary-Ann! I can't believe you! Look what you did!" He hopped over to her side of the bed and leaned down to kiss her lips, then peppered her cheek and neck as he made his way toward her breasts.

She pushed him off with a giggle. "Oliver!" She pointed toward the meal. "We'll get to that in a bit. I went through all this work, so sit down and enjoy it while there's still some warmth to it!" Her tone was scolding, though a truthful twinkle in her eye said never been happier.

Ollie sat down in his designated place across the basket from her. He wasted no time dishing up and digging in. "Mmm." He took another mouthful and savoured the colourful flavours. "Mary-Ann, this is so incredible, it's been *so* long." He met her eyes with loving appreciation.

Ollie couldn't believe how his world had transformed in a little over an hour. He'd felt like a cold, soulless zombie, but now he was warm—not just to the touch, but warm on the inside. He had blood and veins and a heartbeat—so many things he'd forgotten. He set the basket out of the way, then turned to see her standing close beside him, offering a glass of wine.

The whole week of sleepless abandon was behind him. Now he had a belly full of good home cooking, his girl, and a glass of wine.

"There's more," she said, stepping over to the nightstand and moving all the clutter onto the bed. "I was trying to figure out how to do this so we could be comfortable." She looked up at him, with cheeks flushed and a sweet, insecure smile. "This is the best I could come up with." She pulled the nightstand screeching across the floor until it was in front of the window, then invited him over to sit on it and face the small window.

He was confused but he obeyed. Once he was settled, she grinned and ran over to the light switch by the door, then flipped off the lights.

The blackened room felt like empty space as he sat transfixed before the brilliance outside: such beauty, such power, separated by a simple pane of glass.

"Around here"—she exhaled softly as she sat beside him—"winter has the best sunrises."

Ollie reached around, guided only by the gentle brush of his fingertips, until his hand came to rest on her hip. His hand spread wide, caressing, exploring. The feel of her warm curve sliding beneath the fine silk soothed him further. The gravity between them grew heavy. He pulled her close, and she conformed to his every dimple as she laid her head on his shoulder. No two people had ever been so joined.

Through the tiny sliding-glass window rose a sight of such beauty, no sane person would ever consider...

Winter sunrise in a Northern mine.

Above, the dark sky hung saturated in a vast sea of starlight. The wintered forest floor reflected the brilliance of the heavens, and the treetops sparkled with snowy white pillows. On the distant horizon, the budding blue twilight backdropped the spiked peaks of the boreal forest.

They sat together, silent, floating in a mindless drift. The food, the wine, and the nourishment of a loving woman pulsed blood through Ollie's parched veins. Her presence hydrated his soul.

He shut down everything but his eyes, watching as the pioneering blue hue turned to a fiery orange. The trees tipped to it, subtly turning toward the rising sun, their god, the creator, simple in their wisdom.

During the winter season, the sun always rose in the far southeast but stayed low, hovering across the southern horizon throughout the day. Four hours of sunrise to four hours of sun set. Then darkness.

162

Ollie's mind wandered as he stared at two extreme, opposite states of light fade together in such peaceful brilliance. On a molecular level, it was complete madness: an infinite population of molecules, for one brief second, were landing in such a fashion as to reward them with this... to remind him of this. His eyes strained for focus, trying to isolate just one, visible in the stillness. *What are the chances?* he wondered, calculating the impossibility of one single molecule ever occupying the same exact millionth of a pinprick of a point in space more than once in its existence. If that were true, then it would lead one to believe no single moment in time or space would ever appear visually the same. Even breath, sound, and taste—never the same. That would mean at some point, in some life, one could honestly say they were there—at that one point, in that right instant— when it was at its absolutely most beautiful time it could ever be... forever. A unique fingerprint on time.

Every point, every time should be admired... because it just might be that one perfect moment.

The stagnant air held the essence of home cooking, sunrises, crystal snowfall... and her. Her warmth became very present with the strength of her beating heart. The scent of her perspiration teased him from forbidden regions of her body, taunting, begging...

He turned from the morning light toward her. She looked up from his shoulder, and her eyes found his. They were connected, they both realized it at that instant. It wasn't a joke, a fling, or puppy lust. Even the all-reigning title of "love" wasn't enough to describe the energy between them.

Without a word or gesture, their lips drew together. Hers were full and swollen against his as he breathed from her, and she from him. Without breaking contact, he stood and carefully positioned himself before her. He placed his glass on the nightstand and felt for hers, but as she passed it into his hand, it slipped and shattered on the floor, creating a blood-red pool of crystal shards. Neither strayed from their purpose; what was happening was happening, and nothing could disrupt.

His hands shot with confidence around to her bum, and he hoisted her from the nightstand.

She wrapped her legs around him and exhaled with sinful pleasure. "Oh, Ollie" she purred in his ear, laying waste to her natural prim and properness.

He eased her down to the bed. As he rested his weight on top of her, she squeezed him tighter, rallying for control. Her unchained need shivered through her and he was defeated, his mind exhausted by the attempt to abide by rules of respect for her, and he surrendered to simple instinct.

He moved from her lips down to her neck, kissing and licking and frothing, a predatory buffet of pure, selfish desire. The thick silence stirred with her frantic breathing and pleading moans.

He pushed up from her, then pulled and tore at her dress without pause, madness consuming him as he clawed to her bare flesh. He stood only long enough to remove his shirt and pants, then kneeled before her, bare. She sat up and lifted her dress over her head, then released the catch on her bra. She lay back down wearing only an exotic garter and stocking set, minus the panties.

He looked upon her with focused hunger. His mouth watered, and he drew in a strong, quenching breath of air. Fresh oxygen and the stench of her sex stoked his obsession.

He lowered his face to her stomach, breathing her, his lips brushing lightly, the sudden breeze of his warm breath causing her body to ripple.

The pulse of her heart touched his lips through her smooth midsection. The smell of her flesh, the pheromones leaking through her pores, turned his eyes back in his head like a feeding shark. He kissed her skin, then his senses picked up on an even more ripe fruit. Slowly, purposefully, he began moving down.

***

Mary-Ann's heart skipped, then kicked up, pumping a tidal flow of blood to her sexually alert parts, swelling and preparing her for his assault. Her muscles clenched, quick and slight, as down he crept. She whimpered, her breathing turning short and quick, mirroring the pace of her beating heart.

His every movement on her skin left a shivered wake in his passing. Down past her navel he went, crossing into her neatly trimmed pubic area. Her back arched as a tsunami poured between her thighs. Her legs closed with shy resistance and she looked down at him, running her fingers through his golden locks.

He lifted his head slowly and their eyes met, and what she saw bordered on madness. He kept his eyes trained on her, lending his assurance and pleading with her not to deny his pleasure. He placed his hands on her inner thighs and pressed her open, his gaze daring her to resist.

She leaned her head back, closed her eyes, and surrendered to him. Like stepping off a ledge into an endless unknown, she let her legs fall open. Anything

164

once sacred to her was offered to him.

He moved like a striking serpent but then stopped just short, his hot breath telling her exactly where he was. A light tickling of his tongue made her muscles seize, then he pushed in, fully, tasting her for the first time.

Mary-Ann's breath held full at his entrance—feeling him, waiting for his reaction. And then he pushed in harder—deeper, devouring.

She cried out as tremors rippled through her body. Her running fingers turned into fists, clenching tufts of his hair. She moaned in ecstasy at the feeling of him committing to her completely, with no questions, judgement, or hesitation.

He fed from her, gorging himself like a vampire who had not tasted life for far too long.

He lifted himself from her and waited for her eyes to find him. Timid, she looked down and watched as he began to slither up her body. She let her legs relax completely; there were no more secrets. Watching tentatively as he mindfully slid his body through her moist lips, he left a thick wet stripe down his chin, neck, and the entirety of his chest before he found her gushing well with the tip of his very erect and abundant penis.

He towered over her and raised his eyes to the heavens, like a howling wolf. He took a loud, deep breath, and his chest expanded before her.

He tipped his chin down and stared into her eyes, and then, with no other hint or warning, he gave a hard thrust, and buried himself completely.

Mary-Ann let out a shrill cry.

Reaching around with one hand, he grasped the back of her neck with intention while the other took a firm hold on her hip, and he fed her over and over with long, hard, purposeful strokes.

She quickly assisted, digging her nails into his firm, round ass and pulling herself farther onto him.

The energy grew between them as each of their souls fought to possess the other. Mary-Ann felt a rising tide of something exciting her on both the mental and physical realms—something ancient, created with the dawn of the universe, bordering on saint and sin.

She gripped him as the force possessed her everything. Her nails dug into his back… it was coming. Her legs wrapped tightly around his waist, trying to gain control of what was to become of her. She breathed in ecstasy and exhaled panic, and tears began to flow heavily, triggered by emotions she couldn't explain.

PRICE PER BARREL

Pushing deeper, harder, she felt a primal tremor, then her body clenched, and she clutched desperately. Her nails sank deep into the flesh on his back, her toes pointed and stretched until her calves burned. She wanted him in, or out—it felt incredible but so intense. She had lost her air, gasping and heaving with every jolt of pleasure. A spiritual exorcism.

**

Mary-Ann's bucking and squirming excited Ollie's taste for the kill. He wrapped both arms around her, forcefully holding her any attempt at escape as he pounded her harder, relentlessly wanting to rid her of any demons holding her captive to the past. She belonged to him now. Now and for always.

His pulse climaxed, his head grew dizzy. He knew the end was near and never wanted the moment to end. He craved the ecstasy. The trials of an addict. With a sudden explosion, everything left his body—the darkness of the past week, the camp, the missing her—everything he had left was released. Their bodies fell limp and the room grew silent. He kissed Mary-Ann softly and sweetly as he drained and wilted completely inside her. Then, with his last push of energy, he rolled off beside her.

She rolled toward him, kissing him passionately on the cheek and then moving down to his chest and kissing further before snuggling into his arms.

Ollie lay dead to the world, to everything but her nurturing body wrapped around him. The room rested, still and silent. The smell of their love hung pleasantly in the air.

His head fell to the side. On the far side of the room, a large figure draped in robes and dipped in a soft white glow glided through the wall, silently floating toward him.

The phantom towered over the bed, its eyes emitting a gentle smile. It raised a clenched fist over Ollie's head. As Ollie turned to look at its hand, a soft shower of white sand fell toward him in a milky stream, and he drifted off to a deep, peaceful sleep.

36

AJ pushed past the speed limit a little harder than usual on his way home from work that night. Images of his fiancée and that arrogant shit of a real estate agent soiled his mind, with the only sounds being the purring exhaust note and the soft creak of the leather-wrapped steering wheel in his eager hands.

He was pissed; of course he was fucking pissed! Justin fucking McGillivray? His mind had wandered throughout the day, and he'd begun to see things for what they really were. Or maybe he was looking for excuses to see her as something other than what he wanted her to be.

Vicky was a girl who demanded a certain level of attention; he'd known that going in. Before making the move up North, his lifestyle had permitted him to dedicate such attention to her. Now… well, he was letting the job consume him. He couldn't remember the last time he'd treated her to a night out, just the two of them. Of course the entertainment options were more limited in Fort Mac, but there were some decent restaurants around, and a few live plays and bands on occasion—anything that would let her get dressed up so he could take her out and show her off. Make her feel like the beautiful woman she was; she liked that shit.

This wasn't the first brick of jealousy she'd lobbed his way. She'd wait only so long before she began to search for attention elsewhere. Not that she'd necessarily cheat, though—she was just a massive flirt. She wasn't evil… not completely. She just needed him to pay attention.

Why couldn't he spend more time with her? It was not as though he was contributing anything notable to the project. Everything had been discreetly handed over to fucking Charlie. AJ was just attending the meetings now, keeping his mouth shut while his father answered any questions.

That was it, he would just ask— or no, no, he would *tell* his father he'd be working fewer hours from now on. Nothing ridiculous, he'd just cut back to regular working hours. That would free up time for him to spend with Vicky. She was honestly a great woman. They were great together. What they had was great. He loved her—he'd asked her to marry him, for fuck's sake! Relationships took effort, and it was time he started putting some in or he deserved to have her leave.

AJ's mood swung at his new enlightenment. He hammered down on the accelerator.

His phone rang. He fetched it from the passenger's seat and looked at the screen. It was his father.

Perfect timing.

37

Emma held her arms across her chest and kept her eyes trained to the floor ahead as she walked down the quiet, dimly lit hallway to the presidential chambers, the echo of her clip-clopping heels resonating in the hardened surroundings.

She was on her way to see Albert, feeling she had been truly blessed. Sure, there had been some bumps along the way, and there would be more. But time and experience can topple the biggest of barriers, and she had much of both under her belt. *AJ will be all right,* she assured herself. She couldn't blame his poor judgment; he was still just a boy, a young buck—all cock and no brains. It was her job to mind him. Guide him through life until he pulled his head out of his ass.

She held faith that the day would come when he would inherit the professional devotion of his father.

She approached the large official doors and knocked lightly. After-hours meetings had become somewhat routine for them.

"Come in!"

When she poked her head in, Albert was leaning over his keyboard, intensely focused on his monitor.

"Hello, son." She smiled. "Am I interrupting?"

He leaned back and exhaled through ballooned cheeks before he returned a loving smile. "No, of course not, Mother. Come, sit down."

He stood as she sat, then went over to the bar and poured a couple snifters full of Scotch. "So, Mother," he said, always dropping the formalities when they were alone, "what's news for today?"

This was the point where she usually started into the plant gossip—this one's doing that, Bill And Jill are having an affair on night shift, and yadda-yadda. When the onslaught of typical banter was missing, Albert to turned and looked at her. She stared at the desk and bit her tongue.

"Mother, what is it?" He handed her a drink, then took a spot leaning against the desk. He swirled his cocktail, then raised the glass to his nose before taking a hefty gulp. "Mother?" He set his glass down, then took her hand tenderly in his. "What is it?"

She looked up. "Well, I'm concerned."

She watched Albert's brow clench. Then he chuckled softly, picked up his glass and took another gulp, and made his way back over to the bar.

"Mother, you and I both know you're notorious for worrying about things there's no need to worry about. So, just get it out, and I'll fix it. You know how this works."

She straightened herself and took a quick breath. "Well, it's about AJ."

His brow raised with renewed interest. "Oh?" He capped the bottle, grabbed his refreshed drink, and returned to lean on the desk. "Well, go on, what's bothering you about AJ?"

"Honestly, I shouldn't say its him, but rather… Victoria."

"Mother, really, we all know you two don't see eye to eye on… well, everything," He grinned. "But I'll listen. What's going on?"

"Oh, Albert!" She fetched a tissue from a box on his desk and dabbed at her sniffles. I just don't think she's the right one for him."

His expression turned stern. "C'mon, Mother, stop dancing around. Why now? Why are you all of a sudden coming forth with this? What was the trigger?"

"Oh," she sobbed, "I saw her! Walked in on her! We— I was out with them, her and that playboy realtor, Justin." She hissed his name. "We were looking at properties together and I… well, I left them alone for only a moment, to make a phone call. Then I found them… I found them together… in the master bedroom."

Albert gripped his glass. She could see the wheels spinning wildly behind his cold blue eyes. "What? You found them *what* in the master bedroom? What were they doing?" He leaned toward her.

"Well, it's hard to say exactly what they were doing before I got there." She looked down at the crumbled tissue in her hand.

"What were they doing when you found them, Mother?" His tone was flat.

"Well, she was sitting on the bed and had a hold of his tie and she, she was holding him close to her—very close! He was leaning over her—I'm sure their faces were touching—and he was... well, he was standing there!" She made a chopping motion toward her legs. "Right there! Oh, Albert! Her legs were spread and he was standing right between them! She was wearing a dress!" Her trembling hand shot to her mouth.

Albert gave a troubled snort, pushed himself off the desk, and stomped back to the bar, swallowing what was left in his glass on the way. He slammed his glass down and took a moment, rolling the glass around on the countertop.

He poured another drink and pushed himself upright with a heavy sigh. "Well, we knew this about her. Knew she had these"—he tilted his head back— "flirtatious tendencies." He paced a slow, short track in front of Emma. "He loves her!" he bellowed, gesturing with drink in hand. "So what can I do? He's my son; I should support him in his decisions. Isn't that how this is all supposed to go?" He walked over and looked down at her for her affirmation.

"Well, honey, I do suppose that is true. But I think there are special situations where we need to step forward and maybe... persuade him." She studied him, waiting for his response.

He turned from her with another sigh.

She continued, "Albert, dear, think about it—divorce." She stood. "She could take everything he ever worked for. His insurance, retirement savings, his... his inheritance. Oh, and Albert!" She raised her hand to her chest. "If they were to have children, she would have full control over them—over *your* grandchildren. She would get absolutely everything! Can you really just stand by and watch his world get torn apart? As his father? There is a time to be supportive, and there is time to be honest."

Albert's pace quickened, his track length stretched. "All right, so what are you suggesting? We"—he looked at her with exasperation—"we get her rubbed out?"

"No, Albert... *pfft!*" She waved a dismissive hand. "But with his job, you're in a place to... turn up the challenge," she suggested.

He shot back a confused look.

"Well, you're wanting him to show more dedication to his work. This project

171

means a lot. Why don't *you*"—she walked around the desk with her drink—"insist he put in more time? Increase his shift to seven days a week till completion."

Albert scoffed and lifted his glass to his lips.

"Son"—she looked wisely up at him—"we both know what demands his job will have. She should realize it now and determine whether it's something she's willing to marry into. It isn't a bad thing, this. We're just making them see the truth so they can both make a… educated decision." She smiled.

Albert's posture slumped and he sighed. "All right."

Emma smiled reassuringly. "It's for the best, dear, we both know that." She pulled his chair out and swivelled it for him to sit. "Who knows"—she shrugged— "maybe she'll surprise all of us and pull up her socks… or pull down her dress." She smirked.

"Mother!" Albert barked. "That'll be enough."

"If she does, then great, I'll willingly admit I was wrong. But if she splits, best for her to do it now." She patted the top of his chair.

Albert took a heavy seat and swivelled around to face the desk. He set down his glass, picked up the phone, and hit speed dial.

38

AJ slammed the condo door closed behind him, tossed his keys down on the dining room table with a loud crash, then draped his jacket over a chair.

He walked over to the window and looked out at the river valley as he weaved his fingers into his hair and then down his face. He exhaled, then turned toward the shifting light of the television in the darkened living room. Vicky sat in her loungewear on the couch, looking at him in silent, mid-chew of her popcorn.

She blinked, then continued chewing and turned back to her bowl for another handful. "What's up with you?" she mumbled through a stuffed mouth.

He gave her a short smile. "Nothing. How 'bout you? How was your day?" He opened his eyes wide and stretched his shoulders back on his way to fetch a cold one from the fridge.

The call from his father on his way home had not panned out as he'd planned. Instead of eliminating his overtime hours, he was told it was now seven days a week until completion. He was pretty certain it was illegal, but his father told him he could offer a substantial bonus after start-up. Whatever the financial benefit, he was given no option.

He yanked open the refrigerator door and reached in for a beer while listening for Vicky's response.

"Well"—he could barely make out the words through her muffled slaughter of popcorn—"nothing, really, just another boring-as-shit day in fucking Fort Mac!"

PRICE PER BARREL

AJ went to the living room and leaned against the wall, taking a much-needed swig of his frosty beer. His nerves were tense with the falling domino of plans. Half an hour ago, he'd been ready to come home and put some work into saving his relationship. Now… he placed the bottle to his lips.

He finished his gulp with a gasp. "Really?" He looked over to her innocent, questioning eyes. "My grandmother stopped in my office today." He raised his eyebrows.

She set her popcorn bowl on the end table beside her, brushed her hands off on a napkin, then sat up with interest. "And what did sweet old Granny have to say?"

Easy, boy! He clenched the bottle to his mouth for another soothing slug. *Keep it together.* "Nothing, really." He grinned casually. "She just said she ran into you and Justin out for lunch and joined you, looking at some houses."

"Hmph." Vicky ran her hands down her outstretched legs. "That's it?" She looked up.

With a mouthful of beer, AJ huffed a breath out his nostrils, pushed straight away from the wall, and gave his head a quick snap from side to side, cracking some tension. He clopped casually over to the end of the couch occupied by her feet, smiling at her as he reached down and lifted them just enough so he could slide beneath.

"Find anything you like?" he asked calmly, reminding himself he was wanting to save his engagement.

"Well, there was this one place." She tilted her head. "It's gorgeous, and the view!" She held up her palm. "But it's right around the corner from your sweet old bat of a grandmother." She stuck her tongue out.

AJ laughed, then began massaging her feet. For that evening, time needed to be turned back for them. To a time when they were on their own, struggling for direction and having fun with it.

Those were good times, lighter times, and tonight was a reminder. So instead of mentioning the unmentionable and starting the raising of hell, he just sat back with her, talking, laughing, and smiling.

Deep down, he knew these times were coming to an end.

39

Ollie woke mid-afternoon on Sunday. Mary-Ann had stayed the whole weekend, as promised. While he was working at night, she simply stayed in the room, tidied up, and read a book she'd been waiting to get time for. In the morning, she'd meet him downstairs for her breakfast, his dinner. After he'd showered, they'd curl up naked in bed, share some stories, and make passionate love, and then he'd pass out.

He felt bad about sleeping through most of her time there, but his body and mind were starving for rest and it was nourishment only she could bring to him.

He looked over at her, lying naked beside him and reading her novel. He smiled.

She caught his movement and placed her book down on her chest. She gently caressed his cheek, looking deeply into his eyes. "Good morning, sleepyhead," she whispered sweetly. "How you feeling? My sexy, hard-working man."

He looked up at the ceiling and smiled as he searched for an accurate answer. "I... I feel..."—his chest deflated as he settled into the moment—"incredible!" He chuckled and raised his arms straight to the ceiling. He balled his hands into fists and then opened them and flexed his fingers, as if he were newborn.

She smiled and kissed him softly on the shoulder while he continued his story.

"I can't believe the difference in how I feel between Friday and now! Friday, I was ready to crawl in the dumpster, but now... now I feel like I could take on the whole world."

She giggled, then draped her upper half over him, looking at him with her big, beautiful eyes. She breathed out and slipped into a fairy tale. "Like a brave, strong, handsome knight, dressed in shining armour, riding his, um, glowing white stallion?" She giggled and then gave him a big, wet kiss.

He laughed, then pushed her onto her back and took his turn over her. He reached down and gave her hips a quick squeeze, causing a squeal. "Shining armour, hey?" He squeezed her again. "I pictured something more soaking wet, in my bright-yellow fishing coat with matching pants." He smirked.

She slapped him playfully. "Ha, ha… riding your glowing… silver codfish." She broke out laughing.

He smiled at her. "Yes, on my big codfish! Coming to save my princess!"

Her laughter quickly subsided when their eyes met, and their lips moved swiftly and instinctively together. He grew hard against her.

"Oh, Ollie," she panted.

After their good-afternoon round, they lay tightly embraced on the bed.

She watched him stare at the ceiling.

"Whatchya thinking about?" She traced a finger over his chest.

Ollie exhaled, then paused to grasp exactly what it was. He tucked his hand behind his head. "I'm thinking about you… about us." His face scrunched. "I'm thinking about me, and how I've got this great girl. I have a good, dependable job that lets me get done what needs getting done." He took a long breath, then continued. "So I should be happy, right? Why am I not happy? It's like I can't have them both. I can't have the job and the girl. Not here, not the way I want it to be. So… so…" He let out a hesitant breath. "I had this thought." He felt his cheeks flush; he was about to take a big risk. He leaned over her. "Gran was all I had, she gave me energy, love—she was everything!" He stared deep into her eyes as he brushed her hair back from her face. "So, I come all the way out here to save her. I had no other choice. Then I meet you, and you're more. You give me more, so much more. I've never in my life felt the way I do when I'm with you." He kissed her, then rolled onto his back.

"I love Gran—she's been there for me my whole life, and I wouldn't be the man I am without her. But, she's not going to get better." A tear rolled down his cheek. "I know that, and I knew it before I came here. She's better than she was, but it's only for a bit. She'll go down again, worse than she was before. So… how long am I supposed to try and stop it?" He turned his baby-blues back to her. "So, maybe this is it. Maybe this is life's way of telling me it's time to let go, to focus on my future instead of holding on to the past." His chin quivered and he looked deeper into her. "You mean everything in the world to me, Mary-Ann." Tears turned to drizzle as he spat the words he'd been holding in for so long, afraid of the realization, afraid to surrender completely to her. Afraid to let go. "I don't mind saying it neither!"

She dabbed the streams on his face and kissed him tenderly. "Oh, Ollie." They were both crying now. She wrapped her arms around his neck and pulled him down to nestle in her breasts, warm and soft, against the beating of her heart. She caressed his shoulders until he calmed.

When the storm had passed, she lifted his face to hers. "Let's do it, then, Ollie!" she said with excitement, tears still rolling. "Let's leave!"

He looked at her, confused.

"Not right now, of course, but let's put together a plan, the two of us! We'll work days, weekends—whatever it takes—for a year, a whole year. We'll get a good lump of money saved up together, a good start on a house. Then let's get the hell out of here! You and me, we'll head out East. Places are cheaper there, and if we have a good down payment, then we won't have to make much money to live. We'll get work where we can. And, Ollie"—she smiled brightly—"your grandmother could come stay with us! She could stay and we could have a family."

He sniffled. "You want to save up... together? Then you want to move back to Newfoundland... and let Gran move in with us?"

"Yes!" She smiled and nuzzled into him. "She sounds like such a good woman. There's a lot to be learned from her, I'm sure, and it would be an honour."

"But... what about your family?"

"I've thought about that, and my parents will be fine. They have each other, and they'd probably like a reason to head out for a visit. Heck, who knows, if I move out there, they might just follow."

"You, you've thought of that? How long have you been thinking about this?"

Mary-Ann's eyes diverted from his. "Well, I... I was just... I thought maybe..." Her cheeks reddened and she wiped away her happy tears. "I'm sorry, I just thought maybe... It was silly, I should've...please, can we just forget—"

"No!" He placed a finger below her chin and lifted her tear-soaked face back to him. "It's not silly, Mary-Ann, I want to know. I had no idea you were— tell me, please, I wanna know."

She snuffed back her tears, straining to meet his eyes. "I've just been thinking about us, our future. Or, I guess, just fantasizing. I thought maybe we could make a plan to move away from here, away from all this craziness! I just… I'm not very happy here. The work is always here, but it takes so much away from life. It's hard to maintain a life outside of it. Divorce is more common than not up here, and I don't want that. I want to start a family—a strong, successful family. The money doesn't matter much to me as long as we have a roof over our heads." She finally looked him in the eye. "Don't you think… wouldn't it be nice for your grandmother to… meet her great-grandchildren?"

Ollie's heart skipped. What she'd described was just as he'd pictured it. His mind wandered back home, watching his wife in a pretty sundress walking hand in hand with their perfect children. She was so beautiful back home, away from the traffic and the endless working hours. Away from the darkness.

He snapped back to the room, realizing his silence had left her anxious. "I think it sounds like a dream—like my dream come true. If it's silly, then we're both silly." Now it was he who diverted his eyes from her, timid of rejection. "I, I love you, Mary-Ann, and I want to plan our future together."

"Oh, Ollie!" They grasped each other close. "I love you too! Let's do it! Please say yes!"

His lips began pressing confidently along her neck. "Of course, I want it more than anything!"

At that moment, in a work camp nestled in the boreal forest of Northern Canada, Ollie Hynes and Mary-Ann Kibbnok made love… again.

40

Over the next few weeks, Ollie found that the magical serenity Mary-Ann cast upon him during her weekend visits would vanish as soon as she left, letting him fall back, spiralling through forever-sleepless nights.

Pledging their love for each other should have put his mind at ease. Instead, it increased his fear of losing her. She visited every weekend and gave no hint of being bored or of losing interest, but his exhausted mind struggled to accept the facts. He couldn't see how someone like her would stick around with him for a weekend relationship where he slept eighty percent of the time and she was stuck inside a tiny box, waiting on him to become semi-conscious, praying for a future that may or may not become a reality. Not when it could become very real, very fast with a handsome man of wealth.

She always said that she didn't mind, that she actually enjoyed it as long as they were together. She seemed good to the words: she was setting up and mapping out a financial plan for them, and she even suggested they open up a shared savings account when Ollie could get time to head to a bank. When he put all the facts together, it appeared that their love was legit. But he could never believe it.

He'd asked Honey about any possible time off coming their way. *"Take it while it's here!"* he'd said, as excited as a man who'd been handed a blank cheque.

Honey had also grown more liberal with his "little pick-me-up" use around Ollie. Now that everything was out in the open, he enjoyed his hits at the smoke shacks with his buddies while Ollie was out working, or even when they were driving down the road.

Whatever it was, it never seemed to have any type of effect on the guy. He was always up in spirits, alert, and content with life. After weeks of his own dementia, Ollie's curiosity couldn't help but grow.

As they sat in the truck and waited for a crane to exit a yard, Ollie watched Honey spark his lighter and take a long draw. He held it in for a ten-count, and then he blew the silky white wisp out his window.

"What is that?" Ollie finally built up the courage to ask.

"Huh?"

"That stuff you're smoking. What is it?"

Honey took a moment before answering. "It's nothing." He smiled and leaned back. "You ain't been 'round much, have you, kid?"

Ollie turned his head, slightly offended. "I've been 'round some. Just not drugs."

"*Pfft!*" Honey scoffed. "Drugs, this shit? This can hardly be called drugs. It's prescription shit. Doctors prescribe it for patients with depression and whatnot."

"Prescription? I don't know any prescription that comes in a little plastic bag."

"Well, it's not the pill form," Honey protested, clearly no longer able to meet Ollie's eyes. "They get it out of the factory before they have a chance to shape it into the pills. That way it's cheaper and… more pure." He picked off another crumb of the small white rock.

"I don't know any medicine that a guy smokes in a pipe neither."

"It's just another way you can do it, it works quicker this way. They say the pills don't all get into your system because it doesn't digest fast enough. I wanna get the best bang for my buck, eh?"

Ollie leaned his head against his window. "Well, what does it do? It doesn't seem to do nothing to you."

"It's just an upper, like a strong cup of coffee. It makes you feel good, awake, so you can still get shit done."

"So why not just drink coffee?"

"Eh? Coffee's too much… It's too hard on my guts, you know?"

Ollie's guts were churning from the two pots he'd drank that shift. "Can you sleep?"

180

Honey chuckled. "Oh, man, I sleep like a baby!"

It would be nice to be able to sleep. Then on the weekend he could sacrifice some rest to spending better quality time with Mary-Ann. Even go to town together one day, take her shopping and buy her something nice, treat her to lunch at some fancy restaurant. And Honey seemed to be enjoying the night shift a hell of a lot more than he was.

Honey looked over. "Youuuuu wanna try a hit?" He offered the pipe across the cab.

Ollie froze. "No! No, thanks." He shook his head and held his hands up.

"Suit yourself. But the offer's there if you want."

The night went on as usual. Ollie took on the majority of the physical work while Honey stayed in the truck. As visions of taking Mary-Ann for a day on the town danced in his mind, Ollie paid even closer attention to Honey and his magic remedy. He seemed to have no problem coping with the night and suffered no detectable side effects. He had to be getting a good rest during the day. It was pretty obvious that the method he was using worked. And Ollie's strategy wasn't worth shit. Maybe it was the cure he needed?

What would be the harm? Ollie asked himself. *Give it a try, and if it works, then great! If it doesn't, I just won't do it anymore.* His mind was exhausted, his common sense disabled to the point where he didn't even realize what he didn't realize.

He hooked up the hose, then gave the thumbs-up to Honey. A bead of sweat broke on his forehead and he clutched his cramped stomach. He couldn't continue on like he was. He'd be dead before he and Mary-Ann could reach their dream.

He hopped back in the cab, guts still rumbling, breathing staggered.

Honey straightened from his slumber. "Got 'er all packed up?"

"Yeah, good to go."

Honey looked over at him. "Jesus, man! You look like shit! What the fuck's up with you?"

"Nothing," Ollie gasped, wiping at his forehead. "I just haven't been doing too good on this night-shift thing, I don't know what it is. It's been a fucking month now, and I can't eat... I can't sleep!" He looked over. "You sure that shit's safe?"

"Huh? Oh yeah! No worse than taking a couple Aspirin." He had the honest composure of a car salesman. "You think I'd do anything that puts me at risk? You think I'd offer you something that'd put you at risk? You're my fucking partner— you die, and I gotta get out there and do that shit myself." He winked.

Ollie bent forward and rested his elbows on his knees. His breathing steadied as his cramps began to ease. "All right." The words came out involuntarily.

In his mind, he was looking at the Ollie of old back home, dressed in his favourite jeans and blue-striped shirt, with a ball mitt fitted on his hand. That Ollie stood in a field of sun and long green grass, looking so healthy and happy, so… alien. *"Don't do it, Ollie,"* the young man pleaded.

His current self stood in shadow at the edge of the field, his head hanging, the shell of a man he once wanted to be. He was dressed in his work gear, covered in grunge and darkness, holding his hard hat low by his side. *"You don't know,"* the dark one replied. *"There's things I have to get done. I have responsibilities."* He looked into the eyes of his former self. *"It's heavy."* His eyes dropped back to the ground. He raised his hard hat slowly, placed it on his head, then turned and faded away.

"Okay!" Honey gave Ollie a toothy smile. "It's no good living the way you have. You should've said something sooner, kid. We'll get you fixed up right away." He busied himself preparing the pipe, then handed the loaded gun over, careful not to spill it. "All right, man, just hit the lighter and hold it to the pipe. Not too close—hold it above, and then draw the flame to the pipe with your breath. Just breathe in long and steady."

Ollie hesitated as he looked down at the reality. It felt wrong. But Honey was right, something had to change. Everything in his life was so confused. He couldn't continue another night the way he was going, and he couldn't quit; there was too much at stake.

Just try it. You don't like it, don't do it anymore. He exhaled. *Here goes nothing.* He raised the cool steel to his lips. He struck the lighter, then brought it slowly over the pipe and breathed in until the flame tipped down.

"That's it!" Honey said. "Just like that, keep it going. Slow and steady, now, keep pulling. Easy… easy… slow. That's it, suck."

Ollie ran out of capacity and pulled the pipe away.

"Hold it! As long as you can!" Honey's eyes were wide as he watched and waited, as if he were witnessing Ollie's rebirth.

Ollie held it in as long as he could. Other than being starved for breath, he didn't feel a damn thing. Then his will expired and he exhaled a hefty plume. As he watched the smoke spread thin in the air before him, he suddenly became very aware. Before his lungs had emptied, his senses heightened and he turned to the darkness, a vampire in the night. He'd found consciousness, he'd found confidence, he'd found sight, sound, and taste. His scrambled mind focused as he completed the transformation.

Illuminated to a new way of life, Ollie had finally become one with the darkness.

41

Charlie sank into his office chair and put the phone to his ear. "Charlie speaking."

"Charlie, Albert Doyle here."

"Oh, good morning to you, sir. What can I do for you today?"

"What can you do? You just keep on doing what you're doing, and get that plant up and running on time." He gave a friendly chuckle. "Not calling to bust anyone's balls, Charlie, I'm actually getting some positive reports back from some of the contractor leads that things are starting to take shape down there. Looks like turning the reins over to you was the right move."

"I guess that's why you're the president."

Both men shared a laugh.

"So, seriously, Charlie, how are things going?"

"Things are actually progressing quite nicely now. I have to thank you for sending that instrument tech and the programming specialist. They've been doing an excellent job sorting out this… well, mess, for lack of a better term."

"Yes, I know it's not an easy project. First one of its kind," he gloated. "Things are getting hot up here on the front lines as well. The environmentalists are coming on heavy, and the safety board… don't even get me started. Don't you worry about none of that, though. We're doing our best not to let any of them on site, but you let me know immediately if one of them happens to slither past, or if they contact you in any way. You just keep on doing what you're doing, I'll run defence."

"Yeah, I'm glad you're up there to deal with that shit. I'm too fucking old for politics now, no patience."

Albert chuckled. "Not my first time dodging bullets." He changed his tone and lowered his voice. "On a different note, how's AJ holding up through all this?"

Charlie sighed. "I'm not sure what to tell you. He shows up to work on time… sometimes. He goes straight into his office and really has nothing to do with anything."

It was Albert's turn to sigh. "It's unfortunate. I apologize for your being exposed to this… family issue."

"I'm a father, Albert, I understand. I just wish there was more I could do to help."

"There's nothing you can do, and you're not expected to. This is just a coming-of-age time for him; he's facing some realities. It's not just at the site—he's got some domestic troubles. A perfect storm, so to speak."

"Ah, say no more. Women: can't live with them—"

"And I'll just cut you off there." Albert laughed. "As I mentioned before, though, I have to use him for the board meetings, and I'm sure there'll be some press conferences coming up right away."

"Yes, I remem—"

Albert cut him off once more, his tone changing to one of professional hierarchy. "So, I'm going to need you to keep him updated. You know, show him the prints, take him around the site, try to get him a bit more involved."

"Well, see—"

Charlie was overruled again as Albert explained how he needed to keep AJ in decent shape and knowledgeable enough to represent the project. He needed Charlie to babysit. "Just keep an eye on him for me, okay?"

What Charlie wanted to say in response and what he actually said were completely opposite. "I, I'll do my best, Mr. Doyle." Since the request had been more of a command, Charlie didn't feel it a time for informalities.

"I knew I could count on you. Call if you need anything." The call disconnected.

Son of a bitch, Charles! What now? What have you done to yourself now?

With his orders official, he decided to head down to check in on his new side project. *Maybe it won't be so bad*, he thought as he made his way to AJ's office. He did enjoy working with youth, watching them develop. He rapped politely on the door, then opened it and poked his head inside. "Good morn—"

There reclined the young prince, fast asleep. A stiff scent lingered in the musty air. Charlie stepped in quietly and moved around to AJ's side of the desk. The bottom right-hand drawer was open, and a half-empty bottle of whiskey lay at the bottom. A half-full Styrofoam cup sat cleverly stashed behind a family portrait.

Charlie snuck back across the room and out the door, closing it softly behind him.

He exhaled loudly. *Time to retire, old man. It's just time.*

42

The weekend arrived. During the remainder of the workweek, Ollie had continued sampling Honey's picker-uppers—only on a few occasions at first, but by Friday evening, he was indulging a little more regularly.

He felt better—or at least different. He was definitely awake, he didn't have that overbearing caffeine sickness, and he was getting some sleep during the day—some. It wasn't the deep, reviving sleep he experienced with Mary-Ann. It was restless, but he figured it must be better than what he'd been getting before because he was always up and anxious to get to work.

He decided to stock up that night, hoping the effects would last a little longer so he could get some more time with his girl, maybe surprise her with his stamina. Honey had offered to front him a chunk and help him make a pipe from the instrumentation materials, but Ollie had refused; this was staying at work.

They pulled up to the entrance gate of the parking lot for his camp at the end of shift. Honey packed one last big one for Ollie before he hopped out of the truck.

It was morning rush hour, and the foyer was a bustle of workers. Thousands dressed in heavy cold-weather gear were walking and bumping in every direction. The bright fluorescent lights now felt foreign and unwelcome to Ollie, setting him on a stage for the entire world to judge.

He usually made a straight line to the kitchen to fetch some chocolate chip cookies to eat on the walk to his room, but the last hit had flipped a switch to extreme paranoia. He needed shelter and darkness. He kept his head down and pinballed his way through the crowd, his key card out and ready to swipe as soon as he reached the door. By the time he got to his room, his heart was pounding so strongly that all he could hear was the rushing of blood in his head.

He grabbed the handle and was putting the key card up to the reader when two hands came from behind and covered his eyes, inducing instant panic.

"Welcome home, handsome!" a voice once sweet to him sang. She spun him around and began peppering his lips with kisses.

He stared down into her puppy eyes and his jaw fell slack. "Mary-Ann! You're here?" He nudged her inside with a clammy hand and closed the door, locking it quickly. All he needed was some downtime. He'd never been this jacked up before. At night, in the shadows, it would've been fine; he would've had his shelter. But in the daylight, people would never understand.

"Surprise, my sexy man!" She giggled and latched back on to him.

Nope, nope, not right now. Gotta get out of this, get a moment to get your shit together.

She stopped kissing and leaned back, wiping her hand soothingly across his face and studying his complexion. "Sweetie! What's wrong? You're all pale and sweaty."

Her sweetness normally had him melting in her hands, but not that morning. He had become numb to her charm.

"Yeah, yeah." He placed restraining hands on her arms. "I'm really not feeling well… too much… coffee." He shot her a false smile. "I just gotta get out of these filthy clothes and into the shower."

"Oh baby, what can I do to help?" she said, fighting to wrap her arms around his waist.

He snatched her wrists. "Mary-Ann, you know how dirty I am when I get back, you really shouldn't be hugging me." He nodded, with the same unconvincing smile.

She began tickling his ribs and giggling. "Silly boy, you know that won't keep me away!"

He pushed her back. "Mary-Ann, please!" His smile quivered, the sweat continuing to build on his forehead. "Just let me go have a shower and get freshened up, then everything'll be good." He yanked his shirt up off over his head and slipped out of his jeans, then dodged her and disappeared into the bathroom.

Ollie flipped up the toilet seat in case Mary-Ann was listening on the other side, then sat down. He placed his elbows on his knees and rested his head in his hands. He didn't know how much time he let pass, but he waited and breathed and settled until he could get up the nerve to move.

Once he'd gathered the courage, he pushed himself up. His legs burned with pins and needles. He reached back and flushed the toilet, strictly for effect, then stumbled around the small closet of a room to the shower, wincing and buckling with every step.

He tipped the shower handle to hot, and soothing steam soon began to fill the room. He peeled off his underwear and adjusted the water, then stepped in and drew the curtain. The water rinsed the darkness from his body and funnelled it down the drain. The effects began to fade; he could feel himself gaining control. Complete exhaustion settled in.

He counted his breathing—three counts in and three out—as the hot, humid air warmed his insides. With each breath, he relaxed a little more, until finally, his weight was too much for his legs to bear, leaving him sluggish and sloppy, but grateful. Thoughts of his sweet Mary-Ann returned, and he was more thankful than ever to have her. If she found out…

Wanting nothing more than to fall into her loving embrace, Ollie turned off the water and threw back the curtain. He wrapped a towel around himself, mopped up a small puddle of water with the shower mat, and then gathered his dirty socks and underwear off the floor. He grabbed hold of the door handle, took a deep breath, then pushed into the cool, refreshing air of the open room.

He was expecting to have to fend off a full-on smothering attack. Instead, he found Mary-Ann sitting in her spot on the bed, reading.

She lowered the book and looked at him uncertainly as he closed the door with a soft click. She crossed her arms in front of her, her big eyes blinking curiously. "You were in there quite a while?"

Ollie gave her a dopey smile and rubbed his stomach slowly. "Yeah, my stomach." He winced, then busied himself with picking out something to wear. "I feel a lot better now—more relaxed, anyway. That shower felt great." He bent down and lifted some boxer shorts into place, then turned toward her as he fluffed out a black T-shirt with a faded yellow Nirvana logo.

***

Mary-Ann's gaze travelled down the length of Ollie's slender figure, her mind still spinning from her first taste of his rejection. He did look more relaxed, but he still looked grey, drained. And then her bitterness softened at his blue eyes looking so lost, and she opened her arms to him. "Poor boy, come here."

Ollie crawled across the bed and wilted into her. His head came to rest between her breasts and she caressed her fingers through his hair.

"I'm sorry if I seemed a little mad at you. I just… I've never had you push me away like that." She could feel something was different, off. Maybe he was sick? *Of course he's sick, what man wouldn't be after working in those conditions?* Whatever it was, she felt it weighing on them.

"You're a good man, Ollie, working so hard for the people you love." Her eyes began to saturate, but the tears weren't happy. "We all love you so much!" She sniffed and a tear rolled down her cheek, followed by another. She leaned down and kissed the top of his head, feeling his warmth on her lips.

He released a shivered gasp. She couldn't see his face, but she knew he shared her tears. He reached down and rubbed her leg. "I know, Mary-Ann, I love you too… so much!" He sobbed. "I just… I want to do more for you. I just really wanted to go for a walk with you today, out in the sun. It's been so long. I'm so scared to lose you." His chest heaved.

"Ollie!" She slipped her hand to his cheek and rolled him over. She kissed him sweetly, and found it there: weak at first, then stronger. His passion was struggling to return from the blackness. She broke from his lips and slid beside him until she breathed in his ear. "Can you feel me, Ollie?"

He nodded.

"I'm right here, with you. I'm right beside you—the whole way, beside you. We're going all the way to our dream."

He caressed her arm. His warm touch delivered hope.

She sat up and looked down at him, tickling her fingers over his face. "Close your eyes," she breathed. "I have this place I want to tell you about."

He nodded again and closed his eyes.

"We're home—our home—out East. It's springtime, and we're walking in the tall grass along the cliffs overlooking the ocean. We're watching giant icebergs float down from the North. I've heard how wonderful they are." Tears tumbled over her smiling lips. She leaned her head back and closed her eyes too. "We're bundled up in our toques and scarfs and mittens." She shook with a quick laugh, and her tears changed to streams of joy. "Your nose is pink because of the cold.

The wind is cool, but we can feel the strength of the sun. We can feel it returning. Are you there, Ollie? Can you see it?"

"I can see it," he gasped. "I'm there, I can feel it, I can smell it. I can see the sun shining, and you're so beautiful, so happy."

"Then I turn and point to a really big iceberg, and when I turn back to find you, you're down on one knee." They both snickered. She waited a moment until they settled. "Then, you take my hand, and I start to cry, and you ask me to be your wife. I saaaayyyyy"—she opened her eyes to watch his reaction—"I'll think about it."

Ollie's eyes shot open and he jerked his hand down into her ribs and got a squeal.

She leaned down and kissed his cheek. "Then we kiss, and it's the best kiss that ever happened—ever. Better than all the fairy tales in the whole world." She giggled.

"The best kiss?" he said. "Ever in the world? Nothin' like putting the pressure on." He smiled and looked into her eyes.

"Don't forget it; it's ours, all ours! No one can take it from us. I'll be here waiting for you, every weekend and every day I can. When you get lost, I'll be here. Don't forget. Even on the darkest of nights, remember our place."

Ollie's eyes closed above a serene smile. "I won't forget." He felt for her hand and locked their fingers together. He squeezed and held her tight, and then he drifted to sleep.

Mary-Ann wasn't new to life in the oil sands. She'd seen it turn poor men to wealth, and rich men to waste. The bitumen had passed the test of time, surviving millions of years: thick, sticky, toxic, its stored energy from the remains of so much life passed. Mankind, blinded by its riches, was foolish to dismiss it as inanimate ooze. The number of lives taken and great inventions ground to dust in order to mine it—perhaps it wasn't a helpless resource openly available for their taking. It was cold and calculating, drawing men to it from far and wide like flies to sticky paper, and they worked to ensure that what was removed would, over time, be replaced.

Maybe it was the one mining them.

***

By the time Ollie woke on Sunday afternoon, he felt strong and refreshed. His attempt at utilizing his newfound crutch to enhance his time spent with

PRICE PER BARREL

Mary-Ann had been a complete failure. It made nothing better. He finished brushing his teeth and then looked into the mirror, into his eyes, with a stern order. *No more! Not tonight, not ever again, Oliver Hynes! You're a short time away from having the life you never thought you'd have, with the greatest woman you've ever known. Don't screw this up!* He took a deep breath and focused—focused on the place she had given to him. Their place, back home, with love and family. He exhaled. *No more!* He nodded, then turned away.

He finished dressing, then gave his sweetheart a strong hug and kiss. She held him for a moment longer than normal. When she pulled back she smiled sweetly at him, but her eyes were glazed with concern.

"Remember our place." She reached a caring hand to his cheek. "Remember, I'm always here."

He smiled confidently and tightened his arms around her waist. "I will, I promise." He kissed her again, then walked out the door.

At the gate, he climbed into the waiting honey wagon. His simple "hey" greeting carried a disgruntled pitch, and he quickly turned away from Honey to look out the passenger window.

Honey remained silent, shifted the truck into gear, and began their journey.

Many had stood in that place where Ollie now was. *"You can just not do it anymore,"* was the lie they told themselves. It wasn't until they passed through and then quickly turned to pass back that they found the door was missing. Then there were only two options: accept where you are and learn to live with it, or spend the rest of time fighting and searching for the door back. But very few ever escaped. That night would be one of realization for Ollie; realization of that line he had crossed.

As they drove into the valley, Ollie continued to keep his eyes trained out the window, and away from Honey. The sun was holding on longer now, the twilight on the horizon hanging behind the mines across the river. He followed the black silhouette of a haul truck making its way down the cliff and across the bridge. He felt the darkness cloaking over him, the calming hand of shadow resting on his shoulder, welcoming him back. A voice of reassurance whispered in his ear, *"It's all right, Ollie; really, it's not a big deal. What happens at work stays there."* The mental prod triggered an overwhelming pull, and his nerves began to tremble. He clutched the handle of his colossal mug of coffee with a sweaty palm.

Tears began to build and his sinuses stuffed. He clenched with anger. Where

192

was he? What had become of him? Why wouldn't it just let him go?

A tear spilled, blurring the haul truck as he watched it back into its stall. Its bucket began to lift and large frozen clumps rolled from the bed. Thin wisps of dust escaped the mass and dispersed into the air. Then the last bit of twilight faded behind the hills and turned the outside light to black. A broken and faded reflection of Ollie's frightened face appeared in the glass.

A voice broke through to his conscience. *"Remember."* He had promised he would. He closed his eyes tight and searched his mind. He ran, ran through the darkness, looking, watching for the light, their place…where had it gone? There was nothing but darkness. His chest heaved and his body shuddered with a silent sob. He rested his head against the window. *God… help me.*

That's the thing with addiction: You tell yourself *"Never again."* Then, at the next opportune moment… *"Again."*

43

Charlie returned home after a hard day of managing the project and tending to his new babysitting duties. He'd tried to ease in with AJ, making a point of stopping in his office to break the ice with some idle chitchat and a joke or two, but bringing up anything to do with the plant was like hitting the snooze button on AJ. The boy seemed pretty messed up; and the drinking continued.

He stepped in the door and shook off his shoes before heading up to the kitchen, where he found Marge, faithful Marge, warming up a plateful of her good home cooking for him. She'd given up trying to have things freshly prepared for when he got home many years ago. Dinner was at six; anything past then was warmed-overs.

"Oh dear, you look beat." She shuffled over and collected his jacket as he took a seat at the table.

Charlie watched her scurry around, placing his things where they needed to be. It wasn't as if he was a pig. He placed everything close to where it was supposed to be, but never properly, according to her. Oh, the fights it had caused over the years. His boots were on the rack but not straight enough. Keys don't belong on the kitchen table, they belong on the hook by the door. Jackets don't go on chairbacks. For the first time that day, he smiled.

His mind wandered back to AJ. At that time in life when you set out in the big wide world and start making some money, you figure you have it by the balls. No need to follow any rules: shoes by the door, keys stay where they land.

Everyone important in your life seems to be holding you back. Too young and too stupid. *Ah, the twenties. Balls full of spunk, pockets full of money, and a head full of... spunk.* He'd been there, gone through the turmoil. He'd gone one direction to find himself, and Marge had gone the other to do the same. In the end, after Charlie had misplaced his jacket and his keys and all the money had fallen through that hole in his pocket he could never locate, he realized life is easier with two. Two people, combining energy to create one great life.

He didn't know much about AJ's relationship with his fiancée. He'd never met her, and AJ never gave up much personal information. But judging strictly by the young man's current condition and the portrait of the young woman on his desk, Charlie could piece together a credible backdrop.

He was a prince from a family of wealth and power. She was a peasant, blessed—or cursed—with seductive beauty; a trait she used to manipulate her way to a better life. A relationship based on pure physical attraction, and doomed to collapse.

All he wanted was a big fancy house, a high-performance sports car, and a trophy wife. What he was finding now was that working for a living sucked.

All she wanted was the ability to snap her fingers and have everything she ever wanted materialize. In her mind, time was her enemy—all her talent had an expiration date. If not now, then very soon, she'd begin to check every fine detail in the mirror. Her natural immunity to age and gravity would begin to subside with every beat of the heart. The dreaded number thirty, now dawning on the horizon, would begin to poison her mind with insecurities.

They were a couple who would likely never come to the same realization as Charlie and Marge had. When Charlie got up in the mornings, his jacket, boots, and keys were where they should be, and he got on his way with few frustrations. All his meals were prepared, and not from boxes or cans but from fresh ingredients moulded together with her love and energy. And he appreciated all of it. In return, he provided Marge with the necessities and luxuries of life and she was free to adventure within their means. And she appreciated all of it. In times of need, they were there to comfort and support one another. Together, they provided strength to each other and their extended friends and family. And it was appreciated.

Marge finished her fussing, grabbed Charlie's dinner and delivered it to the table, then sat herself beside him and looked on with concern. "Poor, dear, what are they doing to you out there?" She caressed his shoulder.

PRICE PER BARREL

"*Pffffbbbbwahhh!*" Charlie rubbed at his face. "I don't know, Marge." He relayed the story of the new duties.

"Charlie, that's not fair! Why didn't you refuse?" She huffed. "I think you're already doing enough for that project. You're not even the manager, you likely won't even get credit for anything in the end."

Charlie grinned. "You know why, honey? 'Cause I'm a good guy; the word *no* doesn't exist in my vocabulary."

"Well, not for your boss anyway," she teased, smiling sweetly.

He chuckled softly and turned his gaze down to his plate. "Why do we do this shit anymore, Marge? How'd we get to this spot in life? We should be retired."

"Oh sure," she replied, "retired to one of those little trailer park–golf course places down south. We can get up with the rest of the old goats and start drinking at nine." She smiled lovingly, then disappeared into the kitchen, still talking. "What kind of life would that be, Charlie? Not a life for us. You'd be just as annoyed down there as you are up here."

He smiled again at her reasoning. On top of his boots and dinner, Marge had a magic ability to keep his head on his shoulders. Another one of her traits he'd suffer without.

She returned to the table with the tablet computer. She sat with a smile and patted his head. "You do it because you're the greatest, most loving man and grandfather this world has known." She leaned over and kissed him tenderly, then placed the tablet in front of him. She brought the screen to life, scrolled through some options, and hit PLAY.

The proud grandparents held hands as they watched the video. Their grandson took his place in line for a track race. The starting gun popped, and off the boys shot, the camera focusing on and following young Summit. Tears welled in their eyes, and Charlie patted his wife's hand. As if the clip was suddenly in slow motion, Charlie watched the boy's muscles pushing, flexing, and swinging, his chest expanding and contracting. Summit crossed the finish line in second-to-last place, but the fact he could even participate was more than enough reason to celebrate. They cheered, jumping from their seats and into each other's arms. Hugging and kissing, their tears combined into an isolated shower.

They parted to admire each other's smiling, tear-stained faces.

Charlie's eyes widened and his arms tightened around Marge, demanding her attention. "Albert, the big boss! He promised me an extra-fat bonus at completion for all the new bullshit I'm taking on."

Marge nodded in suspense.

"Let's book a trip! A celebration trip!"

Beaming, Marge placed her hands on his cheeks and pulled him in for a big smooch. "I think that sounds just wonderful, Grandpa! Where should we take this trip? Anywhere you want!"

He clapped his hands together, then paced the floor while stroking his chin. "Hmm, the best place to go? Somewhere we can just watch Summit have a blast! Someplace where the smile will never leave his face! The whole time! Disneyland! Let's do it!" He smiled triumphantly, his arms held wide open.

Marge's hands came together in front of her as if in prayer as she looked into his eyes with admiration. "You got it, Disneyland it is. Seven days, all of us, our treat." Her chest heaved, and heavy tears flowed from her smiling eyes. "I love you, my husband."

Charlie's chin quivered as he looked over at her. "I love you, my wife."

44

Several months later, a cool spring breeze ruffled the feathers hanging from the chieftain's handcrafted coat as he stood on the bald hilltop. From this viewpoint, he could see most of the mine area. But close at hand, just at the bottom of the slope, sat the 11-16 Project.

The spot held memories for him. He used to visit the hilltop with his father. It was a special place, unknown to most of his people now, and one of the few natural islands that had survived the violent rape of the land.

It had been known then as a sacred place of prayer, once home to a great teepee. Now, all that remained was a rocky campfire ring.

He liked to visit there when time for reflection was needed. He had seen much change to the land in his life. When he was young, lush green fields of forest impregnated with sparkling marshes had stretched out all the way to the rising sun. Spring had brought the smell of blossoming life in the vegetation and the fresh streams of running snowmelt. Animals waking from winter's dream and the honking and chirping of returning summer fowl beneath the warmth of the strengthening sun had instilled a sense of peace after the trying winter.

Now, it was all gone. Now the earth was black as coal, and it didn't stop at the horizon. Wolves and bears had been replaced by trucks and diggers, singing birds frightened away by blasting canons. The fresh smells had turned to stink. Stink from making the white man's road, stink from toxic lakes stretching farther and deeper than anything natural, stink from fuel for their trucks and other black poison.

He turned to the breeze and closed his eyes. It was still there—diluted, but still there. He knew because he had breathed that air all his life. It was still there, past the empty black desert of ruin. It waited to return, and if given only the slightest chance, it would reclaim this land and heal all its misfortune. Nature was an incredibly real and powerful force, one that most people dismissed. They overlooked it as a governing presence. Nature is an energy that has existed since the beginning. It has built, it has destroyed, and it was once praised and respected.

Now, it was all about their machines. Machines fail, people fail, but nature does not fail. They lied to themselves, avoiding the truth so maybe they would not panic at the reality. They say they are destroying the earth, destroying nature. But nature is infinite. They are only killing themselves.

He looked to the action below, down to the white men. He thought about when they would pay visits to the villages to talk to the Elders. "Deals" they were called—trade of money for pride. At first, his people had refused, but the white man kept returning. They became trickier, dressed in suits and ties. *"The talking ones."* They would talk, and they would smile. Always talking and smiling, but something about them felt very unnatural. As though every move, every word had been scheduled and rehearsed. They brought their toys and luxuries, supplying his people with housing and televisions at no cost. They set them up to live not luxuriously but comfortably: food on their tables, clothes on their backs, and roofs over their heads. There was nothing left for them to do but sit and watch TV. The white men claimed their money back by selling his people addictions—booze and chemicals. They impregnated their ways like a plague. Now, the gravity of comfort held his people heavy as the hands of a hundred dictators. Their dignity had been depleted, and they no longer had the will to stand up and fight!

The chieftain reached into his pocket, dug out his pipe, and began to pack it with his special blend.

How to explain to anyone nowadays why he continued to return to the spot? To speak of communication with spirits and energies were tales of myth told by crazy old men. That's what the television said. But the winds flowed and spirits still called, and he was there to listen. They told to him not to forget about this space, that it was given to him for a purpose and that there would come a time in his life when he would need it. And now, since this new area had started, it was calling him more. He didn't know much about what they were doing down there, but the spirits' insistence of his presence was growing more urgent. He could feel that the white man was nearing completion—whatever was coming, was coming soon.

He lifted the pipe to his mouth, lit it, and pulled in deeply. He held the draw in for a moment of thanks, then exhaled while mouthing an ancient chant to himself. His mind grew dizzy, and the soft words echoed, taking form in a whisper of smoke before being carried away on the breeze.

He closed his eyes and slowly raised his arms to the heavens as he continued his chant, his voice growing stronger and the words coming out faster. He felt his spirit lift free from his physical body. A scream in the breeze; a sudden, thunderous crash; a vision flashed in his mind. The chieftain opened his eyes, and the abrupt weight of his body toppled him to the ground. He lay, panting heavily and struggling to return completely from where he had just escaped to. But there was no rest to be had; the spirits were strong. The wind rolled him over and pushed him to his feet. He gasped and bent over, holding a stitch in his side, then tripped and stumbled as he let the breeze guide him toward the abandoned firepit.

He looked into the centre of the pit, where a lazy pile of snow held on for existence, hiding in the shadow of the lining rocks. There was something there, some hint. He closed his eyes, steadied his breath, and calmed his heart. Slowly and with control, he looked again, and startled at the vision. The centre of the pit had changed. Fire, but not campfire.

It was the fire of hell.

45

"Charlie! It's Albert."

Such morning phone calls were becoming a ritual.

"Oh, good morning Mr.—"

"Oh, cut the shit, I told you call me Albert!" His tone was whispered desperation.

"Yes, all right, good morning, Alber—"

"Okay, forget the niceties, I just need you to listen to me!"

"Yes, sir… Albert."

"How's everything going down there? Is everything on schedule?"

"Well, yes, the mechanical's complete. The electrical and instrumentation's all in place. We're about to go through the start-up and commissioning phase. There's bound to be a few of the routine bugs, but I don't predict any major surprises, other than that this has never been attempted before."

"Okay, good, good. How 'bout AJ? Have you had any time to work with him?"

"Albert, I really wish I could say I've had more success with him, but he's pretty…" Charlie struggled for the most pleasant critique. "Resistant to mentorship."

"So in other words, nothing?"

"Well, no, not nothing, I've managed to get him out for some morning walks. I update him daily on the progress and he seems to take it in."

"Good! Now listen, we have a bit of an emergency. The governing board is coming down hard on us. They want answers in regards to environmental and safety shit. Now, I can answer all of their bullshit questions, but... AJ has to be there, and he has to be somewhat competent."

"Uh, Albert, I don't think—"

"Charlie, this is not a request, it's an order! He has to be there! If he's not there, people are going to start asking questions. This media attention has the potential to build into a real shitstorm! If this isn't handled correctly, it could shut 11-16 down!"

"Yeah, I can give him all the information he needs, but I'm no media specialist, Albert. Isn't there some kind of specific interview training courses you could get him in?"

"No time."

"Wha'?... When is this conference thing?"

"Have him ready and at the gate in three hours! Thanks, Charlie."

The receiver clicked.

God dammit! Charlie slammed down the phone. He stood and wiped a hand across his face, then checked his watch and began pacing. *11:00 a.m. now, plus three is 2:00 p.m... Shit!... Shit! Shit! Shit! Shit!... All right, Charlie, don't panic, get a grip... Disneyland, you're going to Disneyland.*

He stopped pacing, then burst out his door and marched across the empty lunchroom and charged into AJ's office.

Shit! Too late. He sighed and leaned back against the wall as he looked at AJ passed out in his chair. *Sonofabitch.*

It was what it was, Charlie decided. There was no time to waste—he needed to get this kid up, get him schooled and presentable, and get him to the show on time.

Going to fucking Disneyland!

He grabbed the stale pot of coffee and a couple Styrofoam cups from the lunchroom, then set everything on the desk and gently prodded at AJ.

"AJ," he said in a whisper. When he got no reaction, Charlie shook his leg. "AJ? Buddy. Hey... champ?" Still no response. *The kid is fucking out! Fuck!* He shook his head, cleared his mind, and began to strategize.

He grabbed the boy by the shoulder. "AJ!" His voice echoed, loud and stern. "AJ! You gotta get up, man!" He shook harder, until the mass stirred and swatted at him. "AJ, I just got off the phone with your father. There's a press conference in a couple hours, and you gotta be there!" He quit fucking around and threw all the cards on the table. "You have to wake up!" he shouted. "You have to get cleaned up! I have to update you and get you the hell over there in time!"

"Huh?" AJ righted himself, then laid his head on his desk. After a moment, he took a deep breath and sat up, then rubbed vigorously at his eyes. He ran his hands over his hair and looked up at Charlie. "Okay, so what the hell's going on?" He blinked his deeply bloodshot eyes.

The foul whiskey exhaust from his mouth slapped Charlie as hard as if it were still in the bottle. He shrank back in revolt. "Jesus. Shit, AJ, you got a bit of a thing to deal with there. Didn't anyone ever tell you that if you're going to drink at work, make it vodka? It doesn't leave an odour."

"Well, shit, Charlie, you could've had better timing with that." He punctuated the reply with a hiccup.

Charlie watched AJ's lips as he listened carefully to his slurred speech; they were outlined in a thick white film. He looked like a peasant who'd been walking the desert for days.

"Listen!" Charlie filled a cup with coffee, then forced it on AJ. "You gotta work on getting your shit together. You're booked for a media conference in a couple hours."

"What media conference? I didn't know anything about any media conference... Did I?"

"It's been dropped on them last minute, I guess. You get working on yourself."

AJ opened his top drawer and pulled out a bottle of Visine.

"Yes! Good thinking, get rid of those bloodshot eyes. Now, while you're getting fixed up, I'll start running you through some questions. I'll give you enough material to answer whatever they can throw at you, hopefully. Your father will be there, and I'm sure he'll draw their focus."

"My father! Ahhh, fuck!" He pounded the empty cup on the desk, then wiped at his mouth with his shirt sleeve. "Of course he has to be there. I'd be better off without him."

Charlie looked at him sternly. "Maybe some day, but not today."

AJ clenched his jaw and shot out of his chair, then paused and swayed in his spot as he looked at Charlie, acceptance crossing his face. "Okay, I've never done a press conference before, and I sure as fuck wouldn't've picked today to dip my feet."

They did what they could at the office; AJ pounded back the entire pot of coffee, and an equal amount of water. He looked decent, from a distance. Charlie hoped they'd gotten him respectable enough to answer a few quick questions from really far away.

Charlie insisted on driving and got no argument from AJ, who soon fell asleep again. His lifeless body flopped here and there with every bump in the road and he looked nauseous. Charlie found a hint of sympathy for the lad. He was just too young to have all of this forced on him. It was no wonder his relationship was troubled when he was showing up for work seven days a week. Charlie had no idea why. The boy didn't do anything five days a week, so why pay him to do another two?

He pulled up to the plant's main gate and found a mob of a couple hundred people had gathered around a spot in the parking lot. He gave AJ a shake, startling him back to the conscious world.

AJ blinked and yawned, then surveyed his surroundings. "So this is it?... Fuck me." He looked down and shook his head.

Charlie figured the kid probably saw it as another aspect of his life that he would fuck up. He reached over and gave him a playful slap on the shoulder. "Hey, you'll be fine. Piece of cake."

AJ looked dumbfounded out the window. "Yeah."

Charlie checked the time. "All right, big guy. Give your eyes another shot of that Visine." He grabbed the handle on his door and waited for AJ's signal.

AJ nodded.

"Showtime, buddy."

They met around the front of the vehicle. The spring day was spotted with large cumulous clouds and a slight breeze, creating a climate that could change from toques and mittens when a cloud consumed the sun, to shorts and T-shirts when the shadow passed. Charlie gave AJ a reassuring smile as he led him through the crowd, some chatting excitedly, some angrily. AJ followed close behind and kept his head down.

The focal point was a temporary stage composed of a semi-trailer folded down into a platform. Currently it was populated by Albert and some of the company's other higher-ups, and a herd of media was setting up down front. There were more news figures than Charlie had expected—too many for just local

204

media—so he did a scan of the parking area for labelled vehicles. He found news stations from all across Canada. He decided it best not to share the insight with AJ. When they made it to the steps at the back of the stage, Charlie poked his head up and signalled for Albert's attention.

The president came at once. He took hold of AJ's arm and yanked him behind the trailer for a private conversation. "Good, you made it, I was getting concerned." He looked down at his son, who stood quietly with his head hanging. Albert stepped in front of him and placed his hands on his shoulders.

With the two men standing across from each other, Charlie could see how unsuccessful he'd been at preparing AJ. Albert stood tall and proud, his suit was pressed, and his air confident. He emitted the authority of a high-ranking military leader. AJ looked like a drunken project manager, woken from a recent slumber.

"Son!" Albert said firmly.

AJ slowly raised his head to meet his father's eyes, his face burdened with regret.

"Jesus Christ, AJ!" Albert said in a hushed bark. He looked his son up and down, from his bloodshot eyes to his wrinkled attire. "How fucking drunk are you?"

Albert's next reaction surprised Charlie. His physique slumped and his eyes fell to the ground, his semblance transforming to shame.

"We, we did the best we could, with the time we had," Charlie explained. "I think, the more attention he can avoid, the better."

He watched the two men continue to stand in silence, the father's large, guiding hands resting on the shoulders of his lost son.

After a minute, Albert took a deep breath in and righted himself. He shook his boy gently and gathered his attention. He scrutinized AJ, turning his head to either side. "All right." He nodded. "Let's go get this done."

As Albert led AJ onto the stage, Charlie thought, *We're going to Disneyland.*

***

The audience began to chatter and cameras began to flash as Albert made his way to the wooden podium set front and centre on the stage. A couple sets of chairs flanked either side of the podium, and one woman and one man sat on each side of the centre. Both were dressed in proper business attire, and their expressions were a well-rehearsed neutral. Albert stopped directly behind the podium, then pointed at the man and thrust his finger at the seat beside the woman. The man made no argument. AJ quickly took the newly vacated spot, which positioned him in the best place to limit his interaction with everyone.

Albert looked over his troops, then nodded subtly and straightened his jacket. He turned and stepped up to the microphone. "Uh-hum!" blared from the speakers, followed by an extremely annoying, high-pitched screech. A technician appeared, made a quick adjustment, then gave the thumbs-up to continue.

"Testing, testing…" Albert spoke loudly at first and then lowered his volume based on the audience's reaction. "This conference has been called in response to the blatant attack on our organization by anti–oil sands parties, who are accusing us of working over and above the laws of the governing authority in regard to the 11-16 Project." His voice was commanding and controlling. "We're here to assure you that this accusation is unjust. We've been working hand in hand with these organizations and are proceeding and functioning well within our rights." He cleared his throat and adjusted his tie, then continued. "At the request of the media, I have produced myself and the lead project manager." He gestured toward AJ, who sat erect and alert.

Albert then turned toward the other members of the party and introduced them as Mr. Walters and Ms. Sanders, from the legal department. "They are here only to advise us on which questions we are legally qualified to answer, should such a question arise."

"Yeah, bullshit!" called out a faceless, angry female voice.

It excited a similar response from a male voice. "Fucking cowards!"

The audience coordinated a loud, murmuring stir.

Albert pushed his hands down through the air in calming dictation. "Please, people, there's no need for such comments. You'll see we're not here to do any harm to the environment, or the people.

"Before we get going, one word of the wise to the media representatives. You were all issued a general question guideline for this assembly. Please don't waste our time with questions you know we can't answer. Also, any questions that are considered out of line will be issued a verbal warning, and any continuation of such questions will result in the representative either voluntarily removing themselves, or being removed by security." He scanned the crowd for any possible trouble.

"Let's begin. I open the floor for questions." Albert motioned to the three microphones situated in front of the stage, and the media rushed to fill the open spaces.

"Mr. Doyle, Mr. Doyle!" called out a female reporter from the centre microphone.

"Yes, young lady"—Albert pointed to her—"please, go ahead."

The crowd simmered.

"Mr. Doyle, could you please give us some insight into the unconfirmed rumours that Northern Lights is, in fact, failing to cooperate with the governing officials, working outside the legal guidelines, and even withholding critical information."

Albert chuckled, then shook his head and raised his hands invitingly. "People... ladies and gentleman. The 11-16 Project is groundbreaking technology, on a global scale. There's nothing else like this being utilized or attempted on the rest of the planet!" His voice echoed through the anxious silence. "Currently the industry—not just us here at Northern Lights, but all the major players in the area employing SAGD technology—are forced to impregnate the steam with chemical diluents. They have to do this to increase process efficiency as well as profit. A percentage of the chemicals are reclaimed through the extraction process, but there's always a percentage of loss. That not only makes the method hazardous to the environment but also creates a loss to the company, and in turn, to its workers." He slapped his hand down on the podium for effect. "I looked at this system and I thought, *How is this acceptable? In what way does this even make sense? We are poisoning the environment!*"

The crowd gasped.

"We are knowingly poisoning the environment!"

The people looked shocked at what the president of the most powerful corporation in Canada was openly admitting. Cameras flashed madly.

"Oh yes! It's been going on for years! But you know who else is aware of it? Not only aware, but gave authorization to do so?... Your governing bodies!"

A shiver of surprise pulsed through the crowd.

"That's right!" He held up a finger. "Sure, they've done all their testing and have set what they feel to be acceptable levels. But it's still happening. The departments you're all here in support of are allowing this." His confidence frothed. He removed the microphone from its cradle, then stepped into the open and began to pace slowly, watching the audience, ensuring he had all of their attention.

PRICE PER BARREL

"Now, folks! This is where the 11-16 Project comes in. It's designed, specifically, to eliminate the current form of chemical-induced extraction. I myself have gathered together some of the finest minds—a think tank—with one main objective! To increase our production without the use of dangerous chemicals. The solution we arrived at is the one you now stand here to protest! The 11-16 Project is the future, a system to better the way we do business."

From the crowd came a couple of cries of new supporters. "Yeah, that's right!"

"The 11-16 Project is designed to inject compressed air into the area between the bedrock and the oil-rich reserves we're mining. It'll create a slight pressure field that presses down on the oil. At the same time, it replaces the gases extracted through our existing process. The air that's recovered is released back into atmosphere, at the first stage of secondary refinement. That, people," he bellowed, while shaking his fist to the masses, "*that* is progress! The 11-16 Project will increase profit for the company, but most importantly, it'll create a safer, healthier environment for not only our workers but also for the people of the community, and the generations to come!"

The young female reporter pleaded for his attention. "Mr. Doyle… Mr. Doyle!"

Albert acknowledged her.

"Mr. Doyle, please get to the part about your organization's cooperation."

"Yes, of course." He cleared his throat. "There's been a clear misunderstanding about how we're working with the legal bodies. The facts are really quite easy to understand. As the 11-16 Project is the first of its kind, how can there exist a standard set of guidelines?"

The majority of the crowd murmured and nodded.

"Okay… So, then, how does one develop a set of guidelines? They could build their own?" He shrugged. "They could design it, build a scale model, apply it and monitor it for, what, five… ten years?… People, we need this technology now!" He raised a hand to the air. "Why not invite the departments in to work with us hand in hand? We'll build it with them! We'll apply it! We'll monitor it! With them!" He nodded. "We have the funding, we have the property! We agree that KNOWING! Is a responsibility! Are we working with the governing bodies? Yes, hand in hand! Are we working within the guidelines of the governing bodies? How can we? They don't exist. But we are working to build them, together!"

A small wave of applause slowly grew. Albert stopped pacing and held a hand up in modest acceptance, then walked over to the podium and placed the microphone back in the stand.

He looked over his shoulder to check up on AJ. The boy was slumped in his seat and his head was down. A warm wave of nervous heat surged through Albert's body. He turned back to the audience, conscious of his poise, and adjusted his tie to cover an uneasy swallow.

The crowd silenced.

"Mr. Doyle, sir."

Albert looked over at a young reporter who looked a bit out of place. On his face hung a long, dense red beard. He had multiple piercings in one ear, a thick hoop through his bottom lip, and a matching piece hanging from his right nostril. A shaggy curtain of red curls protruded from the entire perimeter of his knitted toque. The bulbous form of the hat suggested the vagrant had a whole hippie-mop stuffed under it. The media logo on his jacket belonged to a small radio station in northern British Columbia. His expression reeked of disobedience.

"Mr. Doyle, if you please, sir, I have a question for the project manager."

"Yes, well," Albert stalled, motioning to AJ, " unfortunately he's feeling a little under the weather. We'd just as soon—"

"No disrespect, sir, but the media—the people—requested the project manager be at the conference. It's really just one quick question, sir… really," the reporter insisted.

Albert kept his hands fastened to the corners of the podium. He held his expression neutral and focused. Though he felt he'd gotten the audience to second-guess their witch hunt, this kid didn't seem to be buying in. Tree-hugging reporters were the most likely reporters to start verbal attacks. But to deny the request would certainly be interpreted as guilt.

Albert smiled. "Yes. Yes, of course."

He turned and looked into his son's nervous eyes, set in his pale, sweat-drenched face, as he slowly approached his seat. He raised an offering hand to his boy, and drew a path to the stand.

***

AJ sat up, wiped his forehead, and then brushed his hands dry on his pants. His head spun, his stomach churned, and his mouth was dry with a sickly paste. With laboured breath, he pushed up from his chair, but his legs wobbled and he stumbled a step. He looked out at the crowd and righted himself, then adjusted his tie. He managed his composure as he walked to the podium. In his peripheral vision, he saw two large video cameras follow him across the floor, and the hoods projecting out were like menacing black holes with the entire viewing audience stuffed inside. He watched the people watching him. The reality of where he was, what he had become, and how completely useless he felt hit him hard.

He stepped up to the podium with the weight of his world on his shoulders. He nauseously surveyed the crowd and leaned into the microphone.

"Hi… Uh-hum… Hello."

The audience watched, motionless.

The hippie reporter gave a brief but mocking laugh.

The onslaught of public attention excited AJ's symptoms, sending a tease of bile into his mouth.

"Yes," the reporter said, and smiled arrogantly. "Mister… well, it's funny, I don't think we've actually heard your name. I've just heard you referred to as the project manager."

AJ stood quietly, his hazy mind attempting to decipher whether he'd been asked a question.

The reporter grew impatient. "If I may, Mr. Project Manager, it's *AJ*, correct?"

AJ nodded like a seasick passenger hanging over the side of a boat.

"The *AJ* being short for Albert Junior, correct?"

AJ nodded again, a wide rim of sweat dampening his collar.

"Your full name being Albert *Doyle* Jr., correct?" He grinned, then struck with bared claws. "Mr. Doyle Jr., how do you respond to the allegations that you were not hired to this position based on your knowledge and capability, and that this new technology project—with potential to cause serious harm to the environment and the people—is your first job of any kind… ever? That you were assigned the position based solely on the fact that you are the son of the company president?"

"…Huh?" AJ dizzied and gurgled.

An upset roar engulfed the spectators, and they quickly switched back to the hats they'd arrived in.

AJ's pulse suddenly halved in strength and doubled in pace. He felt his knees buckle, and the world went black.

***

Albert watched in horror as his son weebled, wobbled, and fell, smashing chin first on the corner of the podium, then continuing lifeless to the floor. The impact sent a burst of vomit reeking of forty proof across the stage.

Albert leapt to his feet and rushed to AJ's side. Luckily, because of the crowd, it was mandatory to have emergency medical on standby. The two EMTs rushed from their ambulance to assist.

Albert pointed at the piece-of-shit reporter, shouting orders for security to have the nuisance removed. He turned back just as the medics were lifting AJ up on the stretcher, and he followed them to the ambulance.

After loading AJ in the back, the medics turned to find a very aggravated Albert staring demonically upon them.

"You two," he snorted. "You know who I am?" He took turns staring them both down.

The paramedics nodded.

"He"—Albert pointed to the ambulance—"is sick with the flu, or you two will never work in this town, or in this industry, ever again!"

They nodded obediently, then rushed to the cab.

Albert faced the crowd. The people were in a frenzy, booing and screaming accusations.

46

Emma was sitting across from Albert's desk with a full glass of Scotch when he stormed into his office shortly after the interview disaster.

He slammed the door, huffing and snorting as he headed straight to the bar, poured a shot, and tossed it back. "Ahhh." He rested his weight against the bar.

Emma looked on, waiting for his outburst, but he simply poured another, then stood entranced by a distant spot on the floor as he swirled his glass.

"Albert... dear," she said cautiously, "the stories going around are awful. How bad was it?"

He took a seat at his desk, his mood now appearing to be one of confident certainty. "It's over! This stupid fucking game we're playing with AJ is over, I'm cutting him loose. He'll be cut back to regular working hours. He'll still have lots of time to learn about the business, and he'll have a chance to live a normal life—hopefully save his engagement."

Emma leaned forward and slid her glass back and forth on the desk. It was exactly what she was afraid of—him losing his nerve and letting her grandson continue on an even more destructive path. She needed to design her offense. "I know, son, but—"

"No!" Albert shouted, slamming his glass on the desktop. He stared at her with fury. "You don't know! He's beat! There's nothing left of him! He's killing himself! Killing his reputation, and his future!... And it's killing me to watch it and know I'm playing a role in it!"

He was throwing the big bombs at her, but it wasn't the first time she'd had to turn his wrath back upon him.

She matched his fury. "How dare you look me in the eye and tell me I don't know! I brought you all the way out here and raised you to what you are today! Me! By myself! You forget that once you were him. Twenty years old, with your brains in your pants! You don't think I spent sleepless nights worrying? Trying to figure out where I'd gone wrong! What I'd done to deserve your shit!"

Albert's stone-cold façade melted and his head dropped.

Emma caught his retreat; guilt was a powerful tool for those selfish enough to use it. She softened, but only slightly. "So yes, I know how hard it is, Albert. How straining it is to look into the eyes of your child when they're set on a personal path of destruction. What you need to realize is how bad he is now, with just the *thought* of losing her. How bad do you think he would be if he lost his whole family? Then what would he be? Lucky to be alive, that's what!" she shouted, making him look up. "That marriage is doomed. If not now, then five, ten years from now, when he's much more deeply invested!" She looked deep into him with caring and concern. "The Band-Aid is half off, why try to put it back on? It'll never stick; not nearly as well as at the start, which wasn't worth shit anyway. I know, Albert, I know… Trust in me, I have never led you wrong. If you don't see this through now, you'll regret it later."

She saw the submission in his eyes and reached over the desk and cradled his hands lovingly in hers. "You don't want to let him down… so don't." She kissed him tenderly on the forehead. "I love you, son, and I'm standing beside you on this. He has to break before he can heal." She caressed her fingers across the top of his head and smiled sweetly, then turned and headed out the door.

As the latch clicked, she heard something thump against the wall and the sound of glass shattering, followed by the muffled sobs of her son.

47

May had bloomed in Fort McMurray and the snow had all but disappeared. The sun rose early and remained until late in the evening. The scent of new beginnings was in the air.

But for Ollie Hynes and Mary-Ann Kibbnok, the dreams and aspirations that gave them purpose and fuelled their passion were being stripped from their grasp.

A heavy wedge of uncertainty had been slowly sinking between them over the months. Mary-Ann was not easily deterred; she believed that there was no force on earth stronger than love and that the man she loved still existed, somewhere deep down. Life had presented him with a challenge, his health had faltered.

Her love and energy used to revive him, but this plague had proven equally powerful. He no longer rested soundly in her embrace, and his appetite for her was fading. He was pale, skinny beyond reason, and heavy bags hung beneath his hollow eyes. What he did with all his time in the bathroom remained a mystery. She'd expressed curiosity, but he wouldn't talk with her about it, saying he just needed to relax. Then he'd roll away from her and pretend to sleep.

Mary-Ann would not quit him though. She could see he was right there, and he was beaten. Could see the pain and suffering of a man who'd fought a hundred battles. Could feel the weight of his burden. She understood she couldn't help anyone who didn't ask for it. It just hurt so bad to watch the infection fester and not be able to help him. All she could do was stand, watch, and pray that someday—before it was too late—he would let her in. She held tight to the memory of him, the man she fell in love with. He was still the same man, and she was a strong woman. They had declared their love for each other, and to her, that meant forever. He was worth waiting for, no matter how bad it got. She would be there, like she promised.

Until he let her in, all she could do was stand beside him, for as long as it took.

***

That Saturday morning, the sky was clear and the boreal was lush and green. The fragrant breeze coming through the window beckoned Ollie to celebrate the day. He decided they should go for a walk through the forest. Sitting stagnant could induce insanity.

He showered quickly, then threw on some simple sweats, a T-shirt, and his grubby old ball cap to shadow his eyes. He knew his smile was forced—it was the smile he wore now—but he couldn't admit to himself that he was losing his battle with the night. His opponent was one of great cunning and power: a massive, constricting serpent invisible to the naked eye. It was nocturnal, just like Ollie. It had glided silkily up and around him like a welcoming embrace. Then, ever so patiently, with every breath and move he made, it tightened a little more, until it was clenching him and he couldn't rid himself of it.

It was nothing, he told himself; it was just because of the night shift. Once he converted back to daylight hours, everything would be good. He was just doing what he had to, to get to where he wanted to be.

He waited for Mary-Ann to slip on her shoes. She didn't smile much anymore. It wasn't until he watched her force one that he became aware of it.

He put his head down and led her quickly down the hall. He had no interest in people. Out the front door and into the morning sun, he continued down the sidewalk and followed a path into the forest. When he was sheltered by the trees, he finally stopped, and realized Mary-Ann was a ways back, hustling in her inappropriate footwear.

He smiled as she approached. "Sorry about that." He took her hand and kissed it sweetly.

They strolled along hand in hand, wordless. The rays of bright morning sun filtering through the canopy were warm, but the silence was cold, and the beautiful spring morning became awkward.

PRICE PER BARREL

Ollie's issue had grown over the months. No longer able to be without, he'd asked Honey to teach him how to construct a simple pipe using fittings from the shop. Then Honey supplied him with enough to get him through the trying days. Health and sleep were now nothing more than a myth. He hardly ate, not even Mary-Ann's cooking. There was only one sustenance now. One greedy little thing that wanted him all to itself, eliminating everything light from his life so they could be together, forever.

Things had changed between him and Mary-Ann, he admitted. The thrill of newfound love had passed, or maybe it had been buried somewhere. Even on their walk, Ollie found it hard to concentrate on her. The tools of destruction were burning a hole in his pocket, making him constantly analyze the surroundings for a place to duck behind. *"It has to be safe,"* the voice whispered. *"She cannot find out."* The bond was strong. With no options for a quick session, Ollie's infection told him it was time to retreat to the safety of the bathroom, where he could lock the door. It was not safe in the light.

He stopped and looked at Mary-Ann, his face glazed in perspiration. "It's really hot out today. I should've worn shorts. Let's head back."

He turned, but she didn't follow. She held her ground and looked up into his evading eyes. "Ollie, we've been waiting to enjoy a day outside together."

He dropped his head.

"Please… Something is wrong, please tell me… please."

"No." He dragged the toe of his sneaker through the dirt, tracing a curved line between them. He snorted a light, dismissive laugh. "There's nothing, it's fine, it's just hotter than I expected, and I'm really tired."

"You promised me a walk when the weather got nice. We haven't been outside camp together since I can remember. We came all the way out here, and now you're telling me you want to go back?"

The voice in his head spoke. *"Oh, come on! Really? Do we have to do this now? What's the big fucking deal with her? All this drama. All I want to do is go back, I worked all fucking night."*

"Ollie?" Her stare probed deep, searching for some understanding.

He dropped her hand and stepped away. "It's nothing!" He rubbed the top of his hat nervously and began to pace. "I just… I mean, I work all night! That's all!… Everything's fine, as fine as can be with me working this shift."

She clasped her hands in front of her and watched tentatively. He could see

216

that tears were beginning to build, and she sniffled.

"Mary-Ann…? I'm sorry, but this is the way it is right now. We both agreed. We both understood this wasn't going to be easy." His tone accused her of being absolutely ridiculous.

"Do you… do you still want that?" she whimpered.

"What? Of course I still want that! I'm doing it, I'm just doing my part…" His voice trailed off and he stopped pacing and turned away from her as he removed his cap and began fussing with the brim. He huffed and placed the cap back on his head, then turned and walked directly to her, hat pulled low.

He grabbed each of her hands, then raised them caringly between their chests as he looked at her tear-streaked face—but only for a second, scared she would see something behind his eyes, something holding him from her.

They walked back, silently, hand in hand. The dark force captivating Ollie's mind weakened a little. Just enough to let him feel the warmth of her touch, her hand in his, melting the frost.

Back at the room, he guided his love gently through the door and closed it behind them. He looked toward the bathroom. The suffocating grip squeezed, his legs fell limp as noodles, and exhaustion hit heavy like a brick to his chest. His grip on Mary-Ann's hand tightened. The man he was pulled her to him; he stared into her eyes without falter.

He leaned in and kissed her lips with a spark that had extinguished long ago. She sobbed and wrapped her arms around him, holding him close.

Warm and nourishing, he felt her energy and he remembered. His eyes began to bleed with clarity, and he could suddenly see where he was and how he had been treating her.

"Why?"

A familiar voice had returned, one of good and reason.

"Get a grip on yourself! Hold on to her!"

He did just that. Squeezing her tightly, he looked down at her. "Can, can we just go to bed?"

She nodded and lifted up on her toes for another kiss.

They changed and crawled into bed, embracing each other the way they used to, hearts beating in unison once again.

Ollie fell asleep, just like he used to, and woke late in the afternoon. He looked at the clock, and leaped out of bed to get ready for work.

PRICE PER BARREL

He was standing on one foot, hunched over to pull on a sock, when Mary-Ann grabbed him by the arm and pulled, toppling him over and onto the bed. She rolled herself on top of him and held his gaze.

"Stay!" she whispered.

"What?" He looked back, confused.

She rolled her weight more fully onto him. "Stay, Ollie!" She remained so focused on him that it prevented him from blinking. "Stay, just tonight... Please, Ollie!"

"Mary-Ann!" He lay stunned below her, awed by her will. "I, I can't just—how?"

"Call in sick! They won't care, you're one of the best employees they've got. It'll be fine."

He paused. He'd never seen her so serious. She was deeply spooked. He knew that to turn away would be a big deal. *She knows. Maybe not what, but she knows something.*

The slithering voice hissed in his ear. *"This is silly, Ollie, she's being ridiculous. She'll be here in the morning. Time to go to work, do your part... reach for your dreams."*

Mary-Ann shook him, bringing his attention back to her. "Ollie! This has to happen! Do this, please! Don't go! Not tonight!" A drop of urgency fell from her eye and landed on his cheek.

As tight as the snake had wound, she was holding tighter. A very clear and powerful voice took authority in his mind, a voice from the light. It spoke clear and loud. *"Ollie! Turning this down would be a big deal!"*

He broke, finally. Relaxing in her grasp, he surrendered.

"All right." He nodded. "I'll call in."

MARC GREGORY

48

Ollie woke the next morning feeling more alive than he'd felt in as long as he could remember.

When he called in sick, Honey was surprisingly pleasant about it, which was a big relief to Ollie, who'd never called in sick for anything before.

The two lovers had found each other again. After the call, they hurried downstairs and grabbed some snacks, then sat side by side on the bed, sharing stories of their past and stuffing their faces. With rest and food, laughter and love, life returned to Ollie with every minute away from the dark.

He'd intended to make love to Mary-Ann that night, but the furthest either of them got before passing out was naked in each other's arms. He woke the next day to the light of an early-morning sun and the sound of birds chirping through the open window. The air was cool and crisp to the point where the very tip of his nose was ice to the touch.

But under the covers he had the warmth of her beside him. The smell of her warmed his soul. He touched his nose lightly to her shoulder.

"Brrrr," she purred, snuggling herself into his arms.

He smiled and leaned in with a kiss to warm the point he'd just chilled.

"Mmm, I like that better," she purred again.

He took a breath, then leaned back and relaxed. He felt in control again, aware of the fact that he'd completely lost it. He didn't want to think about it, so he returned to her warmth. He lay silent, breathing her in and looking around their humble nest. His mind focused on the bathroom door and the horror of what he'd been doing to himself, and to the woman he loved. He'd been dancing with a devil, and the devil was leading. Regret flooded him, and he quickly turned his eyes to the ceiling. *What the fuck happened to you, Ollie? Look at everything you have! You're such an idiot!* He struggled to fight back tears. *You fucked up, boy! You fucked up bad! No more! Now you fly straight! You do right by that girl 'cause your sorry ass'll never find another like her!* It would be just as easy as that, he decided: never again. He had survived, and the only one he could thank for that was the beautiful angel sleeping beside him. Satisfied, he nodded to himself, then turned back to encase her in his love and appreciation.

"Mmm, there's my man." She reached back and rubbed her hand along the length of his thigh.

He kissed her shoulder. "I think today will be a better day for a walk."

"That sounds perfect." She lifted his hand to her lips and suckled it with tender kisses. "Let's wait till the morning rush dies down. I'm still tired and really comfortable." She pulled his arms tighter around her.

They lay there until a sunbeam stretched across the room.

They cleaned up and headed down for a quiet breakfast. Like when they first met, their bodies always had to be connected in some manner, whether it be clasped hands, playful feet, tender lips, or loving arms. The light was truly returning.

After they'd eaten they headed out to the forest again. That morning was a welcome mirror image of the day before, the perfect do-over. They held each other, joked, and played. Their love was on fire again, spring was in the air, and it seemed there was nothing they couldn't take on.

They settled into a stroll as they got deeper into the woods.

"Today's really nice, Ollie. Thank you." Mary-Ann stretched up and kissed him. "I feel really guilty making you call in sick last night because I know you hate that, but… I just thought we really needed—"

Ollie stopped and turned her to face him. "Don't apologize," he said sternly. "I did need this, very much—we needed it. I didn't understand how bad things had gotten. I needed to be with you." He sighed as his eyes moved across the forestscape. "It's just, it's really hard to not… get lost."

"I know." She hugged him. "I'm here for you, Ollie. Please let me be here for you. I really want to."

220

"I know, I can't even begin to tell you how much I love you, and I'm the one who should be thanking you."

They stood in silence, holding on to each other and listening to the budding spring.

"It's so nice today." She smiled, her ear against the beat of his heart.

"I know. I wish it could always be like this." There was a hint of despair in his voice.

She looked up. "What?"

He sighed. "I don't want to go back to work tonight. I can't believe it's just a few hours away. I'm starting to really like being sick," he joked.

She smiled weakly and fidgeted. "Well... maybe you shouldn't..."

"Huh? Shouldn't what?"

"Maybe you shouldn't go back? Maybe you should look for something else. If this job is too hard on you, it's not worth it. We're working toward something, and if this job is causing you to lose focus, then it's no good? We've saved some money; enough so we could live for probably at least a year back East. Maybe we should think about leaving now? Get back to your grandmother while she's still around. We could find jobs. Nothing that'd pay like this, but it's a lot cheaper to live there, and if we're happy, what does the money really matter?"

She was right. For him to continue down this path really didn't make sense beyond the money.

As he considered, a strong force pulled out from the darkness, sending a shiver down his spine. The voice in his head changed. *"Leave? Why would you? Stay, save some more money, why the big rush? You two have a plan. A real man would see that plan through."* It was so strong and so clever. As much as he wanted to turn to her then and confess everything, beg for her help and forgiveness, he convinced himself things were fine the way they were. Maybe it had gone a little too far, but he'd taken a break, and he saw it now and had control. There was no reason he couldn't have it all: the girl, the money, and... the darkness. Just a little while longer and their plan would be complete and they would be gone. No problem. They were overreacting. "I, I guess that could be something to think about."

Mary-Ann smiled. "Our dreams won't happen if we're not there together. No matter how much money we have."

"Yeah, that makes sense. I just... well, it'll be a lot harder of a time if we don't follow through with the original plan. We'd be a lot farther ahead if we could afford a house. I'd hate to go home and fail."

"If we're together, and happy, how is that failing?"

Ollie nodded at the ground. "I suppose it's something to think about. I can't just quit, though, not right now. If we do decide we want to leave, we'll have to put a plan together."

Mary-Ann bounced ecstatically. "Yes!" She kissed him. "Let's think about it! I'll start to look at the costs and put a plan together."

He smiled and brushed a lock of hair behind her ear. She was his angel. "Okay, my sweet, you get going on that."

They spent the remainder of the morning enjoying spring. They returned to the camp for lunch, and then to the room for a nap before they'd be forced to part ways.

They woke late in the afternoon, naked in bed. The sunlight shone fully through the window. The sounds of spring were now muffled by the sounds of trucks and people.

They rolled to face each other. Mary-Ann smiled sweetly and ran her fingers through Ollie's hair. "How you feeling?"

"Good." He smiled. "Really good. Just about time to head back though."

"You'll be all right," she consoled. "My strong, handsome man." She leaned over and kissed him lightly. "You got your health back, and your head on your shoulders."

"Yeah…" He smiled, but there was little hope behind it. The closer the minutes ticked to sunset, the stronger the pull became—so strong that he had no intention of resisting. He wanted it as much as it wanted him. He knew the only way out was to leave. But someone would have to drag him kicking and screaming.

Mary-Ann tickled her fingers along his chest and down his stomach to his groin. She bit teasingly on her lip as he instantly grew in her hand.

Ollie grinned. "What's this?"

She pushed him onto his back and climbed on top. She pressed her body close to his, then slid down and swallowed him between her legs, throbbing inside her. "Something to bring you focus." She leaned down and kissed him.

***

As Mary-Ann pulled up to the gate and looked across to the waiting truck, she saw Honey in the captain's seat, and her blood began to boil. She could swear his eyes narrowed whenever he looked at her. She turned back to her Ollie and pulled him aggressively to her, smothering him with kisses.

He chuckled. "All right, all right, I know, I don't want to go either. Go do your research and figure out how to get us the hell out of here, you crazy woman." He winked.

"Crazy about you!" She threw herself back onto him.

"I'm crazy about you, sexy."

"Be strong, Ollie. Don't forget what you want in life. What you really want."

He nodded, avoiding her studious gaze. "I will… I promise." He kissed her one last time before getting out of the truck, then blew her a final goodbye kiss through the window.

***

Ollie breathed in deeply, slung his backpack over his shoulder, and trudged across the dusty parking lot. Trapped between two dimensions, he couldn't bring himself to look forward or back.

The sun was still high in the sky. Daylight was in abundance now, so maybe, just maybe, if he could just harness enough of the light, he could fight against the darkness.

He opened the door and crawled into his seat.

Honey greeted him with a nod. "Good morning, youngster." He gestured toward Mary-Ann's truck. "Sick, eh?" He winked.

"Y-yeah." Ollie felt his cheeks turn hot as he rubbed his stomach. "Stomach flu, or maybe something I ate."

Honey reached over and slapped him on the shoulder. "Stomach flu! Don't blame you, kid. If I had me a fine piece like that waitin' at home, I'd be mighty sick myself." He chuckled. "No harm done. Last night was pretty quiet. We've been givin 'er pretty good. Sometimes a guy just needs a night to get his rocks off proper. I got your back, brother, don't sweat it!" He shifted the truck into gear.

Ollie's heart settled. He smiled and listened to Honey banter on about his experimentations with love. Or prostitution. Honey really wasn't such a bad guy.

He felt good and strong. He smiled at the bright world. A couple months ago, it was pitch-black at that same time of day. He'd just have to make sure to be extra busy through the night hours to keep his mind off it.

The serpent cradled him, gently rocking him into a false sense of security.

"Silly boy… night will always come."

49

AJ arrived to an empty home that evening. It'd become common for Vicky to be absent upon his return, and she sometimes wouldn't show until late in the evening. She never hid the fact that she was spending time with Justin, insisting they were just friends, that she was capable of having a strictly platonic relationship with men and had many back in Calgary. He knew all those guys, though, and he knew she was a heavy flirt and loved attention. But this felt different.

It was crunch time at 11-16. The push of the green button was officially scheduled for the next Monday. After his media disaster, he'd vowed to never drink again. The fact that his president father had taken it upon himself to cover it up didn't help. It helped the project, it helped the company, but all it did for AJ was show him that he didn't have to worry about anything he did. He could murder someone on site, in cold blood, and good old Daddy would make it all go away. But there were things off site that his all-powerful family had no control over.

He threw his jacket on the dining room table, loosened his tie, and pulled a beer from the fridge. Then he flopped on the couch.

Where is she? Selfish bitch! His mind reeled with scenes of her in various compromising situations, as if his head needed something else to be concerned over.

I work my ass off every day. He cringed. *All of this! Me, my family, we give her everything—more than she fucking deserves!*

224

His mood festered. He stood and walked over to the panoramic view of the city. Twilight was settling, streetlights and headlights came aglow, and tribes of people moved about—families and professionals heading for dinner, transients heading to the casino. She was somewhere among them. He rubbed his face and exhaled.

One more week till start-up, he reminded himself. Then what? Could they patch it up?

One of them would have to beg on hands and knees. Maybe it was time to quit? He fell back onto the couch. He grabbed his phone from the end table, hoping she'd attempted contact him, or at least replied. It was all just a big fucking game to her. Keep him waiting where she liked him: under her thumb. He took another swig of his beer and laid his head back.

Tick-tock, tick-tock. A clock counted in perfect rhythm. He'd never noticed the sound before; he opened his eyes. There it was, on the wall in the hallway, leading to the bedroom. Dark wood framed a traditional face with Roman numerals and heavy forged-steel hands ending in bulking arrows. It was a nice piece, subtle enough to be buried by the simple sound of mindful thought. But when all went silent, it was there to remind one that life was ticking.

Tick-tock. The sound grew abrasive. *Tick*—another second of his existence spent waiting—*tock*.

What a fucking waste! I should be out having the time of my life! I'm young and attractive, and successful! Why the fuck am I even bothering with her shit?

He downed the remainder of his bottle, grabbed another from the fridge, then returned to his spot and chugged down half the fresh bottle. He laid his head back and closed his eyes…

The door shut with a thud. AJ stirred from his inebriated slumber, taking a second to gather his mind and his position on the couch with a warm bottle of beer resting between his legs.

He turned to the door, where a tipsy Vicky stood on one leg, leaning against the wall to remove her high heels. She was one of those women who looked beautiful in sweat pants and a ball cap, but she was stunning in this white miniskirt and matching silk blouse that revealed a black lace bra beneath. As she spun around, the string of her black lace thong protruded from the top of her skirt.

AJ rubbed his throbbing headache.

"Oh!" Vicky stumbled, then braced herself. She looked into the dark room.

225

"You're home! You're awake!" She giggled.

AJ lurched off the couch and tipped back the remainder of his bottle, then walked to the kitchen and grabbed another.

Over the hissing pop of a freshly cracked bottle and the thud of the closing refrigerator door, he asked, "So, where were you?"

Her glance said, *What the fuck business is it of yours?* "Out," she replied snottily.

"Out?" He shot back a smug grin. "Out where? With who?"

"At a club... with Justin."

"Ah, good old Justin, the golden boy of Fort McMurray real estate." He took a swig from his bottle and leaned against the wall.

She straightened and walked toward him, looking him dead in the eyes. "Yeah, with the golden boy." She stuck her tongue out, knocking him with her shoulder as she passed into the kitchen. She opened the fridge for a bottle of water, then tipped back a healthy swallow. She leaned against the counter and looked back over to him as if she was waiting for any more prying questions.

His manner turned submissive at her lack of guilt, and he looked at the floor. She could go from red-hot love to an ice-cold kick to the nuts in the flip of a switch. How does one reason with someone so volatile?

He mustered some courage. "What'd you do?"

"We went out, I told you that. We had fun!... Is that all right with you?" She took another drink and waited.

"Well, what? What did you do?"

She released a heated snort. "Really, you wanna do this? We went out to a club, like normal fucking people do!" She pushed herself off the counter and started toward him, burning his meek stare with her raging fire. "You know what, AJ, if you really gave a shit, you'd fucking be here!" She brushed angrily by again. "I'm done, I'm going to bed." She disappeared down the blackened hallway.

He took another sip and headed back over to the window to look down at the now-muted community. There was a time when he could match her. There was a time when his only care and his only focus was her. A time when time wasn't a factor, a time when he could grab that bull by the horns... a lifetime away. Where had it gone? That world of comfort and confidence, a world where he was the alpha. Out of shape and guided by rules and boundaries, substances were no longer abused to enhance his mind—only to numb the pain.

MARC GREGORY

He turned from the window to the desolate darkness of the room and leaned against the glass. A slow tear rolled down his cheek. With everything he had, and all the power handed to him, he'd never felt so without.

Tick

In an instant of pure hate, AJ hurled his glass across the room to explode head-on with the clock. A heavy frost of shimmering shards sprinkled down. The frame of the clock fell with a solid thud.

Unable to control the flood of emotion, AJ slid down the window to the floor.

The frightened boy wept in the hollow silence.

50

Since the start of the 11-16 Project, leaves and snow had fallen and melting winter had given birth to new forest life. And as if following the law of nature, the new project had reached its final, most crucial hurdle: the start-up.

Charlie plopped down in his office chair. He'd just finished up the critical pre–start-up meeting with his crew before sending them home to rest up for the big event in the morning. He exhaled a long breath; it had been a long go. One of many in his life, and hopefully the last. He was pretty sure he'd told himself that once before... or twice.

He ran his hands through his hair, then cupped them behind his head as he leaned back and stretched. He turned to the window. The clock read 6:08 p.m., but the outside light said noon. Closing in on the summer solstice in the far north, one found how little clocks and buzzers had to do with time.

Wake up on time, be at work on time, get to the meeting on time, only so much time for lunch. Then we forget to check the time, on time, so we need audible rings and chimes to remind us that it's time to check the time.

Knock, knock

Charlie startled from his trance, righted himself, and turned back to his desk. He grabbed a stack of papers and began to shuffle and straighten them.

"Yes, it's open," he grunted.

The door swung in.

"AJ?"

Charlie studied the young man. He looked sober, and he wasn't all dressed up like usual. Though his eyes weren't floating in alcohol, he did look tired and maybe a bit humbled.

Charlie pointed casually toward a spare chair across from his desk. "Come on in, have a seat."

AJ accepted. Leaning forward, he rested his elbows on his legs, bowed his head, and kept his focus on the floor as he rubbed his palms together slowly. Then he clapped softly and looked up. "So, big day tomorrow, eh?"

Charlie smiled. "Yes, finally, the big day." There was an awkward pause, then he continued. "We've completed all our checks. Everything should run... as well as it was designed to." He smiled. "But I've done a few of these, and usually things take a day or two to get running up to snuff. Could be longer for this."

"I guess we'll see."

"I guess we will." He could tell AJ had something on his mind, he just wasn't sure he wanted to get involved.

"Listen, Charlie." He looked up. "I just want to say— well, I know I haven't done... anything, really, to help. I know it's a little late. But I'd like to help this thing start up in any way I can. In any way you need, Charlie." He walked to the window. "I'm sorry. I'm truly, very sorry. I'm just young and spoiled and... and arrogant and just, just fucking stupid. I want to say I'm sorry."

Charlie remained silent.

"No more booze," AJ continued. "You have my word, for whatever it's worth." Placing a hand on either side of the window, he leaned forward and bowed his head and sighed.

Charlie sensed an emotional damn was about to burst. He was finding new respect for AJ, but he felt this was something he should share with someone else. Someone who truly needed to hear it. "I'm glad to hear you're turning your shit around, really."

AJ turned to face him, clearly holding back emotion.

"Listen, son, all us men were boys at one time. I admit I never had handed to me what you have, but if I did, I can't say as I would handle it any better." He grinned. "Unfortunately, there's nothing straight forward about the stairs of life. And there's a lot of them, a lifetime's worth. You can't expect not to stumble down a couple, from time to time—where'd be the fun in that?"

Charlie stood and looked AJ in the eyes. He reached out his hand. "I'm glad to see you're back on board. We're glad to have you."

AJ stepped across the room and accepted Charlie's hand.

51

A dense chill filled the air as the first rays of the morning sun crested the horizon.

The chieftain sat cross-legged in silence on his grassy plateau. Draped in an animal hide blanket, he meditated before a smouldering pit of glowing embers.

On his next inhale, a soft chant whispered ever so slightly on his breath. On the next, it grew stronger, until it existed as a low thrum in the forest, like a ghost on the breeze or a whisper of fog through the trees.

Daylight sliced through the blackness, a deep-blue cusp silhouetting the forest. This morning, though, it didn't appear as a peaceful landscape, but rather as a serrated edge.

At first witness, the chieftain leaned back with an audible gasp. His rocking picked up pace and the chant developed strength.

He would stay sound, listen and follow.

Change was coming.

52

The northern sun was already high when AJ stepped in the door at 7:00 a.m. Tucked under his arm was a tightly rolled sleeping bag and pillow. His smile carried an air of modesty.

The entire 11-16 crew were assembled in the lunch area for the morning meeting, and their random chattering silenced the moment AJ walked in. Not out of respect, but out of sheer shock—he was dressed to work, and sober enough to do so.

Big Harvey Hancock was the first to break the silence with his heavy accent. "Well, I's wasn't told it was gonna be a sleepover."

"Is 'cause you wasn't invited, ya big goof!" Kirby responded.

Harvey looked over to Charlie, who leaned against the doorway to his office. "Why wouldn't ya's invite me? I love a good ol' slumber party. I can fry up a mean slab of bologna, I can."

"You can eat it, too, ya can!" Kirby shot back.

"It's 'cause of me weight, isn't it? You all think I'm fat," he sobbed.

"They *think* you's fat? Who's thinkin'? We're all looking right at ya, and you're fat! No way of getting around it—or you!"

"You shut your mouth, Kirby, or you's gonna be my next meal, ya little shit!" Harvey lunged, causing Kirby to totter in his chair.

Charlie had a chuckle and shook his head. He cut into the conversation to start the meeting.

MARC GREGORY

"First off, I'd like to say thank you to everyone here and all who helped us turn this concept into a reality. We've finished on schedule and, surprisingly, within budget. I'd like to remind all of you of the importance of this project. This is the first of its kind, ever, in the world. There are many eyes watching. We didn't engineer this; our job was to make the equipment function in the manner the powers-that-be intended, and we've completed construction to the best of our ability with the resources supplied to us. Whether or not it works as well in reality as it does on paper is not our concern."

Every person in the room was silent. Every gaze followed Charlie as he paced confidently. Public speaking was not a natural gift but something that had grown over forty years on the job.

"It's been a hard go. There's been nothing straightforward with this assignment; there were no templates to follow, we were the pioneers. And we managed to get here with zero injuries to the people, and no catastrophic failures of equipment. I've been on many projects in my time, and I can say, very confidently, that this achievement is one we should all be very proud of. I am, and I want to say to you all, I've never worked with a finer crew."

Thunderous clapping filled the trailer.

"So, we've finally reached the end, and today's the day we push the button. I'd also like to remind everyone here to please watch your p's and q's because we've allowed one member of the press to be present for kickoff. He should be along any minute, and shouldn't be hard to distinguish from the rest of us."

Charlie cleared his throat. "We've completed the successful run up of the plant in bypass mode. Everything worked as it should, with little to no issue. Today, all we need to do is swing the valve to direct the pressure down the hole and then wait for the numbers to return. The brains upstairs figure we should begin to see an increase in production within twenty-four hours. So please, everyone, take to your stations, and for those not involved with the start-up, please stay outside of the flagged-off area."

He stopped pacing and scanned the crowd. "Play safe everyone. We all know where the stop buttons are. If you feel the need to hit one, do not hesitate. Let's all get home safe to our families. Now... let's get the show started!"

53

Albert admired the vast industrial landscape as he stood at his office window, dressed in his freshly pressed suit.

He took an anxious breath, then sipped from his glass. As he swallowed, he felt gentle hands glide up his back and tuck in his collar.

"Hello, Mother." He turned with a smile, then leaned over to peck her cheek.

She smiled back at her gentle giant. "Hello, my son." She straightened the front of his collar and then gave his tie a quick once-over. "Today is the big day."

Albert gasped, as if he'd been waiting for the opportunity for discussion. "Yes, today is the big day." He turned back to the window.

"You're not going down there for start-up?"

"No." He walked over to the bar to pour another. Before the first drop fell, he had a change of mind and set the bottle back in its place. He pulled down tautly on the bottom of his jacket and turned back to her. "The press is down there—just one—but we had no choice. There's too much interest from the environmentalists." His temper flared. "It's all gotten too far out of hand, the little tree-hugging shits! What do they know about this industry? We put food on millions of tables across the planet! And AJ... Jesus Christ! What in the hell's he thinking? What in the hell was *I* thinking, to put him in charge of such a thing? He still thinks he's partying it up back in the big city. And that fucking trailer-trash woman of his, he's letting her play him like a puppet! She's making a fucking fool of him! He can't even control her. He can't control himself!" He leaned heavily on the desk and his head dropped.

Emma rushed over and placed her hand on his shoulder. "Son." She placed her other hand on his cheek and turned him to face her. "It'll all be fine," she whispered. "Remember, you always come out on top." She smiled and patted his cheek. "This time will be no different, you'll see. In a couple of hours you'll be celebrating."

He calmed for a moment, before he flared once more. "That boy better not fuck things up any more than he—"

Emma grabbed hold of him again. "Albert!" she barked. "I'll listen to no more of this! The project will start up fine! You will be fine! AJ will be fine! The press, the environmentalists, everything! Tomorrow, we will all be heroes. The plant will be producing better than ever, and we can get to work straightening everyone's lives out!" She fussed with his attire again. "Now, do you have a speech made up yet?"

"Yes, yes, I have it prepared."

"Good. A victory speech, I should hope?"

"Yes, Mother, only a victory speech for a successful start-up."

"Good! The other is not an option."

54

Charlie briskly crossed the yard to meet what he assumed to be the reporter. There weren't a lot of slender young Asian men, hair slicked back and sporting a business suit, hanging around. He'd been instructed to keep him by his side, and if something went wrong, he was to notify Albert immediately and not let the "little fucking snitch" leave the site.

"Andrew"—Charlie smiled and reached out his hand—"Mr. Stalkton." The young man turned and Charlie shook his hand. "Charles Bidwell. Welcome to the 11-16 Project. You're just in time." He motioned toward the trailers.

Andrew ignored Charlie's invitation and pointed to the hilltop. "Wha... what's going on up there?"

Charlie looked to see what had caught his interest. A thin plume of dark smoke billowed beside the barren torso of the chieftain. He was bobbing and chanting in some sort of ritual.

"Oh, that. That's the local chief."

"The local chief?"

"Yes, yes!" Charlie smiled confidently toward the hilltop. "Big man in these parts, great guy!"

"Ummm, yeah." The reporter flipped open a notebook and scribbled something quickly, then gestured to the hill again. "And what exactly is he doing? Is it safe to have a fire on the lease?"

"Oh, well, he's... blessing the project. Big fan of what we're doing here. So we've agreed to let him have the fire just this once. Y'know, keeping up relations with the local tribes and whatnot." He guided the reporter away from the media disaster and toward the trailers.

Mr. Stalkton reviewed his notes and continued with his friendly interrogation. "So you're Charles… Bidwell, correct?"

"Yes, that's correct, Charles Bidwell, the project supervisor."

"And a Mr. AJ Doyle? He's the project manager and also the son of the mine president, Mr. Albert Doyle?"

"Yes, that's correct."

"And is it possible for me to meet with this Mr. AJ Doyle today? He's stirred up quite a rumbling in the press world lately. I'd like to hear his opinion on the project, and the company."

"Oh, I'm sure he'll be delighted to meet with you. He's just tied up with some teleconference right now." Charlie's friendly demeanour never faltered.

The young reporter squinted at Charlie as if he sensed things weren't quite as suggested. "How about you, Mr. Bidwell, would you mind answering a couple questions?"

Ah fuck! "Yes, of course, fire away." He never flinched.

The journalist tapped the tip of his pen to his tongue a couple times and then began firing. "Please, Mr. Bidwell, explain exactly how this new pioneering system works, and what exactly is its purpose?"

Charlie had practised a handful of responses over the week. "The 11-16 Project is a series of compressors that feed into each other in order to inject the adequate volume of high-pressure air into the ground, via a deep horizontal well." He paused while the inquiring mind finished his scribbling.

"So, to clarify, the compressors take in air. The air around us right now?"

Charlie nodded.

"They take huge volumes of air out of the atmosphere and inject it… into the ground?"

"Yes, that's correct."

"So, then, why? How is this possibly going to help production?"

"Well, the compressed air is being forced into an area below the bedrock but above where we extract the product. We're basically raising the atmospheric pressure on the product in the ground. So, in theory, the process should help us speed up the extraction as well as making it more thorough, safe, and environmentally friendly."

Andrew jutted his pen toward Charlie, as if he'd just caught a glitch in his story. "Yes, in theory!"

"Well, yes, of course in theory. We haven't proven it yet—no one has. We're the first in the world to try such a thing. It's experimental technology. This isn't news to anyone."

The scribbling grew frantic. "And how do you feel about being involved with a company that tends to employ such questionable and experimental technology?"

"I'm proud to be a part of it." Charlie hoped his bullshit would come with a bonus. "Let's be honest, all these companies go to great lengths to get the oil out of the ground, injecting steam and potentially harmful chemicals to help separate the oil from the sand. You can't get much cleaner than air. So if it works the way they hope, it's a win for everyone. If it doesn't, then at least we're trying, and we'll learn many things in this experiment, things that'll help us improve the process in the future."

A moment of silence fell between the two men.

Andrew squinted at Charlie again. "All right, so what are we going to see here today?"

"Well, I wish I could tell you it was going to be something really spectacular, but honestly, we've run tests on all the equipment, we've run it all together, discharging to the atmosphere. So really, the only big difference is, we're going to swing a valve to direct the air into the well, and wait." Charlie smiled with a shrug.

"So if it's all right with you," he continued, "we've been instructed to keep you down here for start-up, till you're satisfied. Then maybe we can get a word with AJ and send you off to the control room, where they'll be able to fill you in on the results. They're estimating an increase in production within twenty-four hours."

Mr. Stalkton nodded.

It was a plan devised earlier in a phone call from the big cheese. Charlie was to handle the reporter through start-up. If all went well, he could have a meet with AJ and interview Albert.

"So, Mr. Stalkton, if you're ready, I'll call the guys out to get to their stations. We can't allow you in any of the flagged-off areas during start-up, but you can stick with me. There'll be a man in each building, positioned by the emergency stop buttons. We'll watch things from out here and then walk around back to watch the valves swing. After that you can do as your heart desires."

Andrew agreed.

Charlie raised his radio. "Everyone take position for start-up."

All the workers filed out of the trailers, hooting and cheering. It had been a long haul, and many had doubted the day would ever come.

With everyone in place, Charlie raised the radio again. "11-16 to control room."

"11-16, this is control room."

"Control room, we are in position and would like to start the plant to vent to atmosphere."

"Ten-four, 11-16. We are a go for plant start-up, vent to atmosphere. Can we get visual confirmation on the discharge valve position?"

The heavy accent of Harvey Hancock barked back across the frequency. *"Yes you's gots the green light with da valve."*

"Ten-four, all clear, going for start-up."

The air sat still as the seconds ticked to minutes. Charlie reached behind his back and unclipped two sets of earmuffs from his belt and handed a pair to his guest. "You'll need these."

The young reporter accepted them with a quizzical look.

The whining of large electric motors began from inside the buildings. They picked up speed, then other mechanical swooshings and knockings began. Next, a very loud rushing of air came from behind the buildings. Strengthening in force and volume, the "whooshing" grew to eardrum-busting levels. Andrew scrambled to place his muffs.

Once everything was up to speed, Charlie wasted no time yelling the next instructions into his radio. "11-16 to control room! Please proceed to close the atmospheric valve twenty-percent."

He watched for Harvey's signal from around the building indicating that the valve had reached the proper point.

"11-16 to control room. Please close the atmospheric valve to forty-percent."

The routine continued with the pitch of the rushing air changing with every move until, finally, one hundred percent closure was achieved. The whooshing air silenced. Now, the only noise was mechanical, which seemed almost soothing compared to the jet blast.

They were officially live for the first time. All that air was being forced underground. One minute passed, then two… then the cheering began.

Everyone clapped and threw their hard hats into the air. High-fives were slapped all around. Possibly a happy tear or two was shed.

Charlie and Andrew stuck around the site for a short while, listening to the men yelling different readings from the units. The young Pulitzer prospect looked uninterested, and Charlie figured the numbers didn't make much sense to him. After the equipment had run for a while and the excitement had died down, Charlie escorted the guest to AJ's office, where they had a quick meet and greet and a couple of questions and answers, and then due to the lack of apocalyptic explosions, Andrew was eager to get up to the control room. Charlie accompanied him back to his vehicle and sent him on his way.

As Charlie watched Andrew turn off site, a large tanker truck pulled into the yard. It was a surprise to him as nothing had been scheduled and the site was restricted to only those directly involved.

He signalled to the driver to stop, then approached his window.

"You must be lost," he said with a smile.

"No, I don't think so, mister, this is the 11-16 site, right?"

Charlie flinched at the driver's knowledge. "Yes, this is the place, but it's off limits to all traffic today."

The driver rolled his eyes, reached for some paperwork on the dash, and handed it to Charlie. "Listen, man, I don't make the orders, I just drive the truck. My boss says this comes here right now and is supposed to be unloaded to process, or whatever."

Charlie flipped through the papers, scanning until he found the initial source for the order. The signature at the bottom read *Albert Doyle*. He held one finger up to the driver and backed away while continuing to study the papers. "Just wait a minute, please, I have to make a phone call on this."

"Listen, bud," the driver replied, "I don't know why you weren't told about this, but my orders are specific, and I ain't supposed to stop for nothin'! So you go make your phone call and I'll continue on until my boss tells me otherwise."

Charlie rushed straight to his office, picked up the phone, and hit the speed dial.

"Albert Doyle."

"Albert!" Charlie blurted into the phone. "I have some paperwork from a truck that showed up at the gate here. It's full of naphtha and the operator says he has specific instructions to dump into the process." He paused to catch his breath and wait for a response. "Albert"—he shook the papers in his hand—"the paperwork has your signature on it!" he screamed.

Albert finally responded. "I apologize for not informing you of this, but I had to make sure it was kept under wraps."

Charlie heard air brakes hiss. He peered through his office blinds as the truck driver threw the big rig into park and hopped out.

"But why, Albert?"

"Listen, Charlie, I have full confidence this technology will work on its own, but we both know the world is watching. The sooner we can get some notable results, the quicker they'll move on to the next 'big threat' and we can get on with normal operations."

Charlie stalled as he watched the driver and his partner string out their hoses and mumble out an explanation to the slowly gathering crowd of workers. "If the environmentalists ever get word of this, Albert! If anyone outside of us get wind of this!..."

"Precisely why no one was notified. Just keep your mouth shut, and plead ignorance to anyone who asks. You're my man on the ground, Charlie. One last fire for you to fight."

Charlie flooded with rage and disgust—too much for any but one word: "FUCK!!!"

Albert continued to speak as Charlie let the receiver drop from his ear.

"Listen, Charlie, you're done! You did it, great job! You're a hero to this company, and when the bonuses are rolled out, you will not be forgot—"

Charlie hung up.

AJ stuck his head in the door. He followed Charlie's gaze to the window. "What's going on?"

Charlie turned and looked him in the eye. "Apparently we weren't cheating enough, so we're upping our game." He walked by AJ and stepped out to the yard.

He glanced at the crew of guys. Some looked to him with arms out, asking for explanation. Charlie just turned back to the road. He breathed out slowly and his gaze drifted up to the hilltop. The chieftain was looking straight down at him, his painted face still.

The hairs on the back of Charlie's neck stood on end.

55

Albert hung up the phone. One thing he'd learned in his years of leadership was a natural flair for dramatization. He clasped his hands behind his head, leaned way back in his chair, and turned to admire the view: setting the opening scene for the reporter's entrance.

He smiled. The hours had ticked by nervously since the start-up. For the first two hours, there was nothing. Then the numbers started to increase steadily. Now they had a solid eighteen percent return, and climbing. *Success!* He imagined the headlines: PRESIDENT ALBERT DOYLE BEATS DOWN THE ODDS AND REMAINS THE KING OF OIL SANDS!... *King, I like the sound of that. Maybe I should change the placard on my door?* He chuckled. It was over, and he'd won again. *Life is fucking beautiful.*

A soft knock arrived. Albert didn't flinch; this was the position he wanted to be in when the biggest interview of his career began.

He cleared his throat. "Yes, please come in."

The familiar creak of the door's hinges filled the room.

"Mr. Doyle, sir."

Albert took the cue and slowly swivelled his chair around. He lowered his arms and positioned himself rightfully at his desk with the smile of a Cheshire cat.

"Mr. Stalkton, I presume?"

"Yes, sir."

"Well, come on in, son. It's a pleasure."

242

Andrew closed the door and approached the desk, holding his hand out.

Albert stood to accept it. His hand swallowed Andrew's completely. He squeezed just enough to make the young man wince.

"Please, sit down, Mr. Stalkton, make yourself comfortable." He gestured to a plush leather chair, then walked to the bar—a bold move to reveal such a secret to a reporter, but they had success, there was no evil villain story here. "Can I interest you in a drink? I know this is an interview, but it's also a time of celebration. As you can imagine, a project of this importance, this... calibre, comes with a... well, let's call it a truckload of stress." He chuckled. "A big dump truck full, haha." He filled two snifters, then returned to the desk and handed one across to Andrew.

Albert sat down, wearing the gleaming expression of a man who'd ordered the "happy ending" massage.

Andrew took a minute to scribble in his book.

"You're quick to write." Albert smiled curiously. "We haven't even started talking yet."

"I'm just scribbling some notes on the whole... ambiance." He returned a pleasant grin. "Nothing to worry about. Great journalists collect all the details."

Albert settled into his chair, enticed by the sound of the word *great*.

"So, Mr. Doyle, this is your day, your victory. Why don't you tell me where you'd like to begin. After all, this is also your interview."

Given the floor to create the story as he wanted, Albert was not at all shy. He started back at the beginning, the very beginning. The picture he painted of himself was one of a modest hero: robbing from the rich and giving to the poor, sticking up for the little guy, and cheering for the underdog.

The reporter scribbled away with every detail.

Albert was surprised at young Andrew's thirst as he told his story. He had to pause multiple times to refill the reporter's glass, only to watch him gulp it down as if he were at a frat party.

"I tend to remain quite modest about myself in everyday behaviour." He handed the lad his refill, then placed himself back in his desk chair. "But seeing as this is for global news, I think it's best to speak my mind. Maybe it should be part of my duty in life, lending mentorship to the young and upcoming?" His eyes widened. The reporter was taking another heavy swallow.

"Please, Mr. Doyle, we have a lot to cover here, so once you get a train of thought going, try not to lose direction. It's very important we keep the conversation fluid."

Albert cleared his throat. "Yes, of course. As I was saying, I'm usually quite modest in regard to myself and my accomplishments. But maybe, when we look at it from another point of view, perhaps it's selfish of me to hoard my… ingenuity?" He grinned, then continued.

"This 11-16 Project is one of the greatest accomplishments of my career, I will openly admit. Hell, it's one of the greatest feats in the history of the oil industry." He turned to look out the window. "I suppose many will ask, 'How does one man accomplish something so incredible?' Well, it takes balls, straight up! A giant set of balls. Everyone tried to step in my way—environmentalists, safety consultants—but they're also the ones pushing us to run leaner and more efficient. It's the black shit we're all after; like it or not, it puts food on the table for thousands—millions—globally. Politicians and celebrities fly up here in their private jets, take helicopter tours with their cameras, and call us dirty, and then they hug a fucking tree and go home, spitting on us. So, I'll play the role of the bad guy, the one who cuts the tree down and milks the resources so they can fly around our heads and flush. It's not a job for the weak, there are people out there who would love to see me hang." He chuckled. "They keep trying, and I keep dodging. What does it take? Greatness. People can say what they want behind my back, or to my face. This is my land, and my industry… I'm the king."

56

With the numbers in and the project a claimed success, the crew left the site after the first regular eight-hour shift in what seemed like forever. The following week there would be a corporate meeting, where they'd be applauded and awarded with jackets, or maybe some nice watches. Over the last year they'd raked in a pile of overtime, at the cost of a healthy family life. But the experience they'd gained would prove a useful bargaining tool for their future.

The site was quiet, with the exception of the low thrum of the running equipment and the crunch of shifting gravel as Charlie and AJ walked to their vehicles to get their overnight bags. The first twenty-four hours were critical. If anything were to go wrong, it would almost certainly happen then, so they'd agreed to spend the first night on site.

Charlie breathed in, taking a minute to admire how much beauty surrounded him. The sun was out, the birds were singing, the forest was alive and lush. If he could block out the smell of asphalt and the consistent hum of equipment, he could've imagined he was on a fishing trip.

He was still pissed about the chemical injection, but there was nothing he could do about it—the powers-that-be will do what they will. In the end, he felt a huge weight had been lifted from his shoulders. With that release, his mind was free to enjoy thoughts of his family, and the big trip with their beautiful grandson. He smiled. *Worth it.*

He followed the rays of sunlight up through the trees to a small finger of smoke pointing straight into the still sky from atop the bluff.

AJ walked past Charlie and looked toward the same point. "Looks like he's still hanging around, eh?"

Charlie nodded.

"Maybe someone should take him a copy of the performance results."

They shared a chuckle.

Back in the office, they pushed tables off to the side and began crafting together some beds; it wasn't going to be comfortable, but it was only one night. They agreed to take shifts, watching the computer screens and doing hourly walk-through inspections. It was the last hurdle, and then they'd both be on to the next great adventure.

After settling in, Charlie opened his lunch box to see what Marge had packed. In it was a square of leftover lasagne, a nice cupcake surprise, and a letter.

To our wonderful Grandpa. Congratulations on your success. Can't wait to have you back home.

He smiled as Marge's warmth surrounded him.

AJ pulled up a chair to join him. He unwrapped a soggy Subway sandwich and held it up in the air. "Congratulations!" He smiled.

Charlie smirked and held up his plastic fork. "It's been a hell of an adventure."

"I'm sure happy you were assigned to this, 'cause she sure as fuck would've sunk without you." AJ bit into his sandwich.

"Well, thank you. But if it failed, I'm sure they would've just started some noise-making machines, dumped a bunch of chemicals down the hole, and fudged some numbers."

"I guess. In the end it's all really just smoke and mirrors. There really is no way they can trace what's causing what?"

Charlie exhaled. "I'm sure what we've done here will make a difference—it makes sense on paper. It just would've been nice to give it an honest try. Hmph! Honesty and oil." He shot a wink at AJ and then scraped the last of the lasagne from the bottom of his dish, set it on the table, and swivelled his chair so he was facing AJ, who was looking out the window. "So, dare I ask, how are things on the home front?"

AJ sighed. "Home? Not sure there ever was one of those. We're just two stupid kids trying to play big people. This whole last year was my first push at real life. I'd say I failed with flying colours." His jaw clenched and he wrapped up what

246

was left of his sandwich, avoiding eye contact.

Charlie grinned. "Failed? It's really about how you look at it. Maybe some parts of our lives change, we change. But to look at one small point as an overall failure isn't right. You came here straight out of what I assume to be a pretty fantastic playboy-type lifestyle. This is a big first step into adulthood, for both of you. I look at you now compared to when we first met, and you've definitely grown. You're learning, so why don't you stop looking at it as a failure? As for your little lady, she's probably lived a pretty spoiled lifestyle courtesy of you. So she hasn't had to face the trials of evolution like you have, yet. I think another thing you have to realize right now is that—no matter how hard you try—you can't fix other people."

AJ continued to stare thoughtfully out the window. "Evolve." He chuffed. "Evolving into my father is something I've always resisted."

"Your father has some very strong qualities—some good and some bad—and you likely share many of them. I think you should be proud to follow in his shoes somewhat. Just look at what you feel you'd like to do different, and make the change—that's evolution of the species."

"The evolution of a species, all resting on my shoulders." He leaned back in his chair and placed his hands behind his head. "One more night."

"Last one."

57

"Well, get on with it now, Mr. Hynes," persuaded a six-year-old Ollie's grandmother. "The sun's going down, you know."

The warm August sun was setting over the distant shore of the forest lake. Ollie sat on the edge of the dock, dangling his feet over the side so his toes skimmed the surface of the water. He'd been working up the courage all summer to learn how to swim. The water sat still as glass, wrinkled only by the wake of a flock of geese as they built up speed to take flight. Ollie's gaze followed them until they lifted up and over the trees, their lonely honking and squawking fading.

He turned his attention back to the water, where the bugs skated around. He attempted to disturb their path with mountainous ripples created by his toes.

"On with ya now!" his grandmother prodded again. "Pretty soon the sun'll be set, and you'll have wasted another day fussin' about it."

He wanted to—oh how he wanted it. "But Gran, I'm still scared!" He looked over his shoulder at her, hoping she had some solution for him, some secret grandma recipe for learning to swim.

"Of course you're scared, everyone's scared the first time. It's good to be scared, scared keeps you focused." She tenderly brushed the hair back from his eyes.

"But what if I… I drown and I die?"

"Oh, hush! Why would any of that happen now, on such a beautiful night? Don't talk such nonsense!"

"But it happens, Gran!"

"It ain't happenin' to you, Ollie! You're working it up to be more than it is. You see people swimming all the time."

"But—"

"No more buts, child. Life's going to throw some tough times at you. This may seem big now, but I promise you it's nothing. It's the first of many steps to becoming a man. Besides, I'm here and I'd never let anything bad happen to you. You know that. Now off you go!"

He looked over the edge, at the young man staring back at him from the mirrored surface. *The first step to being a man.* He wanted so badly to take this step.

So, without a second's more hesitation, he pushed up to stand tall on the dock, looked at the horizon, took a breath, and leaped in faith.

This wasn't Ollie's first time in water. He'd played in the shallows plenty of times and was quite advanced in his own mind. He and his friends would practise ducking their heads under the water and holding their breath for as long as possible. Ollie always won... well, a couple times he was beaten by that older boy from down the road, Ivan Bridger, but Ollie was pretty sure he'd cheated.

But ducking one's head below the surface in the shallows and jumping off the end of the dock into the unknown were two very different things. The water seemed colder in the deep, and though he stretched his legs far down, he couldn't find the bottom. Instead, his feet felt an unwelcome tickle from the weeds. He always dreaded the weeds—they felt so gross, and local legend claimed people had drown by getting their feet tangled in them. There was also the legend of the people-eating lake monster.

The cold, the threatening weeds, and the lack of footing set in instant panic. Every breath of air Ollie took down with him immediately exploded from his lungs.

Why ain't I floating?!?!?

He could float in the shallows, on his tummy and on his back; he did it all the time.

The water's wrong at this spot, it's thinner! Gran doesn't know—she'll be waiting for me to pop back up, but she doesn't know about the water here.

He opened his eyes wide. Looking toward the surface, he struggled and clawed! But the more he did, the farther he seemed to sink. He kicked, but the sinister undergrowth prevented him from performing a proper stroke.

His burning lungs wanted to suck in for air, but he stifled the urge, realizing this was serious. It was time to stop making up stories of evil weed monsters and pockets of thin water. It was time to fight for survival, or drown. He found a very sharp focus. He kicked down hard through the weeds, pointed his feet like flippers, then cupped his hands and pushed down hard, stroke by stroke, and climbed the ladder.

SPLASH!

Ollie exploded from the surface and sucked in a giant breath. Bulging eyes looked to his grandmother, who was kneeling at the edge of the dock—smiling, clapping, and cheering him on. As quickly as he had surfaced, he sank back under.

But he wanted nothing of it, nothing of that watery grave. With refreshed lungs, he quickly regrouped, found a rhythm, and pushed to the surface again, coughing and sputtering but staying afloat.

He looked back up at his gran.

She spread her hands wide. "Hahahaha! Look at you!"

Ollie finally understood he'd done it; he was swimming. He'd taken his first step toward being a man, and it felt amazing! Like nothing he'd ever felt before.

He cracked a smile up at her and she motioned him to come around the dock. He made a few small adjustments, then started to swim back to shore—still sputtering and gasping to catch his wind, but all the time explaining how he'd triumphed against all the perils.

"And then," he panted, "all the weeds—they were so gross, Gran! They were trying to grab me! And I think the water was a little weird there. I think it's a little thin and cold, it's probably the weeds doing it. We should tell the park to put up a sign."

As he walked onto the shore, she was there to wrap his favourite fluffy towel around his shivering body.

"So how come, Gran? How come you didn't jump in after me?" He looked up at her as they walked along the gravel path. "I was down there for a long time. I bet Ivan Bridger can't hold his breath that long!"

She looked down at him with a caring smile.

Ollie stopped walking and looked up to her as a serious young man waiting for an answer. "Weren't you worried I'd drown? Why didn't you jump in and get me?"

She placed her hand tenderly to his cheek. "Of course I was worried, dear.

I'll always worry about you. But there's a time coming when you'll be a man, all grown up. When that time comes, I won't worry so much if I know you can swim on your own." She winked, then leaned down and kissed him on the forehead.

***

Ollie woke from the distant memory. His tired, dreary eyes focused on his grandmother's picture.

He stirred slightly to ensure his body was still attached to his mind. The blinding late-day sun was pushing through every flaw in the curtain, its snooping rays trying to shed light on his very dark place.

He peered over at the clock: 5:04 p.m. It had been a rough day for him. He'd finally admitted his addiction to himself. He hated it; it had consumed him and was beginning to ruin everything he'd worked for. The best thing for him to do would be to just pack up and get the hell out of there, as far away as he could.

But that little voice was still in his head. It used every gram of reason to convince him to stay, and because his body and mind were so heavily dependent, he could never argue. *Grab Mary-Ann and get the hell out of here*, he would try to tell himself. It was what had to happen. But he could never finish the sentence, let alone apply the action.

A tear dripped from his eye as he lay motionless, still staring at the portrait of his grandmother. What would she think about the man he'd become?

From the drawer it called to him. Each purchase had been bigger than the previous. The only relief he could get from its persistent whining was during his occasional catnaps.

He slid his limp body over the side of the bed and pushed himself up. His legs were shaky—so shaky he had to sit back down. He cradled his head in his hands. How could he break free? The solution was simple in theory. But a twisted web of politics would never let him implement it.

Where were the good things in life? Why couldn't they save him? Why couldn't they see him?

Because all of the curtains were drawn, and all the doors were locked. Only he could open them. But he didn't want to.

Ollie wept into his hands.

A bout of anger hit him and he pushed up from the bed. But he felt so weak—physically he had all but disintegrated. There was no way he was making it to work. With a scowl, he went to the window and peeked through the curtain.

PRICE PER BARREL

The bright sun stung his nocturnal eyes. He blinked a few times, and the blur sorted itself into parked cars and people walking about and enjoying the evening. Some ate ice cream, others bounced basketballs, and small groups huddled for an after-dinner smoke.

He felt life passing him by. It was time to get back in the game. He would fight this last battle, then pack his things, grab Mary-Ann, and run! Run fast, run far, never look back.

He let the curtain fall. He looked down at the dreaded drawer, grabbed the handle, and pulled it open.

Let's get this over with!

58

A few times every year, there was a secret gathering of the elite: a costumed event by personal invitation only, where the uppity-ups could blow off some steam. Albert had called for such a gathering that night to celebrate his victory, a celebration he'd been planning for months.

Albert began preparations for the night's festivities. He hummed and whistled as he methodically fashioned his attire. His disguise for this event would be brilliant. The tailor had been working on it for over a year, and it was sure to be the star of the show.

He slipped on his pants and was starting to thread his belt through the loops when he heard a soft knock at the door. It was past working hours and he wasn't expecting anyone.

"Yes, come in!" he hollered.

The visitor was a surprise, a forgotten delight. Maybe it was time to indulge in a much-deserved appetizer. He smiled wickedly.

59

Mary-Ann's time with Ollie had been shaky lately, to say the least. Some days he was on point and the love between them seemed unbreakable, and the next it was a miracle for him to reply to her messages. She was in a tug of war over him, against some supernatural force. His physical condition was worsening, a state he was quick to blame on the never-ending night, and though she wished that were all it was, she knew there was more to it.

Today was one of those silent days. She'd messaged him several times, asking how he was doing and if she could bring some food up so they could enjoy a nice meal together before he started his shift. But nothing was the only response she received.

She had one last duty at the plant, then she could go up to his room and see what the hell was going on. She loved him, but she hated how he could make her worry.

Up the stairs and down the desolate hallway her shoes echoed. At the door—although she hadn't run in to him for months—she gave a polite knock.

"Yes, come in!"

The familiar baritone sent chills along her spine. Her hand paused on the handle; her knees quivered. She wanted to run, but it was too late. He was celebrating a big victory today, so she hoped he was busy and would tell her to come back later. It had been so long. She turned the knob slowly and poked her head through.

Her fear turned to near rage at the sight of him. He seemed to be in the middle of getting all dressed up, no doubt for some fancy celebration of his great achievement.

He stopped what he was doing and smiled that big, fat, ugly shit smile. "Mary-Ann! My, my, it's been a while since our paths have crossed. If I didn't know any better, I'd think you were trying to avoid me." He returned to fussing with his belt.

"I'm terribly sorry, sir, I didn't mean to disturb you. I thought you'd be gone by now. I, I'll leave you be, I can come back lat—"

"Nonsense, come on in, child. I'm just getting dressed for a little celebration tonight."

She stepped just inside the doorway. "Yes, sir, I heard something about that. Congratulations."

"Why don't you come in and relax. I'll give you the night off from cleaning the office. I've had a very good day, join me in a drink."

"Oh, well, I'm really not much of a drinker, and I really should get—"

"I insist!" His voice had grown demanding. "You know where the bar is. Now quit being ridiculous and fix us both a drink. I need a second opinion on my choice of ties."

She obeyed. She wasn't sure why. Her head spun and her blood rushed. Where was this going to lead?

Her hands trembled as she poured the drinks.

"Mary-Ann, could you please set the drinks down and help me with my belt. There's a twist in the back somewhere."

She watched him wriggle like a turtle on its back.

She huffed and set the drinks on the desk, then reached over to untwist his belt. A meaty paw latched on to her wrist like a steel shackle. He pulled her around to face him as though there was nothing to her.

The shock sped her heart instantly and the rush of adrenaline almost caused her to fall limp.

He locked both hands on her shoulders and squeezed like a vice. There was no escape. She had forgotten his size, his power. Now it was all very clear and frightening as little Mary-Ann melted back into herself.

She watched him suck in a deep breath, as if feeding off her fear, and his body inflated to an immortal size.

PRICE PER BARREL

The tears in her eyes fuelled the fire in his.

"I don't like how you've been so disobedient. I've called for you several times, but you never come to me, there's always some excuse. It seems you've forgotten the structure of our relationship!" he boomed. "I've been through a lot of stress lately, and you show no appreciation to me! Where've you been!"

"I, I'm sorry! I appreciate you! Please, Mr. Doyle!" Her quiet tears turned to hysterics.

He pushed her back against the desk.

She screamed, "No! *No-o-o-o*! Please, Mister—"

"Shut up!" he growled, squeezing her cheeks together. "You remember how this works! Lie back and take it like a good girl! I don't hand this opportunity to just anyone!" He laughed, sounding mad with power.

A whimpering mess, she fell back, refrained from resisting, and tried her best to leave the present. Familiar sounds followed: the ripping of the zipper, the tearing of her clothing, the tinkling of his belt, and snorting breaths, like a pig at feast.

Laid out on the desk, she let her head fall to the side and looked to her saviour, her dark friend, the hunter. But… he wasn't there!

Albert smirked. "Oh yes! Your little friend. I noticed your fondness for him. I'm sorry, but I felt the room was due for a change in ambiance. So I had him chopped up and thrown in the dumpster!" He laughed.

In a burst of energy, she wriggled and squirmed and fought his assault. "*NO!* No, you fucking pig!"

Wop! A big brick of a hand clubbed her across the face and he latched on to her harder. "Shut the hell up, you ungrateful bitch!"

She squealed, shrill enough to shatter glass. Reaching up, she got hold of his pudgy cheeks and dug her nails in deep, with everything she had, and tore at his flesh.

He cried and released his grip. Another heavy hand bludgeoned her, sending her off the side of the desk and onto the ground.

Movement from the side of the room drew their attention. There, in the open doorway, stood Emma—hand placed over her mouth, tears streaking down her horrified expression.

Mary-Ann wasted not even the slightest fraction of a second. She rushed for the door, straight past Emma and away from there… forever.

MARC GREGORY

***

The beast that had possessed the man left. Albert Doyle was a shell of himself. White as a ghost, he raised his hand to her. "Mother... Mother, please, it's not—"

"Don't you 'Mother' me!" Emma snapped back. Her whole body quivered and her eyes sliced him like a razor. "You're not a man! You're no king!... You're a monster!" She burst into tears and stormed out the door.

As she escaped down the hall, her own past came back to haunt her...

The after-party took place on an acreage outside of town. Emma prodded Stephan for some special time alone so she could spoil him. He grinned and grabbed her hand. "Come on, I know the perfect place." He pulled her to the door and pushed her gently outside, then gestured to Andrew, who responded with a nod.

He grabbed a lantern and took her across the dark yard to the barn. Inside, some sheets and blankets lay on straw bales, almost as if someone had planned it. She grinned. She was so incredibly lucky to have such a good man. She threw herself into him, knocking him back onto the makeshift bed. She undid his pants and bent to him, taking him deep until he moaned.

Then she heard the cricket-like chirp of the barn door. She looked back to see Andrew enter quietly.

She whirled around to Stephan. "Not tonight," she whispered. "I want this to be our night together. Just you and me, pleeease?"

"Awe, baby, c'mon. It's a team celebration, after all, and Andrew's part of the team."

At the risk of losing her man, Emma felt it was time to put her foot down and gain some control. She stood up. "If we can't just be alone, I'm leaving!" She turned, fighting back tears. She immediately wanted a do-over, but she straightened her dress and started for the door. As she came up to Andrew, she looked over snottily. "I'm sorry, Andrew, not tonight!"

He reached over and cupped one hand over her breast, digging his fingers in maliciously.

"I'm sorry, Emma, maybe Stephan didn't make himself clear enough. Tonight is a *team* celebration and... well, we just couldn't have it without you." He grabbed her arm and threw her back toward Stephan.

She turned to look at him still lying on the bed of straw. "Stephan, wha'...?"

He jumped up to console her, holding her hand lightly. "Babe, it's all right.

PRICE PER BARREL

We're all friends? We'll have our time alone soon, I promise. Let's just have some fun tonight, don't make it complicated," he said with puppy-dog eyes.

Emma's heart raced. She suddenly wanted nothing to do with the party, or the team.

She broke free from Stephan and tried for the door, but he snatched her wrist, holding her back. She looked at Andrew, who stood watching with a devilish grin, and then the door creaked open again and another player poked his head in.

"Hey, Andy, what's the fucking holdup?"

Emma let out a spine-tingling scream.

Stephan was quick to cover her mouth as she fought against him, and Andrew was fast to the struggle. They wrestled her back to the bed with ropes that had been set in place, and the two guys proved well practised in the art of binding.

With Emma secured, there were some high-fives between the teammates as several more of the crew entered the barn, followed with cheers and bottle-clinking.

The first one ripped open her dress and tore off her panties. Without pause, he forced himself inside her, smiling as if he'd hit a homer. Smacking her and clawing her breasts.

The barn erupted as the crew chanted their team name.

She was angry and scared. The pain to her body new and terrible. But it paled to her humiliation and her broken belief that she was something meaningful to someone wonderful.

Emma turned her head to look for Stephan, but he wasn't there. He wasn't anywhere. Tears streamed, her princess dreams raped from her one by one by… Emma exhaled and drifted into shock.

She'd lost count of how many had relieved themselves by the time it was over and the boys filed out of the barn. All except Stephan and Andrew.

Andrew walked over and squatted, looking into her eyes. "I don't understand why, Emma." He shook his head. "You would've had a much better time if you'd just played along like a good girl. But it's all over now." He smiled sweetly and gently brushed the hair from her face. "Now, we want to untie you, Emma, but we want to get some things sorted out first. Like I said, things didn't have to go this way, but you really didn't give us any choice. So technically, you're partially responsible. When we get back to town, you might feel like maybe you should tell someone." He shrugged. "I don't know, like a teacher, parent, or maybe the police?

258

But I just gotta tell you some things before you go running off. We're a highly respected baseball team, the pride of the town. And then, you're some tramp everyone's seen walking around dressed all sexy-like, begging for the attention. So if you tell anyone about this, if someone questions your bruises, do you think they'll believe that the team did this, or your stinking-drunk father?" He shook his head again. "Now, Emma, the guys have already vowed not to speak a word of this to anyone. We're all friends here, right, Emma? No one needs to know, right?" He stared at her.

Emma slowly nodded. It was a fight she wouldn't win, and it was attention she didn't want.

He smiled. "Good girl. You really are a team player, Emma." He winked.

The two boys released her and helped her upright. It hurt for her to stand. She looked down at her tattered dress, then back to the bloodstained bed. More tears ran from her eyes.

The boys walked to the door. "You can stay here for a while," Andrew said. "Try to freshen up a little, eh? We'll come get you when the bus comes to pick us up." They left her, closing the door behind them.

The bus arrived in the early-morning hours, and the boys brought Emma a change of clothes. Back in town, she staggered home. As she rounded the corner to her house, she glimpsed the all-too-familiar red and blue reflections illuminating the neighbourhood.

As she approached her house, she saw her cuffed father being forced into the back of a police cruiser. "But that bitch stole my money," he shouted in a drunken slur.

A commotion at the front door drew her attention. Two paramedics were wheeling what could only be her mother across the threshold on a gurney.

The police didn't bother to question her. It wasn't the first time they had paid a visit.

60

Alone on his bluff, the chieftain peered over the edge and down to the project. A new steady thrum of running equipment had piqued his curiosity.

Most of the white men had left and the commotion of people had eased. The energy he felt was wrong... a scent on the wind, a taste on his lips, and deathly stillness in the air.

He peered down, through the trees, over the gravel lot, past the steel door where the compressor unit stood, pulsing and thumping. Inside the madness, rods turned on shafts, pistons violently pounded forth and back, bits and pieces clicked and clacked. All the way down to a single, forth-stage discharge valve.

***

Late one Friday afternoon several years earlier, in the compressor assembly facility in Wisconsin, Danny Patrick had been racing the clock, wanting to get out of there ASAP to join some friends at the latest and greatest club to check out the new batch of college tail.

In his haste, the young man torqued the valve cap unevenly, allowing for excess clearance around the seat.

***

At the 11-16 Project, the valve banged and crashed in its housing, disintegrating a little more with every knock. The internal plate heated to a glowing red state, and a very small piece of steel flexed and fatigued, then broke away.

260

MARC GREGORY

Out the discharge port and down the hole into the blackness, the small ember mated with two other necessities to complete one of life's most primitive creations.

Air, fuel… ignition!

61

Albert stood before the mirror in his office's private bathroom, frantically doing his best to clean and seal the visible wounds. Anger, adrenaline, and uncertainty surged through him.

The scene replayed in his mind. The filthy whore… the look on his mother's face. He snapped, pounding fists on the counter with a low growl. He looked himself in the eye. *Calm down. Things are fine, it's a minor setback. You are on top; don't let it knock you down. Celebrate this victory. You can deal with the other shit in the morning. It'll come together. It's what you're built for.*

Repeating his chant, the big man began to deflate. He had to pull himself together. The party was about to start and he must be in the finest of forms. Besides, his costume would hide the wounds.

With a short exhale, he stood and straightened, admiring himself for a moment. He tucked in his white dress shirt, running his palms flat down the front to smooth it. Donning his suit jacket, he stood tall with his head high and breathed in deeply to inflate his ego. *It will work.* With a stern nod, he turned away from his reflection and made his way back into his office and over to a closet, pulled out a hanging plastic bag, and tore it open. He'd been waiting so long to show off his fabulous disguise. It was perfect timing for what would be the grandest celebration of his career: his trophy, and his crown. Now, he'd finally laid eyes upon it, and it was even better than he could've imagined.

He slid it oh-so-carefully off its perch and examined the different straps and fasteners. He tossed it gently behind and around him as one would a jacket, then he pulled down the headpiece like a hood until it covered all above the mouth.

He approached the full-length mirror hung by the door. It was spectacular! Worthy of a king! There he was, the grandest of beasts. A full-length vest and cape made of coarse fur draped over his body, attached to a giant head twice the size of his own. Menacing teeth and large ivory tusks protruded straight out from beside the mouth and then curved up to the ceiling.

Two great alpha leaders! Kings! Together as one!

Snapping back to reality, he checked the time on his phone and realized his limo would be waiting out front. He rushed to his desk and gathered his things, then shuffled out of his office and slammed the heavy door shut.

With a loud thud, the room fell silent.

62

Twilight settled over the 11-16 Project. AJ did his best to sleep in his makeshift bed, while Charlie did his best to stay awake in his chair.

Both men were extremely tired and their senses were dull, but they both reacted to what felt like a low growl or tremor in the surroundings. Something not of the ordinary.

AJ sat up and looked out the back window, then snapped his head around and looked to Charlie, who just raised his eyebrows.

"You ever hear anything like that before?" AJ asked.

Charlie held his position for a moment before he relaxed and returned to a borderline sleeping state. "Probably just the shift operator doing his rounds."

"You mean the guy who comes around every couple hours to scribble down gauge readings on a clipboard? You think that's what that sounds like?"

"I think it's best if we just assume it was," Charlie said with a sleepy grin. "Everything on the monitor looks consistent."

The lonely sound carried through the ground far below the surface and up the hill to the chieftain, who was deep in meditation.

63

Emma sat with Mary-Ann for many hours back in her office, administering some mild first aid and emotional support. All the time, the two cried together and Emma couldn't stop apologizing, clearly shocked and embarrassed by her prized son.

It was early into the morning hours before Mary-Ann felt strong enough to leave. She hadn't heard a thing from Ollie all evening, and her intuition was beginning to insist she get up to his room. A few steps down the hall, she found her stride and picked up her pace. Through the doors and into the parking lot she stumbled. The chill of the night met her skin, and the fresh air filled her lungs. She reached for her phone and saw there was still no response from Ollie. She shook the phone in frustration and then approached a site taxi. She didn't want her company vehicle—they could keep it and anything else tying her to that place. She got in the vehicle and wrapped her arms around herself to contain her shivers, doing her best to stifle her sobbing and shield her face to avoid any questions from prying eyes. Speaking flatly, she requested the site gate.

She hopped out as soon as the wheels stopped, then threw a snuffled thank-you over her shoulder. She headed toward the space where the camp shuttles parked but stopped short when she realized it was empty. She checked the time on her phone. One would be by in fifteen minutes, but she wasn't interested in wasting the time. She looked toward the dark forest. She could be at the camp in five minutes if she followed the crow's path. Normally a trip through the trees at night would be something to avoid, but tonight she didn't care. Through the well-lit lot she hurried, down the ditch on the other side, and into the dense shadow of the forest path.

Out of sight and fuelled by desperation, she broke into a light jog, arms still wrapped around herself, and allowed the tears to flow once again.

It was time. She didn't care about the money, or the plan they had set. It was time to get the hell out of there, to leave this world of darkness behind.

She slowed her pace so she could check her phone for a response. Still nothing. She gritted her teeth. *Ollie, where the fuck are you! Of all the nights to pull this shit!*

It was what they both needed, to get the hell out! Far, far away, they would make it somehow. Anything was better than where they were. Being together was all that mattered.

She saw the glow of the camp's lights ahead and kicked into high gear. Clearing the forest, she rushed to the main door. With a quick, indirect salutation to the night guard, she briskly walked to Ollie's room, her mind spinning with possibilities of what terrible things may have happened to him.

The corridor to his room was quiet and she slowed her pace.

She paused when she reached his room, staring at the number on the door and the small peephole below it. Was he watching from the other side? She quietly peered into the small fish eye, conscious of how foolish she'd look if someone were to see her. She wiped at her tears, straightened her uniform, and gathered herself, then tapped on the door and quickly placed her ear against its surface. "Ollie?" she called softly.

***

Ollie's nervous pacing came to an instant halt.

He held his breath and his heart pounded with an anxiousness he'd never felt before. Sweat poured down his neck, drenching the collar of his shirt.

What in the hell's she doing here? Why? Why now? All I need is this night, this time, this one last battle!

Mary-Ann rapped again. "Ollie?"

His panic went hyper. *She could get in, she could get keys and get in the room! She's coming!*

He tiptoed over to the desk chair and, as quietly as he could, wedged its seatback under the door handle.

But Mary-Ann must've heard him. "Ollie?... Ollie!..." He could hear panic in her voice and she knocked harder. "Sweetie, I know you're there, please let me in," she whispered.

Oh god! Oh fuck! No, no, this can't happen! She can't see this! God, please help, please just let me survive this! Just make her go away till the morning. In the morning my new life'll start... Just till the morning. Tears streamed from his eyes. *Why can't it all just stop?*

He crawled into his bed and pulled the blanket up to his chin. He stared at the picture of his grandmother on the nightstand. *I'll make it through this, Gran. I'll be home safe soon.*

Beside the portrait lay what remained of his poison. He couldn't let Mary-Ann or anyone discover the truth, but he couldn't let himself throw it out. He scrambled from the bed, grabbed the lighter and pipe, and stuffed the remnants in the bowl. It was a lot, but he had to deal with it now. His insides twitched and pulled as he battled with wanting to rid himself of the filth but also yearning for more. He flicked the lighter and held it to the final morsel, his whole body trembling beyond control. When he heard the familiar crackling, he sucked on the pipe, deep and hard. He held it in for as long as he possibly could as he told himself this was the absolute last.

Out of exhaustion he finally let it go, and a large white cloud filled the room. He stuffed the pipe into the garbage can below some existing trash, then returned to his bed and the security of his blanket. It was done. It was all just a matter of time until he recovered, once and for all. The thought of it ending caused his heart to ache. How could it be so hard?

"Ollie!" Mary-Ann yelled. "Ollie!" She knocked more insistently. "Sweetie, I love you, what's going on? Please, honey, please let me in! Whatever it is, we can get through it. I'm here, right here. Please let me in."

Ollie's body had slipped into a catatonic state. It trembled, his breathing was laboured, and his heart pounded so hard he could hear it in his ears and feel it crashing against his ribcage. There was so much happening that he had to shut down.

If she would just go away, he could ride this out. He remained perfectly still, listening for any hint that she had left and so he could relax. The knocking ceased...

Then came a violent jiggling of the handle.

PRICE PER BARREL

Oh shit! Oh fuck! Please, Mary-Ann, not now, please just go away! His body took a large gulp, struggling for air because he'd been unconsciously holding his breath for so long.

"Ollie! Oliver! I know you're in there, I can hear you!" She jiggled the handle furiously.

Violent tension filled the room and seized Ollie's heart; he lay motionless. He had lost all control. Gasping, wheezing, his lungs heaved; he felt froth sputter from his mouth. He stared blankly at his grandmother's photo. To simpler times...

"OLLIE! You have to let me in!... *NOW*!"

The escalating assault from the other side of the door was driving him over the edge. His eyes wide and unblinking, his hand slowly reached out from under the blanket. Reaching... he reached for her, for her hand, the weeds tickling the bottom of his feet, he could see her reflection through the rippled surface.

But he was exhausted. The fight was so hard. Why hadn't she warned him? The surface was right there, so close that sometimes his very fingertip scraped through, but he was so very tired.

The dense water packed around him. He listened for her words, for whispers of encouragement, but there was nothing... nothing.

***

Delirious, Mary-Ann let go of the handle and frantically pounded both fists on the door. "Ollie, please!" she screamed. She backed up a step, and with everything she had, she slammed her shoulder into the door... She collapsed forward, her face pressed against the surface.

Something was very, very wrong, she felt it in her soul. Her nails scraped weakly down the door. "Ollie," she whimpered. Then, drumming up all the energy she had left, she let go of one primal scream, her last chance to get through to him.

"OLLLIIIIIIIIEEEEEEEEEEE!!!!!!"

She squeezed every ounce of life from her lungs, then crumpled to the floor and watched a security guard run in slow motion toward her.

***

The piercing shriek cut through the door and straight into Ollie's soul. His chest heaved with one last mighty pull as he felt the blade puncture his ribs and plunge straight to his heart. The weeds found purchase around his feet, pulling him down, softly, gently, to a final peace as his grandmother's reflection faded into darkness.

64

The limo made its way into an industrial area and pulled to a rest at the front doors of a small, modest building. Other than a finely crafted mahogany door with a crested symbol moulded into the knob, nothing hinted that the lodge was a place of importance. But certain organizations of the city's police community were ensuring that area patrols were non-existent for the evening.

The driver came around to Albert's door. Before exiting the car, Albert took a moment to check that his disguise was securely in place and perfectly proper. With both feet squarely planted, he pushed himself from the vehicle and hurried to the lodge's entrance.

A man dressed in a tailored suit opened the door as he approached, then quickly locked it behind him. The two men stood before each other in coded posture, then exchanged a handshake laced in riddles. The ritual was for both security and respect. Even in his cloak of secrecy, though, Albert's build was very hard to mistake for any other member's.

Formalities aside, Albert continued down the dimly lit hall, past walls resembling old parchment, which were framed in coarsely cut dark-stained timbers that were hand-carved with a perfectly repetitious pattern scrolling down the length. As he descended the stairs, he heard the echo of celebratory laughter coming from the other end of the basement corridor. He went into the first room on the right, a small room used as a changeroom and a place to hang the guests' outerwear. He stripped down to his pinstriped black silk boxers. Despite being known as one of the more modest of men's undergarments, they still left nothing to the imagination due to his mass.

He turned to the full-length mirror on the opposite wall and admired his masculinity.

He was beautiful, and he was disgusting. And he had no problem being either. Life at the top works in that way—when you have that much power, nothing else matters. Physically he was just as he appeared in the mirror: a pig of a man. But they would please him tonight. They would surrender and kneel to him, seduced by the sheer presence of him.

For the most part his mood was positive, but on occasion, the memory of recent events tickled the back of his mind.

Exiting the room, he took a right down the hall, which faded to total blackness until the end, where slivers of light traced the outline of the great double doors leading to the hall.

He reached for the large, brass handles, took a final breath, and pulled the heavy doors toward him, exposing his grandeur to the gatherers beyond.

All heads turned to him. There was a moment of awed silence as people paused to absorb what exactly had just arrived at the party.

He dramatically raised his arms out to the sides, like a king addressing his public. He watched as acknowledgment rolled like a wave through the crowd, and all raised their glasses to cheer his brilliance.

As the shock eased, the party returned to its previous state of merriment and Albert surveyed the room.

It was softly lit by several olde worlde post lamps lining the walls. The ceiling stretched up to a detailed mural depicting the sun and other points of origin. Across the checkered floor on the far side of the room, a throne sat atop tiered steps. And treats everywhere! Sinful treats of every type, to make one feel as greatness should.

A couple men came over to shake Albert's hand and congratulate him on his successes at both the plant and the party. This was his night, his victory. It was he who had called for it and his to design, and he'd chosen a theme suited to blend with his attire, a sort of "Three Little Pigs" atmosphere.

Or rather, twenty to thirty dirty piglets. He grinned.

The gentlemen stood back for a second to take in the girls in their little piggy-pink G-strings, with small curly tails springing as they walked, hoods with piggy ears to match, and pink masquerade masks to finish. They didn't have a clue who any of the men were, and the men didn't really care who they were—rogues, waitresses, and secretaries from all over town trying to make any money they could and work their way up the social ladder. At the end of the day, nothing tipped as well as the gala. They'd been handpicked by specialists, then tied, blindfolded, and delivered to the building. Any attempt to ascertain the location of the event would be met by severe consequences. There was even a circulating rumour that when one party favour had gotten stupid, she'd ended up floating down the Athabasca River in a sack. Everyone had heard the story; Albert encouraged it to maintain respect and order.

Two pretty piggies approached Albert, wedging themselves between him and his comrades on either side of him and hooking onto his arms. One fed him a sip of her champagne as the other rubbed his massive hairy torso.

Dirty little piggies. He smiled and put one paw on the brunette's ass and the other on one of the blonde's breasts. He pulled the blonde close and laid a slobbering kiss on her mouth, then gave them both a playful squeeze. They were very dirty, and very naughty. They accepted it; deep down they were all pigs and he was their king.

Down the middle of the long rectangular room sat the main socializing area. Plush leather chairs bordered tasteful glass coffee tables. Cannabis saturated the air, and many of the patrons were bent over the tables to inhale thick white lines. People were sitting, laughing, drinking, or in various stages of sexual acts.

Running along both sides of the centre area were three beds, each shielded by semi- transparent curtains. These were the "play areas." Albert had one booked for himself, and he led his two pretty piglets there, where they all jumped onto the bed, letting the curtains float closed behind them. As they were finding their positions, a sexy little delivery piggy brought in a small framed mirror stacked with a dozen fat white lines, as well as an ice bucket holding champagne—enough substance to keep them going for a while.

Rolling one of the girls onto her back, Albert scraped his first treat onto her flat tummy and then sucked it in full and deep, leaving not a single grain behind. Then he sat back and watched his two piggies play with each other—kissing, touching, and giggling. As the drugs began to settle in, his senses exploded. He wrapped a giant hand around each girl's head and pulled them down to his prescription-induced erection. At first they resisted a little, but he held them firm until they settled in and obeyed. His power was to be respected.

He sank back into the pillowy plushness of the middle of the bed, stretched both arms out, and stared at the ceiling. The narcotic was enlightening now, and every touch, smell, and squeal from his young servants was amplified tenfold.

He could tell the brunette was less experienced than the blonde one, a little unsure of herself. His heart sped up and his breathing quickened. He reached the peak of arousal and then, with unexpected lightning speed, he gripped the blonde's locks and yanked her down beside him. Like a well-tuned predator, he pounced. The brunette cowered in a corner, looking aghast at his tremendous size and athletic ability. Albert stared intensely into her frightened eyes as he pinned the blonde to the bed with one hand on her neck. He wrenched her panties aside and gave one deep thrust. She bucked and squealed beneath him. The earlier happenings in his office faded to black.

65

By 4:00 a.m., the sun had already breached the horizon. The morning was peaceful, crisp, and fresh. AJ lay sound asleep in his best effort at a bed while Charlie snored, reclined in his chair. Upon the bluff the chieftain sat cross-legged in a deep meditative state: resting, but alert, and waiting patiently.

A sleepy morning-shift operator pulled into the yard in his pickup. He got out of the truck with his clipboard and temperature gun in hand, then made his way to the compressor buildings.

From deep below, a low moan shifted in the ground. Charlie's snores tripped, and he adjusted his position.

A few minutes later the sound repeated, a little more prominent.

AJ woke. He propped himself up on his elbow and rubbed his eyes as he collected his thoughts. But he was none the wise as to what had startled him awake.

He looked over at Charlie sleeping soundly and grinned; they had failed in their last assignment.

This was it, he reminded himself. He stood and quietly pulled his pants on over his boxers. With stocking feet, he padded over to the window to watch the morning shine on what had been his home for the better part of the last year.

They would never know—the people, the public. Production would increase, stocks would rise, and nothing else mattered.

One simple project on a small chunk of land deep on an oil lease that few would ever see had changed many lives in a short time. Charlie's grandson had been spared from his fight with cancer. His own engagement to a woman he'd been more than sure was "the one" had been crushed, along with himself. And his father had been catapulted to the position of king of everything oil sands.

But today—the last day—the sun was rising, his feet were planted, and peace had settled. Life continued. Then a grin stirred. *What the fuck am I gonna do next week?*

A sharp moan shifted the ground, capturing all of AJ's attention. He swore he'd seen a tremor in the leaves in the still morning air. A heavy boulder sank deep in his gut, and the hairs on the back of his neck stood straight on end. Something was very, very wrong.

Doing his best to keep his eyes trained out the window, he reached back and shook Charlie's leg. "Charlie!" The shaking quickly grew more insistent and he turned up the volume. "CHARLIE!"

***

Charlie woke with a start. His gaze wandered around the room as his brain gathered information. "What! What in the hell's going on?"

"You didn't hear that?" AJ was looking down at him, his pale face framing wide eyes.

"Hear what?"

"The noise! The… the sound! The sound from the ground!" He pointed to the trailer floor. "The sound! From yesterday!"

He was in such a panic, it couldn't be ignored. Charlie sat up straight and planted his feet. He held a finger up for silence and listened carefully. "When did it happen?"

"Just now! Right before I woke you up!" He turned back to the window and pointed to the surrounding forest. "The leaves wiggled!" His choice of words, combined with his antics, reminded Charlie of a very overgrown child crying wolf.

Charlie held his palms out to the boy. "Okay, okay! No need to panic, let's just take a moment here. We both just woke up, and we have to take a minute to settle down and discuss what exactly happened." He motioned toward a chair. "Just have a seat, take some breaths, and I'll get a pot of coffee going."

AJ's jaw dropped. "Charlie! The ground is breaking! Or something! We've got to get the hell out of here!"

Charlie brought his palms back up to face the young man. "Just please, *please*, let's just take a moment. We have to calm down and not panic." He indicated the chair again.

AJ calmed a bit and followed the instruction. "I'm not bullshitting you here, you gotta listen to me," he pleaded. "I know you can't hear it now. Whatever, it passed, just like before. You know it happened before, and I'm telling you it happened again! Except it was bigger this time. Something is wrong!... The leaves wiggled."

"I'm not saying you're making this up. But, I mean, are you really sure? It's early, we just finished this big experimental project, pumping new things into the ground. We may have heard something unusual yesterday, but this is an enormous mine, AJ. They're doing things all over the place that can make the ground rumble, y'know?"

Charlie sensed the rookie's self-doubt trickling in when he began to relax and slump back in the chair.

A moment passed, then Charlie got up and looked out the window himself, slowly scanning the landscape for anything unusual. He pointed out to the left. "I'm guessing that new truck belongs to one of the operators. He's in the area, and he hasn't come running out in a panic or anything."

"Yeah, but he's in that building, wearing hearing protection and standing beside a running engine. The floor is shaking in there anyway, it wouldn't be noticeable!"

"So it wasn't that noticeable?"

"Well, it was noticeable in here!"

"Listen!" Charlie turned back, looking AJ straight in the eye. "I'm not doubting you heard or felt this. I just know panicking in this industry can get us killed. So let's listen for a little bit and I'll keep an eye out for the operator. When he comes out I'll tell him what happened and see if he noticed anything, or if he knows of anything happening in the area that could cause something like you described. As of right now, what do we know for sure? We know you heard a sound and maybe felt a tremor coming from the ground. It could be a lot of different things out here. They use dynamite in the mine a lot." He turned back to the window.

AJ's shoulders visibly relaxed. "I guess that could be all it is."

Charlie grabbed the freshly brewed pot of coffee and poured two mugs, handing one to AJ. He sipped his own as he continued to monitor the computer screen for anything unusual and watch for the operator.

A very slight, very slow groan started, like a gurgling stomach. It lasted for a good thirty seconds before escalating into something more powerful. It thrust, and then subsided, seemingly moving around beneath their feet.

AJ froze on the spot, the rim of his coffee cup held two inches from his lips. Charlie watched as the morning sun streaming through the window illuminated the front of his body, leaving a fine line down his side, dividing light from dark. The scene was perfectly still other than the luminous wisp of steam curling from the top of AJ's mug, disturbed only by hushed breath.

... *The leaves are wiggling...* Charlie remained focused on the surroundings in a trance-like state. His mind flipped through potential sources. It was long and drawn out, as if something was heaving. He desperately sought every logical explanation, but the only one he could fathom was that the ground was heaving below them; he swore he could feel it. The pitch of the noise increased to that of the timbers of a pirate ship battling rough seas, and then it died out again, completely.

"Charlie," AJ said calmly, "I don't think that's dynamite."

Charlie didn't flinch at the comment. Using the sleeve of his sweater, he rubbed frantically at the window glass, then moved closer to the pane, and squinted.

Fog... But he was quite certain fog was supposed to roll in. This particular fog seemed to be seeping up from the ground.

AJ appeared beside him, jockeying for position at the window. "What the fuck, Charlie?" His voice was soft and trembling.

Motion from the right caught both men's attention. The door to the compressor building swung open and the shift operator emerged.

Both men shouted and pounded on the window to warn him. The operator lifted his head and raised a hand to the guys, then began to descend the stairs. This excited more urgency from Charlie and AJ, but with the operator's head down to watch his step and his earmuffs still in place, any attempt at communication failed.

They watched the man slow for a split second as he approached the bottom step, which was blanketed in mist. But without knowledge of the happenings and without careful study, the bleeding smoke appeared to be a peaceful fog and he dropped his weight onto the final step.

As if is slow motion, AJ and Charlie watched as the operator swung his left leg past the right to take purchase on the ground. Before his foot touched down, he toppled, face down onto the dirt. No time to second-guess or reconsider, a simple switch had been tripped: alive... dead.

"Jesus shit!" AJ shrieked, grabbing onto Charlie's shoulder. "Is he dead?... Is he fucking dead, Charlie?"

Charlie had seen it during many re-enactments on countless safety-orientation videos. But he'd never witnessed it in real life. *It's H_2S...*

"It's H_2S!" he repeated out loud.

"H_2S! That's really fucking bad, right?" AJ began to shake him. "What the shit! So that's it? That man is fucking dead? We're going to die!"

Charlie grabbed AJ and hurled him up against the wall. He pushed his finger a millimetre from the end of the boy's nose, supplying him with one singular point of focus. "You gotta settle down and get a grip!" He had a will and determination never displayed before. "We gotta stay high—it's heavy, so it'll sink. But it's obviously at face level when we're standing on the ground!"

Charlie raced to the safety closet, where he found two SCBA packs: scuba gear for land. It was supposed to give them thirty minutes of air under normal breathing conditions—likely only fifteen in their current state of panic.

Now he began to wonder how far the disaster stretched. Would they be able to get out, and what the hell was happening?

He lifted the packs and ran back to the window. There were three trucks in the parking lot—theirs and the operator's. Everyone was supposed to leave the keys in the ignition for just such an emergency, but every second counted, so they would focus on Charlie's vehicle since he was sure he'd left his keys in there. Driving with the tank on his back would be challenging, but he'd make it work.

The ground erupted again, causing the two men to grab for support. They looked through the window to see the fumes had thickened. A flicker through the branches caught their attention. Flames were shooting over the treetops. Then the top of a drilling rig began to slowly tilt, as if its collapse were only a matter of when.

Charlie's jaw hung open until understanding revealed itself. "The ground's on fire! The ground's on fire! We started a fire in the ground somewhere! It's coming toward us!"

PRICE PER BARREL

"Holyfuckholyfuck!" AJ was passing into the beginning stages of useless.

Charlie needed to keep him focused. "Here, put this pack on!" He handed him a pack and began donning his own while he explained the plan. "We'll head straight to the truck—*my* truck. We have to get to higher ground—or even over the river might be safe enough, if that's all we can do, but preferably higher ground. But we don't want to get stuck, so no bullshit trying to climb up the side of anything stupid. Stick to the road and go as fast as we can, safely."

He looked over to the commotion that was the boy struggling with his rescue pack. Of course AJ wouldn't have paid any attention in training. Charlie quickly clipped his last buckle across his chest and then grabbed hold of AJ and clipped on his pack.

He placed both hands on AJ's shoulders and looked him straight in the eyes, speaking with calm control. "Listen, we have one chance at this. We can get out of here, we can survive this, but we have to get our heads on our shoulders and remain focused. Smart decisions are what's going to make the difference between life and death. These tanks are good for fifteen minutes of air at best. We can cover a lot of ground in the truck in that time, so we can do this. Put the mask over your face first, turn your bottle on, and then take a breath to open the valve. This will supply positive air, so there'll be no chance of anything getting to you as long as you keep the mask sealed." He held the boy tight until he got a confirming nod. He felt a little better about his partner's focus, but he still wasn't convinced of his consistence under pressure. "I'm driving."

He helped AJ with his mask, then quickly cranked the air bottle wide open as he took a breath and the supplied air flooded the cavity.

With AJ suited up and ready to go, Charlie strapped on his own mask, cranked the bottle, and breathed in the blast of air. The low-level alarm for the bottle rang furiously and his air quickly diminished to nothing. Charlie's pack was dead. Someone must've been screwing with it and never gotten it recharged.

Without a second thought, he looked up at AJ. "GO!"

A muffled revolt came from inside AJ's mask.

"IT'S TOO LATE! YOU HAVE TO GO NOW!... GO! GET THE HELL OUT OF HERE, NOW!" He grabbed the young man, turned him toward the door, then stood back with his nose and mouth covered, waiting for him to open the door and leave.

AJ was trembling. "I can't leave you," he sobbed behind a mask growing heavy with fog.

"SHUT UP! SHUT THE FUCK UP AND GO! I'LL FIND ANOTHER WAY!... GO, GODDAMMIT!"

A sobbing mess, AJ quickly slipped through the door and closed it behind him.

Charlie paused before taking a small breath to test the infestation in the air. Still alive, he raced to the window. AJ was struggling to get in the driver's seat with the tank strapped to his back. He slid the seat back as far as it would go and finally managed to squeeze himself behind the wheel. He closed the door and Charlie heard the engine start. He watched as AJ took off out of the yard and onto the main road.

He did it! He did it! He's gonna make it! he assured himself. *He's going to be all right.*

Then the silence closed in on Charlie, and he felt more alone than ever in his life. He backed slowly away from the window, removed his pack, and let it fall to the floor.

His mind went completely blank, as if there were no further use for it. The finality of the truth began to sink in. This was it. Other than a proper breathing apparatus, nothing was going to get him out of there in time.

He sat down and picked up the radio. "11-16 to control room."

Static echoed back.

He waited for a minute, then called again. "11-16 to control room."

Again, nothing but static.

He slunk back in the chair; he didn't want to look outside anymore. He could hear it—the ground shifting and bucking, the hissing and crackling. He could feel heat building as fire surrounded the site.

Then a dark irony set in, like a plague. His mind let go of the present and strolled through the past. The day she said, "*I do.*" Their first home, the small "fixer upper" on Grace Street. The birth of their boy, the love and pride that swelled his chest. Then his grandson, his prize; the little guy sitting on Grandpa's knee at the game with his cap on, stuffing that hot dog in his mouth—his first one ever... man, he'd loved that hot dog. He just got after it, slopping ketchup all over the both of them. *My little guy...*

He slumped over in the chair and placed his head in his hands. And Charlie Bidwell cried. It was something he hadn't done in so many years he'd forgotten what it felt like. He surrendered completely to his emotion. His family were the ones he'd done it all for, and he would proudly do it all again. Even knowing how it would end.

With his release, Charlie actually felt a sense of relief, a crazy sense of freedom. *So what! So what if life takes me now! Fuck them! I got what I wanted! Trading that little miracle for me is a real shit deal for someone!* A slobbering sputter of laughter shot from his mouth in between sobs.

He lifted his face to the sun streaming clear and bright through the windows. He couldn't stay in there forever, waiting. The office was anything but airtight, and eventually the poison would find him, or the fire would engulf him. He sure in fuck wasn't the man to sit there and wait for it! He couldn't stand for someone to find his remains curled up in the corner, like some coward.

With a surge of newfound energy, Charlie pushed to his feet. He grabbed a forgotten sweater from its hook and soaked it with water at the cooler, then cinched it around his face. It was a pathetic attempt, but it was an attempt. *I just gotta make it to a truck! Twenty steps at the most… I've been through worse.* The experts always warned never to expect to be able to hold your breath through it, but it was the only chance he had left.

With what could be his very last breath, he sucked in deep, filled his lungs to total capacity, and opened the door.

He scurried down the steps and made a beeline for the closest truck. Two steps across the yard, he stumbled. With the cocktail of toxins attacking him from every angle, a threatening cough kicked violently at his insides, begging him to open his airway, and his lungs began to buck. Dizziness crept in and his progress halted. He clutched at his throat as his vision blurred, then turned to blackness. He teetered, and his ears filled with a thundering beat. With his vision lost, he reached for the sky. Then, with what felt like a staggering blow to his chest, his lungs collapse and his body fell limp and weightless.

Charlie Bidwell said goodbye.

66

Up on the grassy hilltop, the chieftain watched the chaos and destruction unfold far below, waiting for the sign telling him what his role was in this event. The ground opened in volcanic craters all around him, consuming perfectly healthy trees like dry tinder. He could not stop it. Nothing could stop it.

Picking up his hand drum, he began his dance to the gods, chanting and asking for their guidance, their wisdom. The white men below were scrambling, some dying instantly in the death they had created. His tempo increased and he looked to the heavens, stretching up his arms, begging for direction.

Then he stopped.

Like a warrior riding to battle, he did a running mount onto his horse, grabbed its mane, and dug his heels in.

Down the side of the hill he charged, letting go an ancient cry. Down to the fire, down to the hell. With a speed worthy of legend, they seemingly glided across the surface of the land. All fell silent but the beating of their hearts. They would complete the task bestowed upon them, or they would die trying.

The chieftain watched as his target exited the building, took a couple of steps across the parking lot, then stumbled and teetered. With another kick of the heels and a cry to the heavens, he moulded himself perfectly to the back of his steed, head hugging the side of its neck.

Horse and man together as one, they streaked across the fire bog and into the smoke. Finally in range, the mighty warrior reached a steel-stiff arm out to the

PRICE PER BARREL

side, pounded his hand into the chest of his target, and heaved him off his feet.

67

Some hours later, Albert woke, the night's events a blur. Three women were sharing the bed with him, and he wasn't certain if any were the women he began the night with. He felt around to ensure his cloak was still in place. Having his identity revealed to some of the unknowing guests could cause a mass headache. He didn't like headaches.

Still concealed, he slowly manoeuvred his way up and around the slumbering party favours. Most were naked, two of them were missing their masks. *Such pretty piggies.* He smirked.

Tossing aside the curtains exposed the main area. Many people were lying back on the sofas, some sleeping, some quietly chatting, and some diehards still enjoying the celebration.

He sauntered casually by on his way to the water cooler; his body craved hydration. It was a hell of a party—the best, from what he could remember.

Some patrons smiled and raised their glasses or gave him a casual salute, which he returned. As he approached the last couch, he saw a couple still engrossed in the festive spirit. A young man in a mask and nothing else was sitting slumped down with his legs spread, letting a sweet piece of ass demonstrate some of her special skills. She wasn't dressed like the others, wearing a black lace thong and a dark masquerade mask; she must be a guest of one of the other gentlemen, not one of the hired help. Albert was impressed. *Look at the ass on that! Maybe I should take me some before I leave. I think I have another round in me.*

PRICE PER BARREL

He followed the long, sculpted legs down from her ass, and some blue pigment on her ankle caught his attention, sparking a memory. He paused, squinting. The blur turned into a blue butterfly.

His blood pressure rocketed as he realized where he'd seen the tattoo before. He let go a demonic growl. Snapping his heavy arm down like an angry god, he grabbed her by the hair and lifted her up as if she were no more than a snifter of Scotch.

He held her head back slightly, turning her eyes to his through his monster's face.

Gasping in fear and pain, she flailed at him.

Though he needed no more confirmation, he reached up slowly and lowered her mask. He growled again, lowly.

Recognition dawned in Vicky's eyes and she screamed, pitching it just right to wake all in a ten-block radius. "HELP ME!" She jerked in his grasp, clawing and kicking, punching his chest—whatever it took and nothing less. "SOMEONE! SOMEBODY FUCKING HELP ME! HE'S INSANE! HE'S GONNA FUCKING KILL ME!" she continued begging seamlessly.

Many came out of hiding to see what all the craziness was about, but they just stood and watched. Not one in the room was willing to challenge the beast, or the man he was—not even the guy she'd been blowing.

Like the mighty Kong in a fit of fury, Albert opened his palm and struck her with the force of a truck, sending her through the air and across the floor into the crescent of light at the entrance.

She was quiet now. Her mask hung from her ear as she weakly pushed up her torso and pulled her bare-breasted body across the floor away from him. She looked back at him and the growing crowd in the darkness, who were peeking at her and whispering to each other. Blood streamed from her mouth and nose, and her jaw hung broken. He had ruined one of her most prized possessions.

With large, purposeful strides, he approached her again, never removing his eyes from hers. He reached down and picked her up by the throat, then pinned her solidly against the wall.

The tips of her toes brushed the floor as she scraped at his face, threatening his cover and causing him to instantly tighten his squeeze with honest purpose.

She gasped for air and focused her efforts on his hand, trying with all she had to free herself. There was no manipulating herself out of this situation. Her grip soon began to weaken.

The entrance doors flew open and in charged four of Fort Mac's finest. They all took steps back when they saw the beast man, and one officer drew his firearm.

They knew he was there, and there was no mistaking that this was him.

"Albert Doyle, you are under arrest! Release the girl, take five steps back, and place your hands behind you head!"

Albert never flinched.

"Mr. Doyle, this is not a request, release her now!"

Vicky gurgled and went limp, and one of the officer's lunged forward, digging his taser deep into the monster's side. The current caused his muscles to clench and twitch, but the giant never fell.

A second officer hit the monstrosity again, and this time his body seized and toppled, falling like a massive timber to the floor.

Vicky fell to a heap, gasping. One officer quickly rushed to her and covered her with his coat.

The other three men jumped on top of the pig before he had a chance to recover, struggling to contort his massive arms behind his back and then slap on a pair of cuffs. It took everything they had to lift him up to his feet.

He quivered until he got his strength back, and then he raised himself up, tall and mighty.

The cop to his right reached up and tore the hood off his head, letting it hang from the back of his neck.

The giant flinched at the sudden increase in light, then turned to the officer. "Just what in the fuck do you think you're doing?" he snarled, his mouth foaming with madness. "Do you have any idea who you're screwing with right now?"

The officer met his stare. "You're Albert Doyle. And you're under arrest."

"Arrest! Arrest for what?" he shouted. "How'd you know where I was? How'd you get in here?"

The officer looked around at the crowd—the ones who were not in hiding. "Guess you all missed the early-morning news?" He raised his eyebrows. "Mr. Doyle, you are under arrest for criminal negligence resulting in injury and possible fatalities." He looked down at Vicky. "Throw in assault and battery of a young woman." He grinned, and then they led the beast from the room.

Moments after disappearing down the hall, a mighty roar echoed from the darkness.

68

At the crack of dawn, Emma sat in her favourite rocking chair, listening to the CBC radio news, as was her morning ritual.

Her cup of tea sat on the small end table beside her, barely touched. Over time, its steam had dissipated as it cooled.

It was the first sleepless night she had suffered in years. She had tossed and turned, then gotten up for some water. But even her little red miracle pills couldn't keep her down, only left her feeling very groggy.

She had assumed her morning position in the rocking chair earlier than normal, hoping the familiar voice of her favourite morning-show host would help sooth her to rest.

Unfortunately, the broadcast that morning was a little too close to home.

"We have a new update on the happenings up in Alberta's own Fort McMurray! It's been confirmed there's a massive fire burning out of control at Northern Lights Energy, an oil sands plant just outside of town. Experts believe the blaze is a result of the controversial 11-16 Project. We did a spotlight story on this several months ago. I'm posting the link online right now; visit our page if you'd like to review it."

Heavily sedated, Emma could hear and understand, but her entire spirit had gone numb.

"Emergency workers are in the area and ready to go, but they're taking extreme precautions because specialists believe the fire is actually in the ground. So, just to bring everyone up to speed on what is suspected to be happening, the ground in the

area, which is saturated with heavy oil, has actually started on fire. The 11-16 Project was designed to deliver compressed air into the ground to increase production, and yesterday was the first time anyone had tried this. Everything was fine until some time during the night. Emergency personnel are unsure how to approach the situation as no one has been trained specifically for this. Helicopters are searching the area and there are reports of many people down and vehicles run off the side of the road; many casualties are suspected. Experts believe the fire has released a cloud of highly toxic gas, which kills instantly. Local police are currently searching for the whereabouts of company president Albert Doyle, the driving force behind the project. We'll continue to keep updating as new reports come in."

Emma's gaze turned to the window and the morning sun slanting through to rest on the spotless hardwood. She had sat in that very spot so many years, she could accurately predict the day of the year by the time at which the edge of the beam aligned perfectly with the fourth slat in the floor.

So many years…

So many years, so many things done and forgotten. She watched as birds played on the feeder that had hung from the tree for… oh, twenty years now. Albert had built it with Albert Jr. when the boy was just five. It wasn't well built by any standard. The bright-green and lipstick-red colour arrangement had been derived from the artistic pallet of her young grandson. Nothing fit or aligned properly, and the stick they had glued on the front for a perch was forever falling off. She never said anything about it. She just looked for it every morning, and when it wasn't there, she took her trusty all-purpose glue out and stuck it back on. It was a couple of months after they hung it before any birds actually visited the feeder—likely scared to death of it. But in time, they had warmed to it, and now she had a faithful flock.

She breathed in and sobbed. Years of wins and losses passed by…

She had kept quiet about the happenings at the after-party all those years ago. School was hard; every time she passed someone whispering or snickering, she couldn't help wondering if they were talking about her.

She would bow her head whenever she saw Stephan or Andrew or any of the other teammates she recognized. And in turn, there was no taunting or teasing from their side—almost as if it had never happened. But some weeks later, Emma's womanly instincts told her the story was nowhere near the end. Queasiness and routine morning visits to the washroom… she didn't need a professional diagnosis.

PRICE PER BARREL

Terrified, she had only one place to turn. It was a dim glimmer of hope, but she had nothing else. If her father found out he would surely beat her, possibly to her end. There was no way to tell who the baby's father was, but she was the mother, and she would provide the best life she could for her child. At any cost.

Her father was serving the last of a two-month sentence and her mother was drunk and still healing from his last beating when Emma pleaded for her help. And surprisingly, her mother sympathized. The two women tore apart the house from top to bottom, scraping together enough money to get Emma out of there.

"You go, Emma! Make your way to Fort McMurray and find your aunt Helen. She'll take care of you, my dear." For the first time in memory, Emma felt her mother's love. She looked up to her teary eyes and saw a smile. "Don't you ever let this world get the better of you! You got what it takes, honey."

Emma broke down in tears.

Her mother kissed her softly on the forehead. "Be strong, my love. Now go! And don't you turn back! There's nothing here for you!" She handed Emma a small suitcase and shooed her out the door.

Emma hated to think what would happen when her father was released. But even with her fear and her guilt, she had done as she was told, and never turned back.

Him... I did it all for him. Everything—blood and sweat—everything.

And he had thanked her, countless times. At the little league hockey championship, on graduation day, and on the day he was handed the keys to the presidential office.

Thank you, Mom!

She raised a limp hand to wipe a tear from her nose, then let it fall back, lifeless.

I just wanted him to be the best he could be... Push, pull, climb, fight to get what's yours. Don't let anyone ever get in your way. He is Albert Doyle, and he is a... a... monster!

She burst out crying, alone in her living room, and it drowned out the echo of the broadcast.

It's my fault... I created this.

The broadcaster's excited voice suddenly commanded attention. *"This just in! Local authorities in Fort McMurray have arrested the president of Northern Lights Energy, Albert Doyle. Pending charges include criminal negligence resulting in injury*

288

or death and an unrelated assault and battery charge."

She kept her eyes focused on the scenic morning through the window and felt around the end table for her bottle of little red pills. She dumped the remaining contents into her hand and let the plastic container fall to the floor. Then she reached back to the spoiled cup of tea. Slowly, one by one, she swallowed every last capsule.

She watched chickadees play in the sparkling morning dew, chirping and flapping for their turn on the perch until one pudgy little fellow won. He settled his full weight on his newfound throne, and as he turned to chirp victory to his friends, the post fell suddenly to the ground.

And Emma Doyle of Corner Brook, Newfoundland, fell asleep.

69

Mary-Ann pressed her back against the wall as multiple security guards rushed past her. It took several hits with their battering ram to gain entrance to Ollie's room. She pushed her way among them and stumbled through the door. He was curled up on the bed with the blanket covering every inch of his body except for his arm, which was flopped over the side, toward the nightstand.

The first officer sat beside him and shook him lightly, then pulled back the covers. His complexion was ghost white, and his lips were a bluish hue.

Mary-Ann rushed toward him, but two guards grabbed her arms and pulled her back, then began pushing her toward the door.

"No! *NO!*" she screamed, fighting for her place by his side. As they got her clear of the door, a female guard began talking to her in a very controlled manner.

"Miss! Miss, you have to calm down." She led her down the hall with a firm grip on her arm. The hall was packed; everyone seemed to be making their way downstairs.

Mary-Ann looked back over her shoulder and saw two emergency medics rush through Ollie's open door.

The female guard tugged on her arm. "Everyone has to evacuate now, miss, there's a problem in the plant. Report to the parking lot immediately for a head count. Miss!" She pulled Mary-Ann to a stop and turned to her with a stern but sympathetic stare. "They're doing everything they can for him, I promise you. I'm sincere when I tell you it's best not to go back there. You'll only interfere. Go down to the parking lot, check in for a head count, then wait by the front door and I'll give you an update as soon as I know anything. I promise!"

Mary-Ann gave a hesitant nod and then did as instructed. They were experienced at this and they'd gotten there pretty fast. *Maybe there's a chance?*

She squinted as she stepped out the front door into the morning light. She found one of the head counters and gave her name, then took a seat beside the front door. The morning sun felt warm on her skin as she did the math in her head, and she believed there was really a chance Ollie could make it. He was young, with a strong heart. And the guard had assured her they were doing everything they could.

Twenty minutes had passed when the door to the camp busted open and a voice of authority ordered people out of the way. Mary-Ann jumped to her feet and turned with a hopeful smile.

The female guard rushed straight to her, grabbed her hand, and pulled her off to the side. She looked her in the eye and went straight to the point. "I'm sorry." She shook her head, then jumped back in beside the gurney as it passed through the onlookers.

The white medical sheet held the profile of a body—his body—covered hair to toe. Mary-Ann stood in complete shock. Her whole body quivered and rivers of tears flowed, but she never made a sound. The words rang in her mind: *"I'm sorry."*

That was the day she lost her hopes and her dreams, as well as her reality.

Two days later she found a quick blurb in the local newspaper: *Newfoundland man suffers fatal heart attack in local camp.*

She never saw or heard anything about Oliver Hynes again.

70

The grassy hilltop glade was a paradise surrounded by what many would describe as the dawn after the apocalypse. The chieftain kneeled beside Charlie and rolled him onto his side as he coughed and sputtered, foam frothing from his mouth as his body dispelled poisons.

Charlie fell back and looked up at the blue sky, a sight he never thought he would lay eyes on again. Then the familiar silhouette of the chieftain leaned over him.

"Where the…? What the…?" He coughed. "What the fuck happened?"

The chieftain remained silent, searching his eyes. Then he grinned, patted Charlie on the shoulder, and stood.

Charlie lay still for a while, waiting for his coughing and hacking to fade from his burning lungs. *How the fuck am I here right now? I walked out of the trailer and I… I was dead! I know I was dead!*

The pain eased, and Charlie's mind quit spinning. He looked up at the fluffy white clouds overhead. *They're like mountains.* A smile crept in as he studied every last bubble, canyon, and crevice, studied the way the light traced out every fine detail of a mountain in the sky. *Funny I never noticed it before…* He chuckled in his state of euphoria.

Upwind of the choking smoke, the air was clean and refreshing. He could feel life return to his every bit; he was alive… by some miracle, he was still alive, and life felt incredible.

As his energy and curiosity returned, he rolled over and saw the chieftain was looking over the edge of the hilltop, his arms crossed over his chest as he quietly surveyed the disaster.

Charlie slowly found his footing and stood up straight—another thing he never expected to do again. It took some effort to maintain his balance for the first few steps as he made his way over to his friend. He put an arm around his shoulders; they were brothers. *He's just such a good guy.* Charlie's soul fluttered. *I really like this guy! He's great! A lot of positive energy.* He joined the man in staring down across the mess.

Any plant life between their hilltop and the river had completely disintegrated, and just a few charred cars remained. The trees surrounding the project were engulfed in flames, and the intense heat was beginning to deform the buildings. It would shut itself down eventually. But would it be enough?

Black smoke billowed from glowing red open veins in the earth, and a thin blanket of white mist covered it all. Charlie suspected it had claimed many good men and women. If he'd ever created a doomsday scenario in his mind, this was pretty much it.

He looked at his new, most favourite guy in the world. "So," he inquired again, "what happened down there? Where, or how, did you…" He nodded toward the project.

The chieftain's simple expression seemed to say, *"How in the hell do you think I got you out?… Stupid white man."* Then he nodded toward his horse, which stood munching grass at the edge of the forest.

Charlie smiled and snorted at the chieftain. "You came and got me with your horse?"

A second passed before the chieftain nodded confidently.

"I'm gonna get me one of those," he joked… kind of.

He accepted that the chieftain lacked interest in sharing the actual story with him, and quickly gave up caring. All that mattered was he was still there.

He heard the *whumping* of a helicopter, then made out its silhouette in the smoke-filled sky as it approached.

A paramedic wearing an oxygen mask raised a thumbs-up to the sky and their rescue basket began to lower. Charlie got in and then watched as the mighty warrior—*"The most awesome guy in the world!"*—kicked his heels into his steed and raced like the wind, disappearing into the trees and never looking back.

PRICE PER BARREL

Charlie never saw or heard of his friend again.

71

Albert sat alone in a darkened cell in the basement of the Fort McMurray Police Station, the pale light from a small single window up near the ceiling outlining the large pile of a man, still dressed in the costume that had been the pride of the ball. Now it just looked stupid.

His attorney, Dale Ingle, clomped down the stairs, escorted by an officer. The uniformed man observed from the bottom of the stairwell while Dale took the few steps to Albert's cage.

Albert jumped up and gripped the steel bars. "Well? What in the hell's going on here, Ingle? This is bullshit, and you know it!"

Dale gave a sigh, expressionless. "It's actually not bullshit, Albert, it's very real." He held some photographs of the scene at the plant in front of Albert and began paging through them.

"A massive fire has broken out on the grounds of Northern Lights. Experts believe the fire started over top of the wells drilled for the 11-16 Project. A heavy cloud of poisonous gas across the ground is preventing any type of full-scale rescue effort. The part of the plant that could be evacuated already has been, but the unaccounted-for number in the hundreds."

Finished with the photos, he lowered them back to his side and replaced them with his blank stare. "So I assure you again, Albert, this is very real. Operations has been unable to shut down the equipment at the site as they have lost communication and the only other shutdown switches are in the buildings, with the running equipment. So at this time, everything's still running. A crew of emergency specialists are planning to physically enter the site and cut power off completely, but of course this has many complications in the toxic environment. We have disaster experts from around the world communicating via satellite on how we can eventually contain and extinguish this completely. Many are under the impression that because the ground has opened up and found its own oxygen source, it may now be self-sustaining. No one's ever dealt with anything like this before, of course, because you were the first to attempt it."

Albert shook his cage. "They can't hold me on this! No one could've predicted this would happen. Get some water bombers on it, for Christ's sake! It's just a fucking fire, there's been hundreds in the area before!"

"Water bombers are on the scene, Albert, they have been for hours. Helicopters are scanning the affected areas with infrared cameras and are reporting that the attempt has had no effect. We're not talking about a simple forest fire—the heavy oil in the ground's on fire. The fuel contained in the ground is endless. The church is referring to this disaster as biblical."

Albert snarled at him. "The church, *pfft*! What the fuck do they know!"

"A Mr. Charles Bidwell was recently retrieved from a hilltop opposite the site," Dale continued. "Apparently he survived only because he was rescued by one of the local Natives." He bowed his head and moved back from the cage. "Mr. Bidwell said your son escaped the site with the last remaining SCBA pack a while earlier. He took their company truck to try and flee the area."

Albert's grip on the cage tightened until his knuckles were white. "Good! He's a fucking hell of a man, that Charlie! So, my son, he's…"

The attorney looked Albert in the eye. "The helicopter circled the site with Mr. Bidwell, and he identified the truck about half a kilometre from the site. It looks like it crashed into an uprooted tree that fell across the road. The chopper was able to get low enough to verify there is a body in the driver's side of the vehicle. I am very, truly sorry, Albert, we are all but certain that your son is dead."

"Nope!" the big man piped up, uncertainty in his quivering voice. "Nope!" He shook his head, looking at the floor. "That's bullshit, they got the wrong truck! How can they tell who's really in there? There's no way they can get low enough! There's hundreds of trucks like that on site! It could be anyone… Nope! Not AJ, you're wrong."

Dale took another step back from the bars.

As Albert watched him retreat, he realized that for once, he had no control over this man; he had no control over this situation. "You gotta get me out!" he pleaded. "I, I'll find him! I'll get him out! Please! I, I'm begging you!" Albert was a caged animal. "I'll come back right after! I promise!... Please... I'm his dad... He's my boy!"

Dale continued to retreat slowly until he'd joined the guard at the bottom of the stairs. "I'm sorry, Albert. I'm truly, very sorry for your loss. But that's not how this is going to work. Not this time." He turned and he and the officer climbed the stairs.

Alone, the big man finally let go and sobbed heavily, no longer worried about who he was or how he presented himself. His hands slipped down the bars until he came to rest on his knees, head bowed in the filtered morning light.

Albert Doyle, the king, had fallen.

CPSIA information can be obtained
at www.ICGtesting.com
Printed in the USA
BVHW031534221221
624592BV00011B/863